CORPORATE ESPIONAGE

CORPORATE ESPIONAGE

WHAT IT IS,
WHY IT IS HAPPENING IN YOUR COMPANY,
WHAT YOU MUST DO ABOUT IT

IRA WINKLER

PRIMA PUBLISHING

PRIMA PUBLISHING and its colophon are registered trademarks of Prima Communications, Inc.

This book discusses a number of alleged incidents of actual corporate espionage. In certain cases, however, the author has changed the names of the persons or companies involved or altered some of the facts in order to protect the privacy of the people involved. In those cases where names have been changed, any use of the name of an actual person or company is purely coincidental.

Library of Congress Cataloging-in-Publication Data

Winkler, Ira.
    Corporate espionage : what it is, why it is happening in
your company, what you must do about it / Ira Winkler.
        p.   cm.
    Includes index.
    ISBN 0-7615-0840-6
    1. Business intelligence—United States.   2. Espionage—United
States.   I. Title.
    HD38.7.W56   1997
    658.4'7—dc21   97-6287
                                                                                    CIP

97 98 99 HH 10 9 8 7 6 5 4 3 2 1
Printed in the United States of America

How to Order
Single copies may be ordered from Prima Publishing, P.O. Box 1260, Rocklin, CA 95677; telephone (916) 632-4400. Quantity discounts are also available. On your letterhead, include information concerning the intended use of the books and the number of books you wish to purchase.

Visit us online at http://www.primapublishing.com

To my wife, Molly,
who took care of everything imaginable
so I was able to write this book

Contents

PART III What You Can Do

Acknowledgments

I T'S IMPOSSIBLE TO THANK EVERYONE WHOM I SHOULD, BUT a few people deserve special mention. I would like to thank Anthony Robbins for giving me the initial idea to write a book. Dr. Mich Kabay, Director of Education of the National Computer Security Association, was invaluable in helping me choose a specific topic and an overall format for this book. I also want to thank Dan Ryan of Science Applications International Corporation for being the first person to clarify the practical application of the basic concepts of information security.

Approximately a dozen people deserve public acknowledgment as sources for the material in this book. Unfortunately, I have to maintain their anonymity. So, you know who you are; please accept my deep appreciation. I also owe Eddie and Nancy an incredible debt for helping me perfect my skills for this line of work.

Finally, I want to thank the Syracuse University Writing Program, which forced me to be a better writer, no matter how hard I tried to fight it.

Introduction

OR WHY KEVIN MITNICK REPRESENTS

EVERYTHING THAT IS WRONG

WITH THE INFORMATION AGE

THE HEADLINES PAINTED HIM AS THE GREATEST THREAT to American security since Khrushchev tried setting up shop in Cuba. Kevin Mitnick: feared by the public as an evil techno-genius, adored by computer hackers as a martyr, dubbed by the press "the Most Wanted Hacker in America." It was said he could compromise FBI investigations with the flick of a finger, break into computer systems at will, modify telephone company records, entrap vulnerable police informants, and forge identities. To stop him, the legend goes, it took another computer genius, Tsutomu Shimomura: the good hacker, "the Samurai," the yin to Mitnick's yang. Shimomura's pursuit and ultimate capture of Mitnick made great copy. It was a front-page story. It led nightly news broadcasts for weeks. It generated several books.

And it was all hype and hysteria. Never was a story less understood by the public or more distorted by the media. Kevin Mitnick wasn't particularly talented; he was just a good liar.

The Mitnick case—or rather, the media and public response to it—exemplifies the widespread misconception in this country that industrial espionage and high-tech crimes are perpetrated by slick James Bond types or genius computer hackers. Nothing could be further from the truth. Oh, there are some brilliant hackers out there, to be sure, but most of them could hardly be called geniuses. And there is no shortage of foreign espionage professionals, especially with no Cold War to occupy them. Industrial espionage is conducted by the SVR (successor to the KGB) and other international intelligence agencies, well-financed foreign and American companies, private individuals, and, yes, those dreaded teenage computer hackers. Nonetheless, just about all corporate penetrations are accomplished with decidedly simple, and preventable, methods.

Most people don't realize how much they could do, without spending a fortune or distorting their corporate cultures, to minimize the risk of an espionage breach in their organizations. Simple things, like turning off computers at night and locking offices, could prevent billions of dollars in losses. I know this from personal experience. Thanks to unlocked offices, neglected computers, and the like, I am able to steal billions of dollars in sensitive information from large corporations in about a day. And they never even know I'm there.

Of course, I tell them all about it, and I give the information back. The target companies are my clients, after all, and their executives pay me to execute what is known as a *penetration test*.

As an information security professional, I help companies protect their information. I am also one of a handful of people (some even say the only person) who simulates industrial espionage attacks to find the client's holes. I also investigate industrial espionage and computer-related crimes. For over a decade, I worked for and with the National Security Agency (NSA), considered to be the most secretive of U.S. intelligence agencies and the world leader in electronic intrusion and information security. Since a transition to the commercial sector, I've been successfully compromising vast amounts of sensitive information belonging to organizations considered to be among the most secure in the world.

Most people assume that I ply my trade with special, high-tech devices and strategies. They envision me crawling around in air-conditioning ducts, evading laser beams and pressure-sensitive floors, parachuting into heavily armed compounds, and seducing lonely female secretaries. Actually, I "steal" most of my information by simply asking for it, looking on desktops, going up to computers that are left on all day, and digging through the trash. With few exceptions, all real-life James Bonds get their information exactly the same way.

That's how Kevin Mitnick did it, more or less. Mitnick's true expertise is in "social engineering," a term used by hackers to describe what amounts to telling lies over the telephone to get information. Hackers often use this technique to learn about modem access points or computer passwords. Mitnick used his social engineering skills to compromise FBI investigations, to trace telephone numbers, to place taps on phones, and to reroute calls from other telephones to his own. He allegedly used this technique on many organizations to set up computer accounts, privileged computer access, and special telephone privileges.

Even Mitnick's attacks against computers had no real technical muscle behind them. He relied on existing hacker tools, readily available on the Internet, that exploited known technical vulnerabilities. Computer security and systems administration personnel should have known about those vulnerabilities and fixed them. The fixes, just like the hacker tools, were readily available on the Internet, at no cost.

One of the reasons for Mitnick's success was that he was able to capitalize on the fact that many people fail to recognize easily correctable security vulnerabilities. One of the special ironies of the Mitnick case is that Shimomura, now widely regarded as one of the world's premiere computer security experts, became involved in the case only after someone had hacked into his personal system. The hacker supposedly targeted some software Shimomura claims to have reverse-engineered from a cellular telephone, the legality of which even he admits is questionable. (Reverse-engineering is like taking a cookie, then working backwards to figure out the recipe and the baking time necessary to re-create it. In the case of software, reverse-engineering facilitates the violation of software copyrights.) Shimomura had left this software, which he must have known was of potential value to hackers and criminals, on a computer system connected directly to the Internet instead of storing it off-line.

The attack on Shimomura's system exploited a known vulnerability. This specific attack had never been reported before, but Shimomura knew the vulnerability was there. He could, in theory, have protected his system against it.

I don't mean to bash Shimomura here—he is one of the better computer security experts, and without him and his talent, I'm not sure Mitnick would ever have been caught—but the bad habits that led to the breach of his system are very common, and the attack could have been prevented with simple countermeasures.

Furthermore, lying over the telephone and using widely available tools to exploit preventable vulnerabilities is not the mark of an unstoppable computer genius. The decidedly non-technical techniques Mitnick used to perpetrate his crimes are used by nearly all hackers, and although they are very effective, they're also easily prevented.

Another major problem, according to Robert Gates, former Director of Central Intelligence and the Central Intelligence Agency, is that most information managers and company owners simply don't believe their organizations will be targeted. If the company is not in the defense industry or if the organization is relatively small, the thinking goes, no one will come after it.

In fact, small businesses tend to be targets *more* often than large corporations, simply because they have more competitors. Studies show that companies of all sizes, from multibillion-dollar corporations to $20,000-a-year, mom-and-pop operations, are victims of industrial espionage. No company or organization is immune from being targeted for attack, and to a small company, a thousand-dollar loss could be much more devastating than the loss of billions to large companies. Here's an example of the most common type of small-scale industrial espionage, described in a letter written to advice columnist Ann Landers:*

A Relative Muscles in on Her Niece's Business

Dear Ann Landers: Last year, I had a flourishing dried-flower business. As my business increased, my sister and aunt helped me out. After a month or two, "Aunt Di" noticed the money I was making and decided to open her own business. That would have been OK, but she started to undercut my prices. She called my steady clients and said she could make the pieces I was making at a cheaper price. Many of her pieces were copies of my original designs.

When my business partner confronted Aunt Di, she became very angry. I tried to reason with her, but it was useless. She called me names and tried to attack me physically.

Ann, my grandmother will be 90 this year. My siblings and I practically grew up with Grandma, and we love her dearly. Aunt Di owns the apartment complex where Grandma lives and she refuses to let any of us grandchildren come visit now. We are heartbroken.

We think what Aunt Di is doing is a disgrace, but we don't know what to do about it. Do you have any suggestions?

—J. F. in Philadelphia

---

*Permission granted by Ann Landers and Creators Syndicate.

The incident may have taken place in just a flower shop, but Auntie Di was every inch the industrial spy, and the results of her actions were extremely damaging to the owners on many levels. Essentially, Aunt Di used her niece's manufacturing plans, price lists, and customer lists to compete against her niece.

In researching this book, I met with many people in the security business and law enforcement, corporate executives, and even a few corporate spies. All stressed that virtually every organization is a potential target of corporate espionage.

None of which is meant to minimize the vulnerability of bigger companies. According to the FBI and similar organizations, industrial espionage costs U.S. companies anywhere from $24 billion to $100 billion annually. In almost all cases of information compromise in the corporate world, average citizens are the ultimate victims. Corporations pass on billions of dollars of such losses to their customers every year, who pass on their losses to *their* customers. Losses to U.S. telephone companies due to theft of services and toll fraud—one of the favorite targets of computer hackers and criminals in general—total over $1 billion a year. By law, this additional expense is passed on to telephone company customers. Likewise, the cost of credit card fraud is passed on to the consumers through higher fees and interest rates. Individuals also pay for the cost of information recovery. If an insurance company experiences a loss of data due to, say, a power outage, the firm will spend a lot of money recovering it. That additional expense is taken from shareholders' and policyholders' dividends.

I do not mean to minimize the importance of computers as potential targets. Although not everyone owns or uses a personal computer, everyone's safety and livelihood depends on hundreds of computer systems performing as expected. The telephone system is now a vast computer network—the largest in the world. Without computers, there would be no 911 service, no exchange of faxes, and no telephone calls to your mother on Mother's Day. New cars can't function without them. Most employees would never see their paychecks without the smooth performance of the employer's accounting software.

But, most important, computers are repositories of *information*—the raison d'être of industrial spies. We're all dependent upon the ability of hundreds of corporations and government organizations to protect the information that resides on their computers. With the worldwide connectivity that exists among organizations, security rests on the weakest link in an international chain.

I'm here to tell you that this is truly a fight you can win, and without the help of high-tech experts like Mr. Shimomura. Your company or organization can be reasonably safe in cyberspace and the world in general—even from the world's best intelligence agencies, organized crime syndicates, and those diabolical hackers—by applying basic countermeasures that anyone can implement.

In the following pages, I've presented a wealth of practical information on the subject of corporate espionage. Part I deals with the essential processes and concepts familiar to corporate spies and the security professionals who fight them. In Part II, I provide detailed and representative case studies of a range of espionage incidents. These stories, all actual incidents that I participated in or learned about from the attackers themselves, show exactly how potentially devastating thefts occur regularly beyond the notice of the media. I'm certain the case studies will infuriate, frighten, and astound. Part III outlines specific anti-espionage countermeasures: simple solutions that are practical and, for the most part, low cost. The actions recommended in Part III are relevant to any organization or individual with any information of value.

In writing this book, I'm not suggesting for one minute that you can achieve perfect information security in your organization or that such a goal is even worth attempting—even if you were willing to spend millions. I'm not advocating the implementation of some kind of corporate-wide martial law. Vital organizations can't function well in a paranoid security death grip. Besides, there is no such thing as perfect security. Every organization is, and always will be, vulnerable to a greater or lesser degree. But knowing that shouldn't stop you from taking steps to protect your valuable information. What you should be going for is *reasonable* security measures that minimize your risk; this is something every organization can achieve. It's all about managing *risk*.

Think about it this way: Fire devastates properties of all types almost every day. It's childishly simple to start a fire; anyone can do it. Yet a relatively small percentage of homes and businesses burn down in this country. Why? Certainly not because anyone has found a way to make buildings fireproof. No, the only reason fires don't sweep the landscape is that people know the steps necessary to keep their properties safe.

More than anything else, I want this book to serve as a safety manual for the Information Age. For the most part, the material is straightforward and nontechnical. But like all information, it's worthwhile only if you use it.

PART I

ESPIONAGE CONCEPTS

Information Is Information

THE THEFT OF SENSITIVE INFORMATION—WHICH IS WHAT economic or industrial espionage is all about—can be highly detrimental to individuals and organizations. Disclosure of sensitive data, such as the fact that someone has AIDS, can ruin people's lives. The damage to corporations can be just as severe. In a 1995 lawsuit, Proctor & Gamble (P&G) and Bankers Trust sued *Business Week* magazine in an effort to prevent the publication from revealing the details of a lawsuit involving the two corporations and some questionable investments; P&G feared the embarrassment and loss of confidence that could have resulted from the disclosure of these details. A Supreme Court ruling was required to resolve the temporary restraining order against *Business Week*.

Information in the wrong hands can destroy a corporation, put people out of work, bankrupt local merchants, and devastate shareholder families.

It's all about information, but not exclusively computer information. If your competitors want your company's strategic plans, they don't care whether they get them from your computers or your garbage. Information is information. The form it takes is irrelevant; it's the content that matters.

The means by which that information is acquired is equally unimportant. It can be obtained verbally, electronically, physically, or visually. It can be snatched from computers, certainly, but a well-placed bribe can be just as effective.

FORMS OF INFORMATION

When I use the word "information," what exactly am I talking about? The classic definition describes information as "organized data," but that's not really very useful in our present context. In these pages, *information* refers to any piece of knowledge that could hurt your organization or help your competition if it were to fall into the wrong hands. That piece could be great or small. It could be a business plan or a phone number, a set of blueprints or a computer password, a high-tech prototype or a business card. While the form of information is irrelevant from a spy's perspective, it is extremely relevant in knowing how to protect yourself. The following sections describe the various and common forms in which information can be obtained.

Computer-Based Information Almost every piece of information generated by a modern company or other organization eventually finds its way onto a computer somewhere. Information is either recorded on a computer to formalize it or actually created in a computer environment. Nowadays, most executives type their own messages and correspondence directly into computers; the dictation-taking secretary is an anachronism. Computers are used for spreadsheets, databases, project design, and tons and tons of e-mail.

E-mail is one of the most potentially vulnerable types of computer information, because most people don't think much about how they're using it. In modern corporate America, most organizations are swimming in e-mail. People use e-mail to convey virtually all types of corporate information, from the most banal interoffice memos to the most sensitive project details. The corporate e-mail "conversation" is dense with information about company problems, personnel issues, and project status. Stop and think about the e-mail you have sent and received during the last week. What would happen if it were intercepted by an unfriendly party?

Nearly everyone understands the importance and potential vulnerability of computer-based information. Most people do take steps to protect their most sensitive computer documents. However, many do not realize how damaging their supposedly nonsensitive computer information can be. E-mail discussing travel plans can compromise potential mergers. Informal notes usually contain as many details as finished documents. Computer-based information has been an extremely fruitful source of information to would-be spies, and it will only continue to grow.

Formal Documents   Companies generate many kinds of formal documents for a variety of purposes. Strategic plans, contractual status reports, manufacturing specifications, production reports—all must be printed out and kept as hardcopy documents. These reports contain critical information that could ruin a company if it were compromised.

Most people recognize the value of formal documents and take appropriate steps to protect them.

Draft Documents   While people instinctively recognize the value of formal documents, they often treat the draft forms of those documents as worthless. They seem to assume that once a finished document is available, the drafts are outdated, inaccurate, and therefore unimportant. Although the draft document itself might be of little use once the final draft has been issued, the information it contains is hardly worthless. Much of it is very valuable indeed, and corporate spies know it. Typically, the draft documents contain the same hard facts as the final document; only the presentation changes significantly. As often as not, the first draft of a document is as valuable to a competitor as the thirty-fifth draft.

Working Papers   Much of the information contained in formal documents and their earlier drafts can be found in the working papers that are part of your day-to-day business routine. Project teams produce action lists, status reports, research summaries, business correspondence, and product specifications. Although the distribution of these documents is generally limited, they aren't usually thought of as sensitive, even though they can contain critical information about specific aspects of a project or organization. These working papers often are not controlled in the same way as formal documents, and people frequently lose track of them.

Scrap Paper   In the process of performing work, people inevitably record thoughts and notes on hundreds of bits of paper. We scribble—on note cards, appointment calendars, and cocktail napkins—anything from a grocery list to the invasion route for a military campaign. If the working papers are neglected, these bits of scrap paper are usually ignored. We don't give a second thought to that Post-it with our computer access code or the telephone message slip with the project supervisor's e-mail address. Yet, once again, these seemingly unimportant carriers of information can contain the same sensitive data as the formal documents that we tend to protect.

Other pieces of paper with potentially unnoticed valuable information include travel tickets, credit card receipts, invoices, and shipment manifests. They may not give a competitor the big picture, but they can help to fill in the pieces. They can give a spy a sense of where to direct his or her attack efforts. A purloined appointment calendar can show me that an important executive meets frequently with an individual from another company, which could indicate a possible merger or joint venture in the offing. That's extremely valuable information. With enough scraps like this, I can put together all I need to know to cause a lot of damage.

Internal Correspondence Internal company correspondence contains an incredible amount of information. Companies produce their own newsletters, policy documents, and meeting minutes, for example, which are filled with project data, details about people, company status updates, and a variety of other information. Often, the people producing these documents have no idea they are generating sources of sensitive information. They don't anticipate the numbers of people who will eventually see the documents.

Unfortunately, I was personally involved in an incident involving an internal memo containing too much information. My work involves identifying vulnerabilities in many publicly known companies, so I use code names for my clients in most of my documentation. Only those people who need to know the client's real name actually know it. This is, or at least should be, a common practice in my business. But in a firm I used to work for, a purchasing officer put out a memo that put a code name together with the client's name. Although I was able to recover all copies of the memo, the information leak could have been disastrous. Chapter 7 presents a case study in which a company newsletter provided an industrial spy with a shopping list of the top technologies being pursued by the target company.

Legal and Regulatory Filings Government agencies and regulations require organizations to publish a variety of information. Companies produce annual reports, patent applications, FDA filings, and a wide range of other documents that are required by law. The content of these filings and releases is usually specified by the relevant government agencies, both foreign and domestic. However, many companies go beyond the scope of these requirements, releasing much more information than necessary.

This situation has spawned the growth of a new industry made up of legitimate businesses that provide a specialized checking service. For a fee, these services simply check new government filings on a daily basis, searching for useful information and passing it along to their sponsors. Of course, industrial spies check these records, too, if they don't use one of the commercial services themselves.

Other Records   Almost every action leaves a record somewhere, especially in the business world. When you travel, you generate records at hotels, airlines, and car rental companies. When you take out a library book, your selection and its due date appear in the library computer. When you place a telephone call or when you receive one, the action is recorded. When someone pages you, when you log on and off a computer system, and when you browse an Internet Web page or look at Internet newsgroup messages, all of it—*all* of it—is recorded. Depending on the security capability of the computer system on which you work, each and every one of your actions may be recorded.

These types of records have been used to convict people of crimes, to provide leads to corporate secrets, and to compromise the most sensitive operations. In many cases, accessing these types of records is completely legal.

The Press and Other Open Source Information   Industrial spies don't always have to engage in illegal activity to begin to compromise a company's information. The data they need to get started can often be found in newspapers and trade magazines. Also, many publicly available databases have a tremendous amount of information, most of which is available to anyone with Internet or library access. Anything that is publicly available is typically referred to as *open source* *information* by the intelligence community. These resources search for or contain important industry news. They report who wins major contracts, which executives are moving to which projects, and a wealth of information that is quite useful in the initial stages of an attack. Every little piece of information helps give a spy a bigger picture. In some cases, spies are able to secure everything they need from open sources without ever having to resort to aggressive activities.

Corporate public relations and marketing departments play a key role in the dissemination of this kind of information. They quite naturally want to give out as much news as possible about their companies to help increase sales and profitability. That's their job. Unfortunately, they tend to go overboard, putting out too much information that makes its way into a variety of public and private databases, which are widely available to anyone with a computer account. Databases such as EDGAR contain complete Securities and Exchange Commission (SEC) filings. There are special-interest Internet newsgroups, where people interested in specific companies or market sectors can post anything that they come across dealing with their "interests."

Formal Meetings   Most organizations hold some kind of formal meeting in which its members discuss a variety of corporate and project issues. The information discussed at these meetings is frequently very sensitive, whether the participants are senior officers or line supervisors. Typically, someone prepares a meeting agenda and materials. Someone else prepares the minutes of the meeting, which summarize everything that went on during the meeting. All of these materials contain information of great value to corporate spies. This does not even address what could happen if the meeting room is actually bugged.

Informal Meetings   Any time employees get together and talk about work, either in person or over the telephone, that gathering could be considered a meeting. The sensitivity of the information discussed at these informal meetings varies greatly. Telephone conversations in particular contain a great deal of very sensitive information. There's something about the device that causes people to relax and let their guards down. Many industrial spies make it a point to tap telephone conversations so they can pick up useful bits of conversation.

Casual Conversations   Perhaps the most overlooked source of valuable information is the casual conversations that take place both inside and outside the office every day. People can't help talking about their work. Sometimes they're just getting together with coworkers for a few beers, and work is the natural topic of conversation; sometimes they're trying to impress others by talking about sensitive company matters.

The smoking areas outside major office buildings are great places to pick up information through casual conversations. I've heard of spies taking up smoking specifically to exploit this vulnerability.

While consulting for a major New York investment bank, I took their employee shuttle from the Financial Center to an uptown office. I couldn't help overhearing two employees sitting nearby discussing a major merger between two large firms that was in the works. If anyone else overheard them and used that information, the bank could have been accused of insider trading.

A secretary I know was having dinner with her husband after work in a restaurant, where she overheard a couple of sales executives from her company talking at the next table. She heard them laying out the details of the sales plan for a new product. This was very sensitive information that was overheard by possibly forty people.

In an incident of foreign espionage, a South Korean businessman set up a social club, to which he invited some of the most powerful people in Washington, D.C., to join. Of course, he had the club building thoroughly bugged. The conversations he taped were considered to be some of the most valuable intelligence South Korea ever collected.

These kinds of incidents go on all the time, and good, patient spies know how to exploit them over time. Over the long term, they can get everything they need just by being good listeners.

CONCLUSION

The form your information takes is utterly irrelevant to the people who want to compromise it. It is the content of the information that their customers, bosses, or spy masters want. Industrial spies don't want your computers; they want the information you keep on them. They're perfectly happy to get information from the easiest and most overlooked sources—including the trash or a vulnerable telephone. As a matter of fact, these sources are even preferable, because they involve less risk to the operative. A good spy always looks for the path of least resistance before trying anything fancy or high tech.

Risk

THE CORE OF ESPIONAGE

SPIONAGE IS THE PROCESS OF COMPROMISING VULNERA-
bilities and avoiding countermeasures in the pursuit of
valuable information. It's about determining needs and satisfying them. Another word for this process is *intelligence.*
When a company is the target of intelligence activities, the
process is called *industrial espionage.* The chances that an
intelligence operation will breach your company's security and
compromise something valuable is called *risk.*

Risk is the driving consideration of all corporate espionage
activities. The strategic decisions of those who would attack
your organization are driven by it; the types of counterintelligence measures, or security countermeasures, you put into
place depend upon it. You can't take appropriate steps to protect your information without first understanding the concept
of risk.

THE RISK EQUATION

In emotional terms, most people think of risk as their chance
of experiencing pain. They manage their risk by balancing

their chances for pain against their chances for pleasure. Unfortunately, many organizations base their corporate risk management decisions on emotion rather than on sound research. "It won't happen to me," or "I have nothing that anyone would want," are all-too-common beliefs floating around the business world with no solid foundation. This head-in-the-sand attitude increases the risk to companies of all sizes, leaving them vulnerable to major losses.

You also don't want to overreact. You should take steps, but you don't want to spend your money on trendy countermeasures that don't fit your organization and deplete your resources without minimizing your risk. Nor do you want to spend more protecting information than the information is actually worth.

Fortunately, there is a scientific way to define your organization's specific level of risk. This formula, called the Risk Equation, has been used by statisticians to establish insurance-related risks for decades. The Risk Equation (shown in Figure 2.1) includes four essential components: value, threat, vulnerability, and the countermeasures in place in your organization. Each of these components will be discussed further in subsequent chapters.

Value refers to the worth of your information, both monetary and otherwise. The value of your information must temper the funding and allocation of your espionage countermeasures. You don't want to spend more protecting your information than it would cost you to lose it. For example, you would not

Figure 2.1 *The Risk Equation*

$$RISK = \frac{Threat \times Vulnerability}{Countermeasures} \times Value$$

normally pay $3,000 to install a car alarm on a $2,000 vehicle. However, multibillion-dollar corporations cannot protect billions of dollars' worth of information with less than a million-dollar security budget, although many firms all too often have tried. (See Chapter 3.)

Threat, simply put, refers to the people and organizations out to get your information. A threat can be intentional or inadvertent, man-made or naturally occurring. While companies do not want to acknowledge or realize it, there is always a threat to the company in one form or another. It's always there. (See Chapter 4.)

Vulnerability refers to your organization's weaknesses or what allows a threat to exploit you. If you have no vulnerabilities, a threat cannot exploit you, so you have no risk. Computers connected to the Internet, unlocked offices, employee ignorance, spotty security procedures—all these constitute vulnerabilities. Vulnerabilities can never be wholly removed from an organization, but they can be managed with countermeasures. (See Chapter 5.)

Countermeasures are the steps, procedures, devices, etc., that you have in place to address your specific vulnerabilities. If your organization establishes a set of countermeasures that fail to address your vulnerabilities, you're just wasting your money. An awareness program that leaves out certain weaknesses in your organization does nothing at all to plug those holes. (See Chapter 14 for an extensive list of countermeasures.)

All these components affect one another. It is their interaction, so to speak, that determines your risk level. If, for example, you accidentally leave a piece of paper in the public library, the information on that piece of paper is highly *vulnerable*. You have to assume that your competitors are interested in everything about your company, so there is a *threat* that someone wants to find that paper and use it against you. If, however, that paper contains only widely available information—say, the address of your company headquarters—it wouldn't have much *value* to a competitor. Consequently, you have *zero risk* to yourself or your business from this piece of paper. Paying a security guard to protect that scrap of paper would not be an appropriate *countermeasure.*

Only when you understand the real components of risk can you put together an effective and appropriate strategy for protecting your organization and managing your risk. By minimizing your vulnerabilities and optimizing—not maximizing—your counterespionage efforts, you can greatly improve your security.

One of the purposes of this book is to provide a proven framework that allows you to develop effective plans to secure your information. Mathematical models of information security–related risk can be very useful to a wide range of organizations. Big companies are familiar with creating such models for nearly every business decision, but the process might be new to smaller operations.

Smaller organizations and individuals can step through the process intuitively, without assigning numerical values. Let's say your company is a small manufacturing firm that has developed a new process for producing a special gear much cheaper than your competitors. This gear can greatly increase your sales and profits, and it could do the same thing for your competitors if they only knew how to make it. Let's also say that there are many companies out there that produce this particular part, many of them foreign. Clearly, you have a threat to your organization that could be called medium to high.

Also, you have identified a few weaknesses in your operation but not a huge number of them, so your vulnerability is medium. You have high value, medium to high threat, medium vulnerability, and you have no countermeasures to speak of. Your risk would be medium to high, and you should increase your countermeasures as appropriate.

Industrial spies—one of your threats—also use a version of the Risk Equation. The risks involved in any one information collection action influence the choice of collection methods. The collection of highly vulnerable information usually involves little risk. The collection of very valuable information, even though it is protected by extreme countermeasures, may warrant a high level of risk. At one extreme, spies may choose to kidnap an executive to secure extremely valuable and inaccessible information as ransom. Most targets, however, do not warrant such a risky operation or such an enormous expenditure of resources. Spies also weigh the costs of detection against the possible benefits of securing the information. Unfortunately, most spies face little in the way of effective countermeasures, so *their* risk is often quite low.

Notice that what I'm talking about in this chapter is *risk management*. Companies functioning in the real world will never be totally risk-free. Every enterprise must exchange information with employees, suppliers, support organizations, the government, and customers almost on a daily basis. You can't do business in a vacuum. Fortunately, you don't have to seal your company into a bubble to keep your information safe. Many highly effective countermeasures are simple, inexpensive, and not particularly disruptive of your day-to-day operations. People are surprised when they learn that the simplest countermeasures often provide the greatest protection.

THE INTELLIGENCE PROCESS

As a trained intelligence analyst, information security expert, and penetration testing specialist, I've compromised organizations, helped secure them, and investigated their multimillion-dollar crimes. I'm convinced that a basic understanding of the intelligence process—that is, the gathering of information about organizations and individuals—is essential to the effective implementation of productive countermeasures. You've just got to stop and think like the bad guys sometimes if you want to foil their plans. The following material may seem a bit like a spy's how-to handbook, but it will help to equip you to better evaluate your own corporate vulnerabilities and choose the best countermeasures for your organization. These concepts are basic, but they are critical to understanding how spies collect information.

Intelligence, like risk, is a science. Each phase of the intelligence process targets different aspects of an organization's risk. In intelligence collection, planning and preparation distinguish the amateur from the professional; unfortunately for corporations, even a little planning allows the most inept, would-be spies to be successful.

The intelligence process isn't strictly a codified procedure, and it's hardly endemic to the intelligence community. Street criminals demonstrate their own version of the intelligence process every day. When a crack addict needs drugs, for example, he calculates the amount of money he needs to make a buy, makes the decision to acquire the necessary funds through robbery, performs reconnaissance of possible victims, chooses one that appears to be the most vulnerable (the one presenting the least risk), commits the robbery when the right opportunity presents itself, and makes off with everything of possible value. After his escape with the goods, he evaluates the approximate value of everything taken and determines whether it will, in fact, pay for the drugs he needs. If he finds his take to be insufficient, he determines how much more he needs, and the process begins again.

The intelligence process is typically divided into four phases: Definition of Requirements, Collection, Analysis, and Evaluation. This group of activities is circular in nature (see Figure 2.2): evaluation of collected intelligence begets new requirements, and each phase of the process requires that the previous phase be well executed. When intelligence gatherers begin with the collection phase without first developing detailed requirements, their actions tend to be unfocused,

Figure 2.2   *The Intelligence Process*

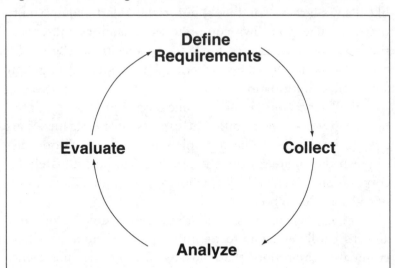

which makes them much more vulnerable to detection. The would-be spies end up grabbing everything they come across, but they often never find any truly valuable information.

The next four sections discuss each phase of the intelligence process in greater detail.

Defining Requirements

Clearly defined requirements provide the foundation for any good espionage operation. Simply put, spies do a better job of finding information if they know exactly what they're supposed to be looking for. The more specific and refined the requirements, the better the results of the effort.

Well-defined requirements are not easy to develop. For example, a foreign intelligence agency might decide it "wants" a foreign missile system in development at an American company. In reality, the agency wants to know about the system's performance capabilities and underlying technology, so it can defend against the missile or improve its own missiles. This is a critical difference. It is almost impossible to get hold of a prototype of a new weapon, yet there are hundreds of other sources for the other information.

Defining requirements is just as tricky in corporate espionage situations. For example, the automotive industry is extremely competitive, and each manufacturer wants to know exactly what the other is up to. Obviously, it would be best for a company if it could get its hands on a competitor's actual car; however, that is not realistic. Accordingly, automobile manufacturers take great pains to hide the details of their new car models in the months before their release; they camouflage the cars, test them only at night, and so on. Their competitors (and car magazine writers) go to equally great lengths to unmask the latest model: they pay people to surreptitiously photograph the cars, they rent airplanes to observe and photograph the cars from the air, and they even infiltrate the testing grounds and plant cameras.

First and foremost, intelligence requirements must be realistic, taking into account the available data, resources, and potential risk. If they could, most corporations would want to know everything about their customers, competitors, and suppliers. Knowing what the government is up to at any given moment could also be quite useful to most American businesses, because they want to know about any pending legislation or regulations that could drastically affect their company. Available resources, however, rarely allow for such omnipotence. With this in mind, companies tend to focus their espionage efforts rather narrowly, very often on specific concerns of their customers—anything that could affect market share and customer satisfaction.

In some cases, initial intelligence requirements can be very broad. "Tell me what I don't know" seems to be almost too vague an objective, but it's often the basis for spirited espionage activity. Usually, fewer resources (people, money, time, etc.) are involved in this kind of information collection activity, and very low-risk tactics are employed. After these fishing expeditions, the organizations in question can develop more targeted requirements.

Requirements drive the tactics and the level of risk that collection efforts assume. In the above case of a vague requirement, intelligence organizations tend to stick to reviewing information that they already have and searching publicly available databases. They search business journals, newspapers, and magazine indexes for useful information. These are extremely low-risk activities in that they require no intrusions into an organization or face-to-face contact. As a matter of fact, most companies and all intelligence agencies engage in this kind of straightforward intelligence gathering on a regular basis.

The quality of information gathered in this way varies, but it can be outstanding. An interview with, say, the target's chief financial officer (CFO) offers even greater potential. The interview could provide better information in a much shorter time period, but the risk is also much higher. Obviously, a face-to-face interview with the CFO potentially exposes the whole operation, while a public data search is almost undetectable.

Requirements define the kind of information that has value to the organization launching the intelligence operation. The information might not even be considered valuable by the company that possesses it. A restaurant's reservation list is practically worthless—unless a terrorist organization wants to assassinate someone dining in your bistro. In such a situation, knowing the target has reservations at the restaurant at a specific time provides the terrorists with crucial information. Likewise, an old expense report can give one of your competitors an indication about a potential marketing lead.

Collection

When most people hear the word "intelligence," they automatically associate it with collection. To many, espionage is the collection process. However, collection is just one (albeit the flashiest) phase of espionage.

To satisfy the requirements, information must be collected. To experienced spies, the information collection process is highly intuitive. Once they understand the requirements of the assignment, they usually know where and how to obtain it. For example, if I want to learn about someone's personal habits, I would look at credit reports and credit card statements, follow the person for a period of time, and talk to the person's friends and coworkers. I might even talk to the person directly. If one of the requirements of the project is keep the effort a secret (not always necessary), I know to avoid people. These activities are second nature to me and to many others.

Sometimes the information is already available. If I want to locate someone, for instance, the person's address might be available through a variety of computer resources, such as the Internet. There's no need for a lot of legwork nowadays—no trips to the courthouses or exhaustive interviews of friends and family. Hundreds of databases in cyberspace provide open source information. Some organizations, such as large companies and foreign intelligence agencies, have their own massive databases, which are stuffed with information about people and companies.

While it may sound more like an art, collection is a science. People have predictable vulnerabilities, and what makes collection an intuitive process is that spies understand this. They are trained to understand this. While some people are obviously better than others, you can train people to be collectors.

An effective intelligence collector finds the location of the information in question before beginning any other tasks.

Sometimes the location is obvious; sometimes it is not. If a specific source of information is unknown to the collector, he or she targets potential sources. Only when the true source is identified does the real collection effort begin.

Spies use a set of well-established collection methods. Some of those methods are scientifically complex, but the vulnerabilities they exploit are the same basic exposures that petty criminals take advantage of. Experienced spies not only predict vulnerabilities, they plan for likely countermeasures. Unfortunately, they often have a better idea of the actual value of the information they're seeking than their targets, who typically take the information for granted, leaving it unduly exposed. Frequently, there's simply no reason to resort to expensive or complicated acquisition methods; the targets make it so easy.

In some cases, surreptitious information collection is an ongoing process. Pierre Marion, the former head of the DGSE (the French intelligence agency), for example, has acknowledged placing people inside numerous American high-technology firms. The DGSE believes that by establishing an agent as a long-standing employee within a targeted company, it creates a breach that pours data for years. While this far-sighted approach yields varying degrees of success, the rewards are usually tremendous.

Long-term collection efforts are rare outside of national intelligence organizations, large corporations, and organized crime. These groups have the money required to place and fund people for long periods of time. They also have the resources required to identify possible agents—people inside the target company who are likely to volunteer information.

Well-funded organizations can afford what you might call espionage luxuries, such as paying insiders, establishing and monitoring long-term telephone and wire taps, and securing the cooperation of regular informants. Large companies are also able to better distance themselves from espionage activities. They can monitor the competition by paying people to pay people to pay people to get information. Organized crime is adept at this kind of layered espionage activity.

Disinformation   Disinformation is a common practice among smart organizations. These groups try to mislead would-be spies by providing them with false data that not only is worthless but is sometimes used to unmask the thief. One of the most common examples of this kind of disinformation may be found in your local telephone directory. Telephone companies place fake listings in their directories to catch rival publishers violating their copyrights. Whenever one of the fake listings in the "official" telephone directory turns up in another directory, the company has clear evidence of an illegal copy.

Disinformation can also damage the recipient of the collected information. The so-called Star Wars defense program of the 1980s is an excellent example of this side effect. During that time, all indications were that the U.S. was putting together a system that shielded it from all incoming missiles. Government officials talked to the press about it, and it is likely that known Soviet spies were fed information that indicated the U.S. had the required technology to accomplish such a plan. Feeling it had to respond, the Soviet Union nearly spent itself into bankruptcy trying to account for the Star Wars program. As you know, the program never materialized to any significant degree. How many companies have done the same to their competitors?

One famous security countermeasure, known as the "honeypot," involves placing made-up information that looks very valuable into an otherwise unused area of a computer. The information is sometimes not only incorrect but damaging to competitors. Since no valid users belong in these honeypots, any intrusions sound an alarm.

Unfortunately, experienced spies know when they are being misled. It's a little like panning for gold: the trick is to spot the precious metals amid the feldspar.

Analysis

Once the information has been collected and delivered to the sponsoring organization, the analysis phase begins. At this stage of the process, analysts pore over documents and comb through reams of data, sorting out the pieces into useful reports. This can involve translating information from foreign languages or computer formats. When the requirements are clearly focused, this process is very straightforward.

Intelligence analysis falls into two major categories: standard intelligence analysis and traffic analysis. Standard analysis involves the examination of the actual content of the collected data to determine its potential value.

Traffic analysis is the process of examining data flow. Information flows through a variety of media, including telephone systems, computer networks, and the mail. If I watch someone's mail over time, just reading the envelopes, I can learn an incredible amount about that person. Return addresses on letters can reveal employers and religious affiliations. Magazine subscriptions indicate personal interests. A credit card bill can reveal something about a person's income status. Children's magazines indicate the approximate age and number of children in the household. Letters from colleges give an educational history.

Even airline reservations provide valuable information. From a corporate perspective, knowing which companies visit which research facilities can tell me which companies want to commercialize the latest research. Following travel trends can point out likely licensees. Trips by a researcher to other companies can reveal an unhappy employee who is trying to find a new job—a potential spy.

The more effort an intelligence organization puts into collecting data, the more effort it has to put into the analysis of that data. Spies involved in long-term efforts constantly feed information back to their primary organizations. Much of that information is nearly worthless, but valuable bits hide within. It takes experienced analysts to know what information is valuable and where to find it within the flood of the collected materials. The extra analysis does sometimes pay off. While searching for one chemical formula, for example, espionage analysts might stumble onto even more valuable specifications.

The final products of analysis are written reports that organize the information into a useful form. Writers of these reports tailor them to the needs of their recipients.

The driving concept for the analysis effort is value. Analysts must know what is valuable to the people they report to, and more important, what could be valuable to them. Good analysts always look beyond the scope of the current collection effort and strive to get the most value from whatever is collected.

Evaluation

After analysis comes the evaluation phase. Although it sounds a lot like analysis, the evaluation phase is quite distinct. Evaluation refers strictly to the process of determining how well the information collected meets the particular requirements of the espionage effort. If the information satisfies all requirements, then all collection efforts may stop—the spies got what they were after. If the evaluation is part of a long-term collection project, then requirements are adjusted as they are satisfied and new information is evaluated.

A good evaluation also notes when the collected information uncovers other potentially valuable targets. After providing their customers with their desired secrets, good industrial spies market this extra booty to new customers. They also use the additional information to entice their current clients to do more business with them.

Evaluation also serves another purpose: it is the reality check for ongoing espionage activities. Only through careful evaluation can ineffective collection efforts be stopped. On the other hand, highly successful activities receive increased resources at this phase and may go on forever.

Sometimes people tamper with the evaluation process because of personal biases. Spies have pet projects, and they hesitate to reduce their resources in the face of a negative evaluation. Others might hate a particular project and search for any excuse to kill it. Fortunately for potential victims, tainted evaluations occur frequently, causing fruitful espionage efforts to be canceled and bad ones to continue, draining valuable resources.

Again, evaluation is a determination of value. The evaluation process focuses on whether the requested value has been attained as well as whether something else of value has been discovered. Value puts the whole process in motion and can stop it in its tracks.

CONCLUSION

Without perceived value of information, there is no threat. Why would people come after you if you do not offer them anything? People do not define requirements and fund collection efforts if there are no rewards. Without thoughts of value, there is no basis for analysis and evaluation. Obviously, different people have different perceptions of what is valuable. To foreign intelligence services, almost everything has value. Industrial competitors, on the other hand, only care about their business' standing and their competitors. As Chapter 4 discusses, different threats have different motivations and define different requirements. This causes varying levels of damage to a corporation.

Normally, intelligence agencies want to know only about capabilities of products. Competitors, on the other hand, want to dominate a target. Despite the fact that intelligence agencies can do more harm, they do not cause nearly as much damage to the target.

Collection, the active phase of espionage, relies upon compromising vulnerabilities and avoiding countermeasures. Each phase of the intelligence process is a different aspect of risk. With a clear understanding of risk, you can understand the real threat of industrial espionage.

Value

ETERMINING THE VALUE OF THE INFORMATION IN YOUR organization is an essential first step toward the development of an effective security plan. If your information isn't worth anything—either monetarily or otherwise—then it won't matter how vulnerable you are to attack. No one normally spends time and resources collecting worthless data. Espionage professionals do not define requirements and fund collection efforts if there are no potential rewards for their efforts. Without perceived value, there is no basis for analysis and evaluation. You could have an open warehouse full of unlocked filing cabinets stuffed with documents or post your information to your Web site with a thousand links to it and still face no significant risk if the content of those documents has no value.

Of course, the chances that your information has *no* value to *anyone* are slight. If you have competitors who want to know what you're up to (and what business in America doesn't), then at least some level of risk exists. Often, smaller enterprises face the most risk, because their information is valuable to so many competitors. Southwest Airlines certainly must protect itself against a few serious competitors, but a local pizzeria has to protect its secret sauce recipe from thousands of pizza parlors and would-be restaurateurs.

Individuals and organizations have different ideas about what is valuable. Foreign intelligence services have greatly varying requirements, and almost everything has value to them. Industrial competitors care only about their business' standing and what their competitors intend to do. This would include competitors' manufacturing and strategic plans, production capabilities, and so on.

As I suggest in Chapter 2, the value of your information must temper the funding and allocation of your espionage countermeasures. You don't want to spend more protecting your information than it would cost you to lose it. But in your calculations, you will want to consider more than just the monetary value of the information you seek to protect. Every business must consider three types of value: monetary, hidden, and adversary/competitor.

MONETARY VALUE

When we talk about monetary value, we usually apply the concept primarily to physical assets. Every physical asset has a market value that can be calculated readily in dollars and cents, usually in terms of replacement costs. Cars have resale value. Art has an estimated market value. Houses have an appraised value. Insurance companies thrive on pinpointing these kinds of values and limiting claims to the penny. However, the monetary value to your organization of your physical assets is much greater that the mere costs of replacing them. Unfortunately, this value is often much less obvious and is often quite difficult to calculate accurately. The numbers don't always present themselves right away.

When an airline lost my luggage on a flight from Baltimore to Phoenix, for example, the loss cost me more than the price of my suitcase and its contents. There was the cost of telephone calls to the airline to check on the search for my bags, the gasoline to drive to the luggage shop to buy a new suitcase, clothes, and so on, the cost of notarizing the forms to send to the airline to validate my loss claims, and the time it took to do it all. All in all, I spent around $1,000 in additional expenses.

When a bomb was set off at the World Trade Center in 1993, anyone watching the evening news could see that several million dollars in physical damages had resulted from the explosion. But the businesses located in that devastated building lost more than their physical assets. They experienced devastating losses of business, relocation expenses, and computer and other equipment rental expenses.

HIDDEN VALUE

Information is not a physical asset, which makes the calculation of its monetary value rather difficult. Is its worth found in the time it took to create it? Or is it as valuable as the price someone will pay for it? People who compile and sell mailing lists to direct marketers know the value of the names on those lists. It might have cost hundreds of thousands of dollars to compile them, but after the lists are created, they are worth millions to a competitor in ongoing sales. The value of the laptop on which the list is stored is nothing in comparison.

Many companies carefully calculate the monetary value of their assets without considering their hidden value. You might have a floppy disk on your desk that would cost you about a dollar to replace. If, however, that disk contains your company's business plan or the essentials of a key process, how much would it be worth to you then? It might even contain a less-sensitive file that took hundreds of hours to create. What would it cost you to re-create that file? Often, work like this is irreplaceable—which means that one-dollar disk is *invaluable*.

In most cases, *confidentiality* is not considered to be a major value issue. Yet what about information that could hurt you should it fall into the wrong hands? What happens when private information is compromised? When large companies sue each other, they often try to keep the specifics of the suit secret, because such details could hurt them. The alleged revelation that tobacco companies have actively sought to hide health-related information about their products has been very damaging to that industry on a number of levels.

Public or customer *confidentiality* is of inestimable value to your organization. Distrust of Internet confidentiality is stalling the development of Internet commerce. People don't believe that their credit card numbers and other private information will be safe in cyberspace (never mind that it is probably safer to give out your credit card number on-line than on a cordless telephone). Distrustful consumers are costing on-line merchants billions.

The *integrity* of your information is another hidden value. Whether the data in question has been purposely modified, inadvertently corrupted, or is just plain wrong, the loss of information integrity can cause irreparable damage in many industries. I recently stopped in at a small bicycle shop to look for a certain type of bicycle helmet. The clerk checked the store's computer system and informed me that there were none in stock. As I headed for the door, I spotted the helmet I was looking for on a shelf. I told the clerk, who apologized and sold me the helmet. I had almost left and spent my money elsewhere. How many other companies have lost business because their computers didn't accurately reflect the state of their inventories? How many companies have promised to deliver products they didn't have?

The Toys "Я" Us chain relies on its ability to track precisely the items that are and are not in its stores. This is especially true during the period between Thanksgiving and Christmas, when the company sells the entire contents of each store five times over. The company utilizes a computerized point-of-sale system to manage its inventory. If that system shows that more products have been sold than were actually moved out of a particular store, then the shelves and stockrooms in that store quickly become overstocked; if the system shows that fewer products have been sold than in actuality, then the shelves quickly become bare and sales are lost. Millions of dollars per month in revenues depend on the integrity of the Toys "Я" Us inventory system.

Banks rely on the ability of their computer systems to accurately transfer trillions of dollars a year. More important, the public trusts these systems not to lose any of its money. If that trust were ever lost, the banking industry would collapse, and the banks know it.

The *availability* of information is another aspect of value. No matter how sensitive, how reliable, or how safe a particular piece of information is, if you can't get to it, then it's not only worthless to you but could actually cause devastating results. What would happen to a mail-order business if its telephones were to suddenly stop working? What would happen to a manufacturer if its blueprints and schematics were lost? What would happen in a war if missile targeting information were rendered unavailable?

The SABRE system drives most of the major airline support systems. If the information provided by the SABRE system were suddenly unavailable, we wouldn't be able to make flight reservations or pick up a boarding pass. All planes would be grounded, and the airlines and everyone who depended on them would lose millions. If the Toys "Я" Us computer system went down at the wrong time, it would cost the company millions. The shutdown of a robotics system at an automobile factory, even for a short time, would be financially devastating.

The hidden costs of a loss are often the most damaging to an organization. Although your competitors are probably not concerned about the hidden value of the information you're protecting, disgruntled employees often are. They know where and how to hurt you the most. To others who would also seek to hurt you, this is important information.

Information Resource Management

Only about a decade ago, the value of an information systems (IS) department in a large company was determined by the estimated monetary value of its computers, peripherals, software, and the salaries of personnel. Typically, IS was considered to be a physical resource that should be managed like every other physical resource. Accordingly, the IS departments were subordinated to the CFOs.

During the late 1980s, businesses began to understand that the value of the information and the services provided by the computers was greater than the computers themselves. This was especially true in the banking community. The field of information resource management (IRM) swept the business community.

Most large companies now employ chief information officers (CIOs), who are given strategic responsibility for information resources. A CIO often enjoys status equal to the CFO and sits in on all executive meetings. Companies with CIOs on staff understand that computers represent much more than the monetary value of the hardware and software. They've come to recognize the tremendous amount of hidden value that must be protected with adequate funding for appropriate countermeasures.

ADVERSARY/COMPETITOR VALUE

Information that might seem totally worthless to your organization can be extremely valuable to a competitor. Broken products tossed out in the dumpster can give a reasonably resourceful competitor an opportunity to reverse-engineer the product (see Chapter 8), cutting into your market share and profitability. If the competitor is very resourceful, you might find yourself out of business.

Sometimes the value is irrelevant to your organization but affects the situation around you. When I throw away food and a vagrant picks it out of the trash, I am not affected in any way; I have lost nothing. Some restaurateurs, however, might argue that every meal a vagrant pulls out of a dumpster is one more meal they don't sell, or they might say that the presence of the vagrant scares off customers—both could result in lost revenues for the restaurant in question.

Workers inside a company often deal with sensitive information they don't think of as valuable. Items such as price and customer lists fall into this category. All too often, familiarity breeds indifference, and these critical lists become nothing more than another piece of paper. If people lose that paper, they just print up another copy. This casual attitude toward valuable data is commonplace in most businesses, and it inevitably costs companies millions, if not billions, of dollars every year.

Many companies counter this dangerous practice with data classification, in which they classify data by estimating how much damage would result if a competitor were to get a hold of it. The Defense Department has been doing this for years, classifying information as Confidential, Secret, or Top Secret, and criminally prosecuting people who do not treat information appropriately. In the nondefense sector, you can't hold the same threat of criminal prosecution over your people for not treating your information appropriately, but you can impress on them the importance of respecting your classification by firing anyone who doesn't.

VALUE AS A TOOL OF RISK ANALYSIS

The value of your information is one of the tools you can use to determine how much you should spend on security countermeasures in your organization. You'll want to look at the costs to your company of short-term, long-term, and permanent losses of sensitive data. What you're after is a reasonable balance of reasonable countermeasures and potential losses.

Start by putting together a list of the information you have; you must first know what you have before you can decide what it's worth. You'll also want to compile a list of the people who use this information or are affected by it. How many salespeople rely on it? Are there third parties who depend on it? Will the loss of this information create a ripple that causes a loss to another company that can sue you? Will the loss of this information cost you the trust of your customers and, ultimately, their business? Will your losses be noticed by Wall Street, causing a drop in the value of your company?

Next, you'll want to answer two important questions: Which piece or pieces of information at your company might have the greatest value to a potential threat? How much would you lose if an adversary were to compromise that information? In an ideal world, you would ask these questions about all the information at your company, but in most cases, that could be an overwhelming task. Some companies might reasonably base their answers on a worst-case scenario, in which a competitor could put you out of business with the right data.

Obviously, the smaller the business, the easier it is to answer these questions. But remember: the harder the question is to answer, the more important it becomes.

Take care to consider your answers carefully, taking into account monetary, hidden, and adversary/competitor values.

Many people contend that the entire value of your company is at stake no matter what information is threatened. In reality, the losses are usually not that dramatic. For example, in a recent controversy, a descendant of the inventor of Coca Cola is rumored to be considering selling his family's secret formula. Although the Coca Cola Company has relied for decades on this secret formula to make its featured product, the company will not crumble if the recipe gets out. Coca Cola has name recognition, promotional resources, and other products. The company may lose some market share, which could amount to millions of dollars, but it will survive.

All companies, no matter what their size, have competitors who want their information. By determining which information they want the most, you help to define the threats your organization faces. Value is the reason those threats exist.

CONCLUSION

Foreign companies accept industrial espionage as a fact of life and deal with it as a regular part of their business activities. Unfortunately, most U.S. businesses fail to realize the value of their information to others. If an American company is small or not in the defense industry, its managers often reject any notion that someone would attempt to penetrate their organizations. All too often, U.S. companies fail to consider the full value of their information and consequently fail to protect themselves from serious losses. They increase their vulnerability through inaccurate application of inadequate countermeasures. In this Information Age, at a time in which the value of the data often surpasses the value of the computers in which it is stored, companies must think strategically and from an adversary's perspective.

4

Threat

IN RESEARCHING THIS BOOK, I SPOKE TO BOTH SCOTT Charney, chief of the Department of Justice Computer Crime and Intellectual Property Section, and Robert Gates, former director of Central Intelligence and the Central Intelligence Agency. They both concurred that one of the biggest problems companies face in their efforts to secure their sensitive information is their lack of awareness of the threats around them.

Accurate assessment of the level of threat against your organization is critical to the success of your counterespionage and security plan. You must have a clear understanding of the different kinds of threats you face, their origins, their potential for damage, and the extremes to which they may go. Threat is an essential factor in your risk reduction formula, and you must consider it carefully. If you don't, you'll simply be flying blind when it comes to prioritizing countermeasures and determining your information's real value.

A *threat* to your company or organization is a person, organization, event, or condition that could hurt you in some way. Industrial spies, for example, who want your information pose a threat. Whenever the information you possess has value to someone else, you have a threat on your hands. Let's say that you have the schematics for a new computer micro-processor locked in your desk drawer; I own a competing microchip manufacturing operation. Voila—I am a threat. I don't even have to contemplate launching an attack against you to be a danger to your organization. The fact that your information is valuable to me is inescapable. It simply is valu-able because we're in the same business, which may inspire the actions of others I don't even know. If I didn't exist, and you had no other competitors, there would be no reason for any-one to go after those schematics. They would have little value outside your organization, and your threat would be minimal.

In some cases, the threat you face may stem not from what you have but from who you are. The U.S. government has many enemies who don't care about its valuable assets per se; the adversaries' fundamental goal is to hurt the government or at least monitor what it is doing. Pharmaceutical operations frequently use animals to test their products, and groups such as People for the Ethical Treatment of Animals (PETA) mon-itor these companies constantly, trying to get their hands on information that will further their cause. Groups opposed to improving U.S. relations with Vietnam watch companies con-sidering doing business in that country.

Some threats are indirect. Your organization might possess information about another targeted group, which could make you a secondary target. In a recent case, a Nigerian credit card fraud ring launched an attack against the U.S. Social Security Administration (SSA) by co-opting insiders to look up infor-mation on the agency's computers. They weren't interested in the SSA itself; they wanted information about the people listed in the SSA computers. A crook might steal a woman's purse to get the keys to her office building, then use the access to attack a neighboring organization. Your suppliers might be attacked because of the records they keep about your operation.

What is important to consider is that the loss of informa-tion can be unrecoverable. The act of writing a book, document, or report requires someone to express original thought, which is never consistent from one moment to another. If you assume that the first time somebody puts information together they are not under as much stress as when they have to re-create the work, then you might assume that the quality of the new work suffers. In many cases, you won't have the opportunity to re-create the lost work at all. If somebody leaves the company or even dies, then that person's work is impossible to recover.

In the sections to follow, I discuss the major potential threats to your organization, both inside and outside, foreign and domestic. When assessing the level of threat in your company, you will need to consider each of these categories. Different types of employees—past, present, and future—can cause harm. As well, a threat may be posed by foreign entities, in the form of foreign competitors, foreign intelligence agencies, hostile and friendly nations, and third-world countries; this may include organized crime and terrorism. You might also face unintentional harm created by suppliers and customers. And you should be aware of hackers, who could invade your company electronically at any time. Before you get too excited about "evil" organizations and people out to get you, though, you should know that the biggest threats to your organization are plain and simple mistakes and acts of God.

POORLY TRAINED WORKERS AND ACCIDENTS

Everyone wants to hear about the hackers and the industrial spies, but the truth is that the biggest threat to U.S. corporations is human error, the most deadly source of which is the ranks of their own employees. This is the most basic kind of threat your organization is likely to face. People make mistakes, and those mistakes are the most likely things to hurt you.

The majority of the errors made by employees are the result of poor training, but some highly trained personnel also screw up from time to time. Highly trained workers have more privileges and responsibilities, so they can do more damage when they err. Computer files are accidentally deleted with frightening regularity in almost every organization. Most of these incidents are minor, since most users have access to a limited number of files; when a systems administrator hits the wrong button, however, he or she can delete every file on the computer system.

Every computer professional at some point in his or her career has accidentally caused a major outage. I personally watched a very skilled programmer, who was setting up a demonstration for one of the top people in his company, accidentally delete the entire database when he attempted to clean up the system to allow it to run faster. He erased all critical information on the system. These things happen.

Programming errors pose another potentially devastating threat. The errors occur in virtually all business sectors and cost companies billions of dollars a year. A one-line programming error almost resulted in the downfall of the Bank of New York. A single line of code out of hundreds of thousands of lines caused the bank's computer system to crash. At the end of the day, the bank had a $5 billion shortfall. They had to borrow the money from the Federal Reserve Board to cover the loss until the error was worked out. The computer was up and running the next morning, but the interest owed on the borrowed money was reportedly $23 million.

"To err is human," the modern saying goes, "but to really screw things up takes a computer." However, don't underestimate the power of noncomputer human errors. Little mistakes can add up to major problems. People make mistakes all the time. Papers are misplaced. Car keys are lost. Sensitive information slips out in casual conversation. In most cases, these small mistakes are inconsequential, but they can add up, and you should include them in your overall threat assessment.

ACTS OF GOD

Next to human errors, acts of God are responsible for the greatest financial losses to businesses in this country. Floods, earthquakes, lightning strikes, fires—all cause billions of dollars' worth of damage every year, including losses from damaged equipment, lost productivity, and lost and corrupted data.

The losses from natural disasters can mount very quickly in this Information Age, when we're all so dependent on electricity and major computer systems. In the summer of 1996, nine states in the western U.S. lost power when a fallen tree took down a power line. Poor contingency planning caused a chain reaction among power stations throughout the West as different power companies tried to cover the outage areas. The way in which the various power company computers interacted caused a series of unanticipated events that led to a major system crash.

Although not an act of God, poor facilities can also wreak unexpected havoc. Damaging power outages can result from bad wiring or from exceeding the power limitations on inadequate electrical systems. I once gave a computer hacking demonstration to a German news crew in a laboratory that was running over a dozen computers simultaneously. The camera man plugged his high-wattage power converter into a wall socket and overloaded the electrical system. The entire lab went dark. Critical systems on uninterruptible power supplies (UPS) continued to function, but several usually less-important systems that were not on a UPS crashed. Hours of work were lost, and hours were spent on repairs and recovery. The loss in manpower amounted to over $1,000 for this relatively small incident. These kinds of accidents occur daily throughout the country, and the cost adds up quickly.

Fires and floods can pose a significant threat, depending on the region or country in which your business is located. Flood damage can result from heavy rains and hurricanes and also from water pipe breaks, sewer backups, and sump pump malfunctions. In some regions, heavy rains can create damaging mudslides. When the loss of equipment from such natural disasters is combined with the loss of information and productivity, the total can easily reach billions of dollars.

The death of a key person can be more damaging than the destruction of a computer system. When an Air Florida flight crashed into the Potomac River outside of Washington, D.C., in 1983, Fairchild Industries lost several indispensable executives who were on the plane. The crash of the Air Force jet that killed U.S. Secretary of Commerce Ron Brown also killed the CEOs of several U.S. corporations. The effect on the companies was devastating.

Hours and even years of work are lost to acts of God every day. In most cases, these natural disasters are not utterly ruinous, but they are costly in almost every case. Consider carefully the geographic location and physical facility of your organization. Bad weather and bad wiring can represent a significant threat.

INSIDERS

Although acts of God and human errors cause much more damage than corporate spies ever will, attackers do cost U.S. firms a bundle—over $100 billion annually. You might not realize it, but the most deadly of these spies are company insiders, most often your own employees.

People with physical access to your company pose the greatest threat to your security. As Scott Charney told me: "Insiders do insider things." They have the time and the freedom to search people's desks, read private memos, copy documents, and abuse coworker friendships. They know things about your operation because they're on the inside. They typically stick to low-risk espionage activities, and if they're smart, careful, and patient, they're rarely caught.

Most important, these people know where and how to hurt you. They know your prized secrets, they know your competitors, and they usually know how to hide their actions. Insiders constitute a formidable threat that is much too common. What is perhaps most damaging about insider espionage is that it goes unnoticed. Your competitors are beating you to the punch, you're losing market share—and no one knows why.

Employees

Current and former employees can pose the most destructive threats you will ever face. One of the things that makes them so dangerous is that they're often very difficult to spot. Two documents were pointed out to me by an observant coworker when I was working at NSA that illustrate exactly how difficult detection can be. Both documents described a worker as follows:

- Shows an interest in what coworkers are doing
- Always volunteers for extra duties and assignments
- Works late hours
- Rarely takes vacations

One of the documents, written by the personnel office, was giving advice on how to get promoted at NSA; the other, written by the office of security, was listing the signs that a coworker might be a spy. In almost all cases, a spy appears to be one of your hardest workers.

Employees turn on their employers for many reasons. They do it for money, for love, to get even for perceived wrongs, and even because of political ideologies. They can be cool, sophisticated pros, like Bill Gaede (Chapter 8), or petty criminals, like the Maryland convenience store clerk who participated in his own kidnapping to facilitate a robbery of his store.

When greed is the motive, companies that perform large volumes of automated electronic funds transfers are frequent targets of employee theft. The general public would be surprised at the number of companies that perform these kinds of transactions. Retail store chains, direct marketers, large wholesalers, insurance companies, and investment firms, among others, regularly send millions of dollars through computers around the world. I personally know of two separate incidents, one at a bank and one at a direct marketing firm, in which employees created false electronic records that would have resulted in large amounts of money being sent to their personal accounts from corporate funds transfer systems. Diligent computer operators in both cases noticed the theft in progress and called in security. Unfortunately, most operators are not so diligent.

Throughout the country, there are hundreds of cases a year, which never make the headlines, involving insiders trying to steal money and information from their employers. The following sections describe the various types of employees who may be a threat to your organization.

Disgruntled Employees Many employees are of the opinion that they deserve more recognition and respect than their employers show them. The disgruntled employee is almost a cliché in this country, but a frustrated worker can pose a real threat to your organization. It's usually not about money for these folks—what they want is to feel important, and that makes them dangerous.

Disgruntled employees are easily manipulated by outsiders and are considered an important resource among professional spies. Such employees commit industrial espionage for the specific purpose of stroking their own egos. They seek approval and respect, and their handlers know how to give it to them. A good spy master will tell disgruntled workers that someone as important and smart as they are can get their hands on anything in the company. To prove their worth, they will often go to extreme lengths, compromising some of the company's most valuable information.

In many cases, employees with an ax to grind just want to hurt their employers. They're mad at the company for a variety of reasons: they're not getting paid enough, they find working conditions to be unsatisfactory, they don't get along with coworkers, or they don't like the boss. What they want is revenge. They plan out their attacks meticulously and focus on how best to hurt their employers. In some cases, their revenge involves selling information to a competitor; more commonly, it manifests as acts of sabotage.

There's a popular story in computer security circles that serves as a good example of the potential damage a disgruntled employee can do. It goes like this: A computer programmer, anticipating that he will be leaving his job under unfriendly circumstances, modifies a computer program that does the company payroll. When the program runs, it checks to see whether the programmer is on the payroll. If he's not, it deletes all employee records. In a more recent case, a systems administrator in Annapolis, Maryland, encrypted a small company's entire computer database. Nobody could read or access the data until he gave them the password. He claimed that the company owed him money, and he refused to give up the password until he was paid. The company eventually called the police.

Thrill Seekers   Sometimes what dissatisfied insiders crave is excitement. They commit espionage for the thrill of it, to break the routine of their boring lives. The prospect of secret meetings, dead drops, and the like captivates these wanna-be James Bonds. Whenever I give talks about the type of work I do, many attendees volunteer to work with me for free. After my articles about the work are published, I receive resumes and calls about possible job openings. This type of work intrigues most people, but few are willing to cross the line into genuine espionage activities. It's those few you have to worry about.

Departing Workers Another version of this threat is employees who are leaving the company. These folks are sometimes tempted to curry favor with their new employers by snatching sensitive information on their way out. They've either already secured a position or they anticipate securing one, and they want to demonstrate their worth and knowledge to the new boss. Because they are trusted insiders, they can provide your competitor with a variety of sensitive trade secrets.

The recent lawsuits filed by General Motors (GM) against Volkswagen illustrates this type of insider threat. In court documents, GM alleges that Jose Lopez, GM's former worldwide purchasing chief, stole boxes of documents before leaving to accept a position as Volkswagen's production chief. The documents specifically contained pricing information as well as information on a secret GM project, referred to in internal documents as Plant X, a factory management style of the future. The lawsuit implies collusion between Lopez and senior Volkswagen officials, including Ferdinand Piech, Volkswagen's board chairman. (As of this writing, GM continues to seek legal redress of its grievances against Volkswagen in the courts.)

In a recent case involving China, Andrew Wong, an Ellery Systems engineer and Chinese national, was accused of stealing computer software from his employer. Ellery alleges that Wong sent the software to China with the expectation that the Chinese government would set him up in his own company. Wong was acquitted in 1996, but Ellery still suffered the effects of the loss.

Former Employees   Former employees can pose a serious threat to your organization. They can seek to hurt you out of vindictiveness, to get a payoff, or to impress a new boss. They can hurt you unintentionally, simply because they know what they know. Although they no longer have direct access to your sensitive information, they know your layout, your procedures, your habits, and your weaknesses. Chances are, they know your operation better than many of your current employees. Perhaps most important, they know your competitors, which means they know who would value your information enough to pay them for it.

Much of the damage caused by former employees is indirect and, from an espionage standpoint, unintentional. Good salespeople, for example, want to offer the lowest prices and the best products. If they know the prices of their former employer's products, it is inconceivable that they would fail to use that knowledge to undercut the competition and land a new client. They're not out to hurt their former employers; they just want to do a good job and make a sale.

This type of casual espionage is all too common, and companies have come to expect it. With the current state of employee turnover in this country, most competing firms have employees from many, if not all, of their competitors.

Some former employees, however, maintain contact with their old workplaces solely for the purpose of gathering information. In many cases they abuse old friendships with former coworkers. The damage these unscrupulous people can do to your organization is considerable.

On-Site Nonemployees   Nowadays, just about every organization employs at least a few temporary workers and consultants. In some organizations, these so-called contingency workers make up a significant part of the workforce. The growth of corporate outsourcing practices has increased the number of on-site nonemployees with physical access to many organizations.

Large companies typically outsource their security and janitorial services. They don't want to invest their resources in the training and maintenance of this group of specialized workers, so they hire others to do it. It's a good business move, but it's very bad for security.

Think about it: janitors and security guards do the bulk of their work when everyone else has left the facilities. They have wide access and virtually free reign, and nobody questions their presence in even the most sensitive parts of the building (*somebody* has to scrub the floor in the prototype development lab). An article in the Winter 1994 edition of *2600: The Hacker's Quarterly* (a magazine for hackers) gives detailed advice on getting a job as a janitor for the purpose of gaining physical access to a targeted firm. If the hackers know this, you can bet that much more organized threats know it, too.

Companies also outsource many white-collar positions. Temporary employment services provide clerical workers for short-term support. Technical vendors provide on-site support. Depending upon their assignments, these nonemployees could have access to the most valuable information in a company.

Ideologues   Employees frequently cite ideology as the real motivation for their industrial espionage activities. Bill Gaede (Chapter 8) took information from Advanced Micro Devices (AMD) and Intel for the Cubans; Jonathon Pollard, a U.S. Navy analyst, stole information from the U.S. government for Israel.

These ideologues claim that money is unimportant— they're doing it to help a struggling nation, to even the playing field. Good spy masters know how to encourage this stuff in their moles, allowing them to believe that the money is a sign of appreciation and not the reason for their actions. (Interestingly, in 1991, Russian spy agencies were directed to ensure that all of their recruits were spying for monetary motivations. The Cold War was over, and the agencies feared that their moles would withdraw support once they realized the new nature of the country they were spying for; a reliance on money would keep the moles in line.)

Activists   Activists also use ideology as a motivation to infiltrate companies and become very dangerous insiders. These people are much more earnest in their intentions and are willing to go to greater extremes. They gladly risk jail, and sometimes their lives, for their causes.

One of the most common activist espionage tactics is securing employment at the target company. They act as normal insiders, trying either to obtain incriminating evidence against the target company or to sabotage or hamper the company's offending activities. They are much more likely to take risks than the average insider, and they usually have no fear of punishment.

When activists seek to cause damage, they want the damage to be severe and highly visible, so that the company is hampered and the public hears their message. These people are much akin to terrorists, with the only real difference being that activists directly target their victims without intentionally involving people not associated with the victim.

People for the Ethical Treatment of Animals (PETA) targets any group that mistreats animals. This includes cosmetic firms, pharmaceutical companies, and even McDonald's restaurants. Any information that could hurt or embarrass any of these companies is fair game for this animal rights organization. The group MC-1 targets any information that damages or embarrasses companies attempting to do business with Vietnam. In another case, a group of hackers obtained jobs at America Online (AOL) to gather information they could use against the service. AOL is despised by many people in the hacker community for a variety of reasons, not the least of which is that many hackers believe AOL is responsible for a flood of "clueless" people gaining access to the Internet. The hackers in this case have been accused of a variety of crimes, including credit card thefts, giving people free accounts, and creating false accounts to cover other hacking activities.

COMPETITORS

The first threat that comes to mind when most people think about corporate espionage is the competitor. Virtually all business enterprises have competitors; they are a fact of life in capitalist countries. What many people don't realize is that smaller companies, by virtue of the markets they serve, have more competitors than big corporations. Boeing, for example, is one of the largest aircraft manufacturers in the world; few companies around the world can compete with such a huge operation. A local office supply store, on the other hand, must coexist with dozens of competing enterprises: other office supplies stores, department stores, computer stores, and even supermarkets selling similar products. Competition is definitely livelier for smaller concerns.

Basically, a *competitor* is any business that seeks to increase its market share or profits at the expense of your business. Competitors need not behave maliciously nor act illegally to pose a threat to your enterprise. All they have to do is seek to improve their wealth, inevitably at your expense.

Your competitors profit in many ways from information collected about your business. A supermarket manager, for example, would love to know about a competitor's profit margins, supplier discounts, and upcoming special sales. Is the store planning to expand, extend its hours, or respond to an unforeseen market trend? The answers to these questions are worth millions.

Large companies face large competitors with great resources. Small mom-and-pop stores have more competitors to worry about. Midsized companies face the greatest threat in terms of competition: their competitors have the resources to pursue them, and there are plenty of them out there. More important, midsized companies are often less cognizant of the threat. They feel that they're not big, like defense contractors, so no one would want to spy on them. These operations often have the most to lose in a highly volatile marketplace. For example, Erol's Videos was put out of business as Blockbuster, a "megachain," crept unnoticed into its market areas.

One of the best examples of midlevel corporate espionage involves the Starbuck's Coffee chain. The owner of Japan's largest gourmet coffee chain learned that Starbuck's was planning to enter the Japanese market with a number of stores. He immediately began studying this potential competitor. He hired a real estate firm to determine where Starbuck's was most likely to put its stores. He flew to the U.S. and visited every Starbuck's store on the West Coast. He examined the stores for consistency and quality of service and product. He then developed marketing and sales campaigns to cement customer loyalty before Starbuck's arrival.

In the Starbuck's example, the Japanese coffee shop owner used entirely legal methods to collect intelligence on his competitor. Your competitors can ask vendors and customers about your capabilities, talk to your former employees, and even hire private investigators to find out whether you are fulfilling your contracts, all without breaking the law. Organizations specialize in providing information to companies about their competitors without engaging in illegal activity.

The results of the legal intelligence-gathering activities of your competitors can be devastating. When American Airlines decided to go head-to-head with People's Express, the original "no frills" airline, it monitored the smaller carrier twenty-four hours a day. Whatever discounts People's offered, American matched immediately. This intense monitoring resulted in the demise of People's, which had once been an extremely successful business.

Of course, some of your competitors won't stop at legal intelligence-gathering methods. They'll resort to a range of attack techniques—simple breaking and entering to sophisticated computer hacking—to steal everything from your customer lists to your expansion plans. Some will break the law without knowing it.

Some companies engage in the highly questionable practice of paying private individuals to acquire information about their competitors for them. According to a former Russian intelligence officer, many U.S. firms secure the services of private investigators through third parties. They hire people to hire people to hire people to get information on their competitors through illegal means. Their intention is to separate the illegal actions from the end user of the information. The Russian officer told me that this practice is common in many multi-billion-dollar corporations, but smaller companies do it as well.

Foreign Competitors

Despite some notable exceptions, most U.S. businesses operate legally and ethically within a system of widely understood laws. Most foreign businesses also adhere to a set of rules and laws, but Americans should never assume that those rules are the same—especially when it comes to the standards by which they judge and treat foreigners.

The threat from foreign competitors can be particularly troublesome for a number of often confusing reasons. Italy, for example, readily cooperates with countries, such as the U.S., in the prosecution of industrial spies, even Italian ones. However, the Italian government provides an exemption where health concerns are involved. When acts of industrial espionage involve biotechnology or pharmaceutical products, the Italian government refuses to cooperate on the grounds that the actions are health-related.

Multinational corporations know exactly what they can and can't get away with, and they become experts at covering their tracks. They use the same tactics and methods as your domestic competitors, but they also count on at least some protection from their homelands. Expecting this type of support, foreign business owners are often emboldened to commit more egregious acts of industrial espionage than U.S. firms. Furthermore, foreign countries sometimes engage in additional espionage actions on the companies' behalf, providing foreign competitors with additional funding and capabilities that American firms don't usually have.

I certainly expect governments to support their own businesses. Americans can't impose their ethics on others. Governments and their intelligence agencies are expected to act in the best interests of their countries and not in the best interests of Americans. Although this does not have to be a "one or the other" situation, that is how countries typically perceive it.

FOREIGN INTELLIGENCE AGENCIES

More than 100 nations engage in corporate espionage activities directed against U.S. companies. Many of them rely on their countries' intelligence agencies for direct support. Foreign intelligence agencies are the best-equipped organizations to infiltrate businesses of all sizes. Governments fund them, and they are never held legally responsible for their actions, which gives them tremendous resources and immunity. The only thing that holds them back is the fear of creating a political embarrassment for their government's leaders.

Most countries today have an interest in ensuring that their businesses are strong internationally. The U.S. has traditionally done this by using its influence and intelligence agencies to negotiate favorable trade and business treaties.

U.S. intelligence focuses on foreign countries to develop an optimal negotiating position. This is exactly what Japan recently accused the U.S. of doing. According to a variety of newspaper reports, Japan claims that U.S. intelligence agencies targeted the Japanese trade delegation during the recent American-Japanese automobile trade negotiations. Japan claims that the U.S. intercepted sensitive communications between the delegation and Japanese leaders, giving the U.S. an unfair advantage. The U.S. denies these accusations. I believe that most Americans hope that these allegations are true. We *want* the U.S. to use its intelligence agencies in this way.

But, unlike most other countries, the U.S. uses its intelligence agencies only to pursue national interests. The U.S. government does not provide intelligence data to American businesses. On some occasions, the FBI has alerted American companies when they are apparently being targeted by other nations. For the most part, though, U.S. intelligence stays out of the business arena.

Not only do many foreign governments target U.S. firms with their intelligence agencies, they even fill information requests from local businesses. In other words, other governments engage in corporate espionage on a regular basis. The threat to your organization from your foreign competitors often has the muscle of a government spy agency behind it.

Hostile Nations

When hostile nations become involved in corporate espionage, they are less concerned about political embarrassment. In other words, they are not as concerned if their actions are discovered, which makes them more of a threat by far than a friendly nation. They are then willing to assume more risk of exposure and resort to more aggressive and effective tactics. The former Eastern Bloc and other communist countries are known for their generally aggressive tactics. These formerly communist countries realize that economic matters are now more important than military matters, and they are making economic espionage a top priority. The following four sections discuss those traditionally hostile nations whose intelligence activities could potentially pose the greatest threat to your organization.

Russia   Russia is the largest and strongest country emerging from the former Soviet Union, and it has acquired most of the Soviet Union's wealth and resources. It has also acquired most of the Soviet Union's debts. Despite the tremendous availability of natural resources and intellectual talent, the Russian economy is in turmoil. And despite the appearance that Russia is now a friendly country, it still remains America's greatest adversary.

John Deutch, former Director of Central Intelligence, has said that Russia is still the most active nation engaging in espionage against the U.S. Additional news reports claim that not only has this espionage continued since the demise of the Soviet Union, it has increased. Although much of this espionage activity involves military intelligence, most of the Russian focus has moved to industrial espionage. This trend will only increase as Russia's economy continues to struggle.

Virtually all American businesses are potential targets of the Russian intelligence agencies. Although the KGB has been broken up into many separate intelligence agencies with different functions, Russian intelligence is still alive and well. Most of the KGB activities Americans are familiar with were assigned to an organization known as the SVR. This organization continues to use KGB resources and spy networks that have been developed over decades. The GRU, the Soviet military intelligence agency, which is considered even more diabolical than the KGB, has remained intact despite many political upheavals, and it is as strong as ever. Few U.S. businesses escape Russian scrutiny.

What should be of major concern to most midsize and large U.S. firms is the fact that the Russian government has been thoroughly infiltrated by organized crime. During the first free elections in Russia in the late 1980s, the only people with the money to campaign for office were successful criminals, and many secured key political positions. Other organized crime figures bought the newly privatized Russian companies previously owned by the State. Representatives from these companies sometimes sit in on meetings of the Ministry of Defense and the Ministry of Defense Industry, where they can request and fund intelligence operations to profit their companies. In the post–Cold War world, these agencies have evolved into purely profit-driven organizations, and they are widely considered to be extremely ruthless.

These new Russians capitalists realize that it is much cheaper to steal technology than to develop it themselves. They also have the distribution mechanisms to sell goods made with stolen or pirated technologies. Since they also have significant control of the Russian government, they are extremely unlikely to suffer any punishments for their actions.

Russian intelligence agencies have tremendous assets at their disposal. They have well-established networks of moles and operatives throughout the world. Each agency strives to have at least one mole in every important American company, and indications suggest that they have accomplished their goal. A former Russian intelligence operative boasted to me that with at least one person inside, the Russians can get anything out of a company. They train these moles and provide them with any resources they need to be successful. Chapter 9 describes the Russian recruitment and collection process in detail, as it actually occurred in one case.

Today, despite its previous focus on military activities, modern Russian intelligence agencies utilize a decidedly capitalistic model for intelligence gathering. Through the auspices of the Ministry of Defense, Russian intelligence generates a very large document that lists and identifies every requirement of its intelligence agencies. This vital intelligence document is divided into four major parts: Political Structure, Military Structure, Industry Structure, and Collection Requirements.

The Political Structure section focuses on the U.S. and world political infrastructures. It identifies governmental structures and includes the names of individuals in key positions, from very low levels of the hierarchy to top officials.

The Military Structure section of the document closely parallels the Political Structure section, except that it focuses on military personnel and organization. This section describes the purpose and capabilities of each military unit and lists unit leaders. Depending on the strategic importance of the units highlighted, it may also list personnel all the way down to the platoon or squad levels (basically, units of ten to forty people).

The Industry Structure section identifies all businesses that could be of military or political importance to the Russian government. Russian intelligence agencies keep lists of American businesses by market sector, type of information each company might have, and key company personnel. Companies of all sizes have something to offer the Russian intelligence agencies, whether or not they appear to have anything to do with the military or politics.

No business functions in a vacuum—every business has suppliers and customers. While one business might not have anything of importance to the Russians, it might have customers and suppliers that do. In turn, the customers and suppliers also might not have anything of importance, but *they* might have suppliers or customers that do. Intelligence agencies know that many of their primary targets protect themselves against possible attacks. To bypass the protection mechanisms, these intelligence agencies frequently compromise third- or fourth-party organizations, who have weak or no security, to obtain access to their primary target. While the third parties might not suffer a direct loss, they will eventually be affected, perhaps by paying more for the services received or by losing a customer.

All organizations are potential targets. Consider the pizza delivery services in the Washington, D.C., area, which are frequently the first to know when a crisis is going on, because their late-hour pizza deliveries increase to government buildings such as the Pentagon. A small mom-and-pop grocery store in the middle of Arkansas might sell to a frequent customer who happens to be a friend of President Clinton. A gasoline station thought to be in the middle of nowhere could be a regular stop for a congressman. The agency representing me for this book has four employees, yet they represent dozens of people, some of whom (like me) have access to sensitive information. The possibilities are endless, and the Russian intelligence establishment prepares for this.

The Collection Requirements section of the document lists every piece of technology the Russian government and its agencies want. It is essentially a buyer's guide for intelligence operatives. The items the document lists could be anything from information about the production output of a given piece of machinery to the schematics of the machine itself. They might want to acquire a specific computer chip, or they might want the manufacturing instructions for that chip. Every listing in the Collection Requirements section includes a tracking number, a description of the item listed, possible sources for the item desired, and the maximum price the agency is willing to pay for that item. If an operative acquires the item for less, he or she earns a percentage of the money saved, and everyone in the operative's chain of command is rewarded. Flash updates to this section of the document are sent out whenever the intelligence committees get together to address any new and critical needs.

In the modern Russian intelligence community, there is open competition among agencies for both financial gain and prestige. If the GRU consistently beats the SVR to the targeted information, then that agency is rewarded with increased annual budget allocations. This performance-driven approach is the source of much conflict among the agencies.

Besides the traditional human espionage methods, the Russians employ many other more technical means of collecting information. They tap telephones, monitor truck lines, bug buildings, and use spy satellites, special airplanes, and naval vessels. Some Aeroflot jets are configured with communications collection devices. Every foreign firm with offices in Russia just assumes that all of their offices are bugged and all of their telephones are monitored.

Another way Russian companies collect industrial information is by pursuing joint ventures with foreign firms. Russian enterprises do employ many brilliant scientists and businesspeople, making them very promising business partners. However, the U.S. National Counterintelligence Center (NCIC) warns that these joint ventures are frequently fronts for industrial espionage. The Russians frequently exploit these business relationships to gather information well beyond the scope of the agreement. Additionally, they will use a relationship with one firm to develop a relationship with another firm, expanding the scope of their collection efforts.

The Russian industrial espionage process is very effective and highly profit-driven. These people are very good at getting exactly what they want from U.S. companies. Although the U.S. economy will not crumble from these attacks, certain businesses and industries might suffer drastically.

China China has one of the largest economies in the world. Despite the apparent widespread lack of technology throughout the country, China is focusing on the acquisition of new technologies to bring its economy into the twenty-first century. They have a population of about one billion people, and businesses throughout the world are battling to break into

China's growing consumer market. The Chinese government is pursuing a series of economic reforms to allow for this foreign expansion into the country. However, unlike Russia, China is not simultaneously pursuing political reforms. This allows for highly planned and controlled economic growth that will not be ruined by a weak central government.

Industrial espionage has always played an important role in Chinese economic development. For many years, China has used its military intelligence capability and tactics for economic purposes. However, the Chinese tactics are somewhat different from those of the Russians. Russian expatriates often do not maintain strong ties with the country they fought so hard to escape; many despise the Russian past and the government and want nothing to do with it. Despite their government's repressive, totalitarian society, people of Chinese descent frequently feel an ethnic devotion to their ancestors and their homeland. Chinese intelligence agencies know this and exploit this devotion at every opportunity.

Chinese intelligence agencies focus their recruitment efforts on Chinese nationals traveling and living abroad, as well as people of Chinese descent who are citizens of other countries. They find these people mainly through social clubs, which they join. They cultivate friendships with potential agents and try to recruit them for espionage activities.

Chinese intelligence also relies heavily on university students studying abroad. Every Chinese student who wants to study abroad must be approved by the government, and most of the students' financial support is provided to them. Since China places such a high priority on technology, the vast majority of Chinese nationals studying in the U.S. and around the world major in science and technology. In many cases, these students work on state-of-the-art research projects and gain access to cutting-edge technologies. After their education is completed, some of these students return to China and become teachers; others may work in Chinese research facilities.

Some Chinese students, however, are encouraged to stay in the U.S. after they graduate and get jobs in U.S. companies. Over a period of time, they may be approached by intelligence operatives, who ask them to provide China with sensitive information on different technologies or businesses. Other Chinese nationals are required to return home after graduation, where they might be trained as intelligence operatives and sent back overseas to obtain jobs in strategic companies.

Not all Chinese nationals traveling, studying, or working overseas are intelligence operatives or agents. But China herself does consider them to be a primary industrial espionage resource, and with so many Chinese citizens traveling abroad, the intelligence agencies need only exploit a small percentage of them to pose a considerable threat to U.S. companies.

Like the Russians, the Chinese also use satellites, spy ships, airplanes, embassy collection, wiretaps, and telephone monitoring in their intelligence gathering activities. It has the largest military in the world, with an intelligence capability to match.

China also takes full advantage of the size of its economy. Every industrialized country in the world wants to sell its products to the Chinese people, and the Chinese government knows it. Accordingly, as part of normal trade negotiations, China forces foreign companies that want to establish businesses in China to train Chinese citizens in their U.S. factories, build factories in China, and place Chinese citizens in key management positions. Many companies are willing to agree to these conditions, even though they constitute a major security threat, because of the immense Chinese market.

Chinese nationals specifically placed inside American firms are bound to engage in espionage activity. The Chinese don't even seem particularly interested in covering the tracks of their operatives. In many instances, these placed workers simply "disappear" after several months of employment. The assumption among intelligence professionals is that once the operatives collect everything they need, they simply have no reason to return. All technology inside U.S. factories built in China must be considered totally compromised.

The Chinese also use a bait and switch technique to get into facilities to which their operatives normally do not have access. Creating a "scene" is another common tactic (not only of the Chinese but of other intelligence agencies as well—see Chapter 11). Chinese government operatives infiltrate Chinese social clubs and exploit relationships there. They urge members to do all they can to provide new knowledge and job opportunities for other members. They then convince their compatriots to arrange for tours of company facilities where they are employed. In case the companies check the identities and backgrounds of visitors, Chinese operatives use the names of other people; then, at the time of the visit, the intelligence operatives show up in the others' place, and unwitting companies allow the unapproved guests through. If a company rejects the new visitors, the operatives create a scene, trying to portray it as a racial or international incident in the hopes of intimidating the company into letting them in. They also use this ploy to get into restricted areas, saying that the company is trying to hide something. I personally know of such instances in three companies. It is no surprise that in 1996, the Defense Investigative Service put out an alert about the above practices.

The Chinese infiltration efforts have been very successful in this country. They have cut significantly into the international market share of U.S. businesses in several high technology areas, including weapons sales. This is a multibillion-dollar loss to U.S. firms. It also involves national security interests, since China has been willing to sell weapons and restricted technologies to nations and organizations that are openly hostile to the U.S., including Iran. The availability of cheap labor and the low cost of acquiring technology makes China extremely competitive in the international market. It might also become competitive inside the U.S. market, depending on the results of the latest trade negotiations.

Iran To most Americans, Iran is a backward nation with a single modern industry: oil production. The Iranians may seem medieval with their beards and veils—merely Muslim fundamentalists who despise technology, people who want to return to the old ways and shun the modern world.

The Iranian government is happy to foster this impression. It hides what they're really up to. Iran is an extremely rich country that does want to modernize—not necessarily its society but its military. Iran is almost constantly at war with neighboring Iraq, and it spends its oil money in a relentless pursuit of advanced weapons technology, including nuclear, chemical, and biological weapons. Iran has one of the best-financed intelligence capabilities in the world.

Russia continues to train Iranian intelligence operatives and to provide them with the necessary collection equipment. Using the standard intelligence collection methods, such as theft, wiretaps, and bribes, Iran collects information from high-technology firms throughout the world. It also exchanges information with other hostile intelligence agencies, such as the Russian GRU. It also hires former Eastern Bloc experts in the nuclear, chemical, and espionage fields.

To obtain certain technologies, Iran secures the cooperation of the companies of U.S. allies, such as Germany. These companies have their own technology capabilities and are not subject to rules that limit the acquisition of "controlled" equipment. Consequently, these companies are able to use their ally status to acquire technology supposedly for themselves, then sell it illegally to Iran. Iran uses these companies as intermediaries to front their activities. Iranian scientists specify their requirements, and when money is no object, they get what they want.

Although Iran's use of technology appears to be limited to noneconomic gain, its espionage activities pose a major threat to U.S. companies and the world in general. Should Iran develop a working arsenal of weapons of mass destruction and/or significantly improve their military capability, the Mideast could be thrown into turmoil, and the world's oil supply could be threatened.

A more critical aspect to consider is that Iran considers the U.S. its greatest enemy. Iran calls the U.S. the "Great Satan." It sponsors terrorism to punish the Great Satan and her allies. Iran looks for new ways to hurt the Great Satan, and weapons of mass destruction would be ideal for this purpose. With this type of leverage, it would no longer be intimidated by U.S. military capability and would pose an uncontrollable threat.

Cuba Cuba is also high on the CIA's list of countries engaged in industrial espionage. Unlike Iran, Cuba is a third-world country, with a third-world economy. With the breakup of the Soviet Union, Cuba has lost its primary supplier of money and technology. Compounding its problems is the U.S. economic boycott. With America taking the lead, other countries have avoided economic involvement with Cuba. The Cubans are financially isolated by much of the world, making economic growth very difficult. Necessity has caused Castro's government to shift its focus from military to economic growth, with the acquisition of technology a top priority.

With few legal options, Cuba resorts to any means necessary to acquire new technology. Like Iran, Cuban intelligence operatives are trained by Russians. Using their education, they try to infiltrate companies to steal technology. They also bribe people, tap telephones, commit blackmail, and recruit communist sympathizers. They also use foreign companies to bypass the Cuban trade embargo. In several cases, the Cubans have acquired technologies to trade with their allies.

It is unlikely that Cuban thefts of American technologies will significantly impact the market share of U.S. firms. However, Cuba is a major supplier to the black market. The affect on the overall economy is minimal, but it can significantly hurt individual American companies, depending on the specific technologies that they acquire.

Friendly Countries

America's greatest foreign competitors are its traditional allies—countries that compete with the U.S. not only in the world economy but also in the American marketplace. In many ways, countries friendly to the U.S. pose a greater threat to your organization than openly hostile countries.

When I asked Robert Gates about friendly spying, his answer boiled down to this:

- Japan does it all the time, but almost everything it does is legal, so it doesn't try to hide it, and there is little we can do about it.
- France does it all the time and has been doing it for over 200 years, and it doesn't really give a damn about what anyone thinks.
- Israel does a lot of illegal things. While it prefers that its actions go unnoticed, it doesn't really care who knows, because the Israeli lobby in Washington is too strong for the U.S. to do too much about it.
- Germany performs some illegal actions, but it doesn't have much leverage in the U.S., so it keeps its lawbreaking to a minimum.

The allied nations listed above and discussed in the following sections are highlighted because their activities are more extreme than others. However, just about every other U.S. ally also targets U.S. companies, using a wide variety of methods to collect information. Although many employ only legal methods, you can count on a significant amount of illegal activity as well. The citizens of many countries expect their governments to help their businesses and their economies with espionage support.

Any business with foreign competitors either abroad or in the U.S. must recognize that those foreign competitors pose an information security threat. In the U.S., too many managers don't believe that anybody would spy on them; to foreign companies, just being a competitor is more than enough reason to target a company. It's a cultural thing. You can't expect other countries to think and act like Americans.

Keep in mind that there are well over 100 countries engaged in one form of espionage or another against the U.S. Pierre Marion, former head of the DGSE (French intelligence) said it best: "Everybody spies on everybody."

Japan   Perhaps no country has integrated industrial espionage into its culture to a greater extent than Japan. Japanese businesses watch their competitors, both foreign and domestic, almost as well as they watch themselves. The larger companies have entire units devoted to competitive intelligence. They're responsible for learning what their competitors are up to, what their capabilities are, how much profit they're making, how much product they're producing, what new directions they are going in, and what unique processes they've come up with. They study every publicly available document containing information about their competitors, including newspapers, magazines, annual reports, and government filings. They regularly check the patent and trademark office, looking for new filings there. Japanese companies want to know everything about their competitors.

Although Japanese companies usually rely on straightforward collection methods, such as reviewing open source information, they can be extremely creative in their collection methods. One interesting tactic involved a questionnaire sent to several U.S. firms by a Japanese company. In each cover letter, the company claimed to be considering using the U.S. firm as a supplier, but before the firm could be seriously considered, it would have to complete the enclosed questionnaire. The questionnaire called for a detailed summary of all corporate locations, the names of the key people at each facility, the types of products developed, the volume of the products produced, and a variety of other sensitive information. Chapter 11 summarizes the efforts of a Japanese film crew to obtain detailed information on U.S. biotechnology firms. Both of these actions were completely legal—and successful.

As the earlier Starbuck's example shows, Japanese executives take an active role in the information gathering process. They will covertly visit their competitors. If they can't find the time to do this on a regular basis themselves, they will send their subordinates. They also pay people to monitor other companies. They even pay delivery people to report on the packages they deliver and pick up from certain companies.

The Japanese government has no intelligence capability of its own. According to John Quinn, a former CIA operative and expert on Japanese business and intelligence practices, the Japanese government relies on the country's businesses to supply it with intelligence on other countries. The government has set up the Japanese External Trade Relations Office (JETRO), which is reportedly staffed by visiting corporate intelligence professionals. Although JETRO was supposedly established to improve Japanese business relations with other countries, most U.S. counterintelligence professionals consider its primary purpose to be intelligence collection.

Even though Japan is an important American ally, it represents a significant threat to U.S. companies. What international business has not been affected by a Japanese competitor? What domestic manufacturer has not had its market share cut by a Japanese company? Most Americans assume that the

Japanese succeed because they are more creative. The truth is, Americans generate many times more new technologies and technological breakthroughs than Japan. The Japanese just "acquire" the technology and develop new ways of using it. The fact that they don't have to put as much money into research and development allows them to spend their money on more competitive issues and to offer their products at lower prices.

France   France has twice been identified by the CIA as one of two U.S. allies that commit acts of corporate espionage against American companies as frequently as U.S. adversaries. Perhaps no U.S. ally has been more flagrant in its intelligence-gathering activities than France. To a great extent, the French are proud of this distinction.

The French government has been using its intelligence capabilities to support its domestic businesses since the reign of Louis XIV. French companies regularly approach the DGSE (the French foreign intelligence agency), and request intelligence support. Each company must justify its request with specific financial criteria. If the DGSE considers the request valid, it uses its resources to get the desired information.

One of the most important tools of the DGSE is French hotels. It is widely reported that the agency has recruited many domestic hotel employees to facilitate its intelligence collection activities. These employees let DGSE operatives into hotel rooms while the occupants are out. They also bug the telephones of visiting U.S. businesspeople during their stay. The NCIC has reported at least one case in which hotel telephone taps resulted in a French company beating out a U.S. competitor on a multimillion-dollar contract. Many of the major American companies warn their employees traveling to France that their rooms must be considered bugged and videotaped.

France's espionage activities are by no means limited to domestic operations. Pierre Marion has said that France has successfully placed moles inside many U.S. companies, including IBM and Texas Instruments. These are long-term operatives, expected to advance through the ranks of the company and to obtain access to the newer developments over time. France has probably targeted non-U.S. companies as well. The U.S. is not singled out by France, who believes that "there is no such thing as an economic ally."

Peter Schweizer reports in his book, *Friendly Spies,* that France bugged the first-class cabins of some Air France jets. This invasion of privacy, while considered outrageous to Americans, is looked upon by the French people as a normal part of business (the French justifiably think that high-paid executives on business trips are the only people who *regularly* fly first class).

U.S. companies should keep in mind that many French corporations are actually owned by the French government. French government-owned businesses are often used as collection tools. The U.S. Government Accounting Office (GAO) recently released a report to Congress accusing foreign-owned firms of abusing their ownership of U.S. government contractors. These companies, including the French company, Loral, bought out American firms with classified government contracts. The U.S. allowed the companies to acquire the U.S. firms with the stipulation that the foreign owners maintain a complete separation of information. The GAO reviewed the implementation of the requirements and found them severely lacking. France, among other countries, uses these companies to gain access to very sensitive technology. To France, spying for industry is the same as spying for the government.

France also bears the distinction of actively supporting the computer hacker community. France has long recognized the importance of computer hacking in the collection of information. It has developed and trained a world-class group of its own computer hackers. It also supports the underground hackers, mainly to help hide its own activities and gather information. Very reliable sources report that the DGSE runs the QSD computer bulletin board system, which is one of the best-known places for hackers to exchange information. France monitors postings on QSD to gather new techniques. Dr. Eugene Spafford, professor at Purdue University and one of the world's leading computer security experts, says that France also finds new computer vulnerabilities and releases them directly to the hacker community. This allows hackers to use very advanced techniques while inadvertantly masking the illegal activities of the DGSE. If the average hacker can compromise a computer system with a very advanced attack, then the companies hacked by France likely assume that the attack came from a teenage hacker rather than a well-trained DGSE operative.

The French operate one of the most capable intelligence agencies in the world. Although they do gather military intelligence information, there is little doubt that their primary goal is economic intelligence. The military information they do gather is usually collected for sale to other parties. They use the information they collect to give French companies an advantage. If your firm has ever competed against a French company, you have been a target. If you have ever produced the same product as a French company, you have been a target. If you've ever been a target of French intelligence, your whole company was threatened.

Israel Israel shares with France the distinction of being named by the CIA as one of the two leading allied perpetrators of industrial espionage. Unlike France, the Israelis very strongly prefer to keep their espionage activities under wraps. They are very dependent on the U.S. for military and political support, and they don't want to antagonize their ally. However, the Israelis also believe that the very existence of their country is at stake, and they will do everything possible to protect themselves.

According to many intelligence sources, Israel has the world's best intelligence capability, man for man and dollar for dollar. Knowledgeable sources believe the Israelis to have the third best intelligence agency in the world, trailing only the U.S. and Russia. Although they lack the worldwide presence and many of the assets of the larger nations, the devotion of Israeli operatives and agents to their country and their cause make their intelligence organizations one of the best in the world.

Israel's primary espionage target is military technology. Israel wants advanced weapons to improve its ability to defend itself and to sell to its allies. Israel always seeks to strengthen its economy and trade balance so it is less reliant on foreign aid.

To obtain information, Israel uses many of the same techniques that are often associated with more hostile countries. For example, Israel places people inside companies through contractual negotiations. This was the case with Recon/Optical, a U.S. defense contractor that specializes in state-of-the-art optics technology. During the mid-1980s, Israel hired Recon/Optical to develop better optical technologies for its military. As part of the contract, Israel was allowed to have two people on site to monitor the progress of the work.

After several years, Recon/Optical realized that the on-site observers (who were reported to be Israeli intelligence officers) were stealing information about not only the contracted technologies, but also non-related technologies. Recon/Optical had put millions of dollars into those developments, and the Israeli agents had stolen almost all of them. They apparently gave the technology to Electro-Optics Industries Ltd, which was able to offer it at a much lower price than Recon/Optical, since the company had spent no money on development costs. The Israelis nearly put Recon/Optical out of business. Although the company managed to survive, it laid off over two-thirds its work force, ruining many lives and devastating the surrounding community.

Like their French counterparts, Israeli intelligence has had significant success in recruiting computer hackers. The

Mossad and probably the LAKAM (both Israeli intelligence agencies) support hacker activities, much like the DGSE, and occasionally try to recruit the more talented hackers.

Similar to the Chinese, the Israelis also utilize ethnic targeting to recruit many of their agents. Many Jews have a strong devotion to Israel, even though they may never have been there. To many, supporting the country means supporting the Jewish faith. Some U.S. citizens volunteer to serve in the Israeli army. If a person is willing to give his or her life for Israel, then stealing a little information is a small thing. Although the number of American Jews who actually commit espionage for Israel are extremely small, they do exist. Jonathan Polland, for instance, was a Naval Intelligence analyst who sold top secret military information to Israeli agents.

Although the Recon/Optical and Jonathon Pollard cases are among the few Israeli espionage cases to hit the media, it is extremely likely that Israel is every bit as active in this arena as the French and the Chinese. They probably have agents and moles inside many U.S. and foreign high-technology firms. They probably bug hotel rooms and tap telephone lines. Their agents are very bright and very motivated, and they usually get what they want. These are people who have infiltrated the very closed ranks of Arab terrorist organizations; to them, breaching a multibillion-dollar U.S. corporation is a walk in the park.

Many American Jews justify Israeli industrial espionage actions with the argument that Israel has always been America's strongest military ally. What they don't recognize is the economic impact of these actions.

Germany   When the GAO testified before Congress on foreign economic espionage in 1996, it hid the identities of U.S. allies engaged in this activity. It is widely believed among those who study espionage that Germany was one of those unnamed countries. Germany maintains a very large intelligence organization, called the Bundesnachrichtendienst (BND). Although its primary focus was the Eastern Bloc, the BND has always engaged in a significant amount of industrial activity. After the breakup of the Eastern Bloc, it shifted most of its Cold War resources to industrial efforts.

The BND continues to monitor international communications and tries very actively to obtain information that can help German companies. The agency has supported Siemens, one of Germany's largest companies, by infiltrating high-technology companies around the world. The BND infiltrated the Nixon White House, and it is likely that it continues to target other people and organizations that have access to sensitive trade information. There is little doubt that the BND has enjoyed many major industrial espionage successes.

Much like the French DGSE, the BND has a strong computer hacking component. In *Friendly Spies*, Peter Schweizer describes Project Rahab, a BND effort to hack into computer networks and compromise systems in the Global Information Infrastructure. It hoped to develop the capability to break into corporate and government computer systems at will to ensure its political, military, and economic survival.

Project Rahab's reported successes include infiltration of the SWIFT system, which is one of the world's major financial networks. SWIFT facilitates the transfer of trillions of dollars a day among financial institutions around the world. If the reports are true, Germany can monitor most of the world's financial transactions. The value of this intelligence is tremendous, and Germany is no doubt using this information to its advantage. It's also likely that the BND is using its capability to steal information from private companies as well.

As Chapter 10 shows, the Germans also rely on the more traditional espionage methods, including seduction and blackmail.

Perhaps of greatest concern to U.S. citizens is the apparent willingness of German businesses to funnel sensitive information and technology to nations that are hostile to the U.S.

German companies have been accused of providing technological help to such hostile nations as Iran and Libya. Alarmingly, a great deal of this technology involves nuclear and chemical technologies. Some of that technology was reportedly stolen from U.S. firms.

Third-World Countries   Third-world countries present a unique threat to American businesses. There's a certain desperation in the espionage efforts of these struggling nations. They are known to pursue their targets with any means available. Winn Schwartau, author of the book, *Information Warfare*, describes the dilemma faced by these countries this way: "They can spend billions of dollars and wait almost a decade to develop technologies on their own, or they can spend less than a million dollars to steal it tomorrow."

Given their limited resources, these nations don't present much of a risk to large organizations. Instead, they present a real threat to lower-technology companies, in particular, companies with older technology that utilize outdated machinery and cheaper resources. Think about it: even if one of these countries could get its hands on the latest technologies, it wouldn't have the money to acquire the other resources necessary to use them. You might acquire the latest copy of the Windows 95 computer operating system, but if the only hardware you have is an old 286 computer, you wouldn't be able to use it. The outdated machinery can be purchased for a very low cost and might even be available for free. So what would really be valuable to you is an old version of Windows 3.1, which you might find in the trash.

Surprisingly, many third-world countries rely on high-tech espionage techniques to acquire this low technology. Computer hacking is one of the cheapest ways to infiltrate a company. It can be done from anywhere with just a little bit of knowledge and without paying for on-site operatives, spy masters, or expensive travel. The Internet provides a wealth of free hacking resources for impoverished countries.

Obviously, these countries use some of the more traditional espionage tactics as well, but they don't have nearly the capability of the first- and second-world countries. Their economic successes amount to nibbles as opposed to bites, although some of the successes are at the expense of U.S. businesses. Again, midsized businesses that use low technology are most at risk from this particular threat.

ORGANIZED CRIME

Dozens of major organized crime rings are thriving throughout the world today. These criminal organizations include the traditional Italian Mafia, the new Eastern Bloc mafias, and drug cartels. There is even a growing criminal phenomenon known as cyber-cartels. All of these kinds of criminal organizations are exclusively profit-driven.

For the most part, organized crime presents a relatively minor industrial espionage threat. However, there have been widespread reports of the Eastern Bloc mafias acquiring the expertise of former Soviet Union operatives. Some of these operatives have probably gone to work for the more established organized crime rings, where they provide their employers with information about companies entering markets controlled by the criminal organization. They want to know what the company could possibly provide them and how to optimize their extortion demands. This type of information is worth billions to these crime rings, and they are willing to go to extreme measures to get what they want. When they learn about a company's strategic goals, they know what the company is after, and they use the information to leverage a deal in their favor.

Some crime rings contract out their intelligence capabilities to other organizations. A business might hire a criminal group to steal information from a competitor, especially if it doesn't want its government to know or its government has refused to help.

In some instances, a criminal organization might want to expand into a new area and use some espionage techniques to gather information about potential "customers," rivals, and law enforcement.

Organized crime rings are also developing their own computer hacking capabilities. Although they usually hire the computer experts they need, they have also reportedly resorted to intimidating people into cooperating. Through underground sources, I have learned of at least one incident in which a hacker received an "offer he couldn't refuse." (I should point out that he was apparently paid well for his efforts and probably did more work for them after his fears of bodily harm were put to rest.) Criminal organizations also have their own experts with outstanding capabilities. Admiral William Studeman, former Deputy Director of the Central Intelligence Agency, stated that the drug cartels have the technical capability to wage a very effective information war against the U.S.

The initial purpose of computer hacking in many criminal organizations was to facilitate money laundering. They sought the help of computer experts to enable them to make large financial transactions that went relatively unnoticed. The drug cartels and other organized crime rings then developed the capability to perform this money laundering themselves. Eventually, the Mafia-type organizations realized that not only could they launder their own illegally gotten gain but they could steal it as well. Today, criminal organizations steal this money from banks throughout the world.

On September 17, 1996, the Russian news agency Tass reported that the Central Bank of Russia lost over 250 billion rubles to electronic theft in 1995 alone. In October 1996, the U.S. Senate Select Committee on Investigations released a report stating that U.S. financial institutions reported an annual loss of approximately $800 million to electronic theft. This study was somewhat flawed, and I believe this figure is very low. I know of three U.S. banks alone whose total annual losses from what is referred to as "misrouted transactions" is more than double that figure. When you add the probable losses of the other top ten U.S. banks and the larger Japanese banks, the total must be well in excess of $10 billion annually.

Misrouted transactions are electronic transactions made against customers' accounts supposedly without their knowledge or permission. When a victimized customer proves that he or she did not authorize the transaction, the targeted bank reimburses the account and tries to recover the money from the place it was sent to. If the receiving bank claims that the money is no longer available, the bank usually considers the money lost do to a misrouted transaction. The investigation stops, because an investigation might prove that the money had been stolen, which would require the bank to report the theft, causing what would be a flood of very negative publicity. Banks consider misrouted transactions a part of the business process and do not have to report them. As one banking official told me, "What we sell is trust. If we lose people's trust, we are out of business." This fear among bankers keeps organized crime operating in the black.

In recent years, organized crime rings have begun targeting nonbanking organizations as well. In January 1995, the *Washington Times* reported that Russian crime rings alone have stolen over $1 billion from U.S. businesses through computer networks. The tremendous potential for profit through computer hacking has apparently created a new type of crime ring. These *cyber-cartels* have no physical presence, and their only activities involve the electronic theft of funds. There is no real proof that these organizations even exist. Yet it is widely believed within many underground communities that their members include former computer gurus from the KGB and other Soviet intelligence groups as well as young American hackers who have decided to make hacking their profession.

Unless a business is a direct target of organized crime, it has very little to worry about from this threat. These groups are probably a greater threat to private citizens. Organized crime rings are more likely to break into government databases containing personnel information than into companies. Such databases, like the one at the Social Security Administration, have extensive information on an individual's background. Criminals have been known to break into the SSA computer system to learn whether someone might be an undercover agent. Private citizens are also paying for the losses the banks incur from misrouted transactions.

TERRORISTS

Terrorist organizations resort to industrial espionage for a variety of reasons. They use it to identify possible targets for their terrorist actions. They gather information on new weapons through espionage techniques. Sometimes they use computer systems to launder money to fund their activities. They have even been known to use stolen technology to make money.

Information is a particularly valuable commodity to terrorists. For example, knowing the route that somebody will take to work allows a terrorist to plan an attack or a kidnapping. Building blueprints, which are usually widely available in government offices, help terrorists find the best places to plant bombs. The list goes on.

Businesses are very unlikely to be victims of espionage committed by terrorists. Terrorist attacks are extremely rare, and the damage is very limited—unless, of course, they blow up your building.

PETTY CRIME

Petty crimes can cause major problems for large corporations. When I ask my audiences how many people work in companies that have experienced thefts of computers, just about everyone raises a hand. In some cases, the entire computer is stolen; in other cases, only specific parts, such as memory chips, are removed. There has been a tremendous increase in laptop computer thefts in recent years.

The problem here isn't so much the loss of the hardware, although that certainly adds up. The computers themselves are often not nearly as valuable as the information they contain. A $2,500 laptop can hold information valued at over $1 million.

Furthermore, these kinds of thefts leave the motives of the thieves unclear. Was the computer taken by a petty criminal interested only in the value of the hardware, or was it part of a more sophisticated intelligence operation targeting the information the computer holds? Petty crime confuses the issue of industrial espionage. The targets of a petty criminal and those of an industrial spy are frequently the same, as are the short-term affects of the theft on the company. Luckily, the long-term affects of petty crimes are much less devastating .

In either case, the company is forced to replace the lost equipment and information. The affects and recovery costs associated with this kind of crime are still very large—and it always seems to happen at the wrong time.

SUPPLIERS

Although your suppliers might not intend to compete directly with you, they are frequently trying to increase their profits, which ultimately decreases your resources. This relationship must be looked upon as a kind of threat, albeit an often unconscious one.

Your suppliers are selling you products, and in many ways, they behave as all salespeople do. Consider the process of buying a car: As you walk into an automobile dealership, the typical salesperson will gather intelligence about you. He or she will glance outside to see what kind of car you're currently driving and will notice the clothes you're wearing. Are you with a family or by yourself? Do you speak intelligently, or does it seem as though you're trying to sound intelligent? Car salespeople are trained to gather this type of intelligence to figure out what you can spend and how gullible you are.

While you're off on a test drive, you leave a copy of your driver's license with the dealer; the dealership could check your credit records while you're gone. The salesperson with you on the test drive gathers more information by asking questions. By the time you get back to the dealership, the people inside know you better than you know yourself.

Similarly, suppliers want to know as much about you as possible. They want to know about your future plans so they can determine whether you will be likely to seek out other suppliers or need other products. The training of IBM salespeople is widely discussed in the computer professional community. Supposedly, IBM trains its people to scan office bookshelves to determine the technical level of the people they are dealing with. They are taught to read upside down so they can decipher notes on a potential customer's desk. They're encouraged to look for awards and pictures of families to find a basis for better rapport. They also look for information about other suppliers you may be considering. Before they even arrive at your office, they have researched your company thoroughly to determine your needs and anticipate questions or objections. When they're with you, they're probing with leading questions.

In many cases, all this probing leads to better service. Sometimes, though, it undercuts your own bargaining position.

Even the suppliers of very small businesses often go to great lengths to improve their bargaining positions. If you own a mom-and-pop store, for example, suppliers can antici- pate or manipulate your needs based on information they get from you, your competitors, or other suppliers. If a supplier knows that you are not looking for other suppliers, it might not offer you the lowest rates available. If you are known to be shopping around, you might get better rates.

Some people might say that this surreptitious intelligence gathering is just business and not espionage. Whatever you call it, you must be aware that your suppliers are constantly gathering information about your organization. What they learn can help or hurt you.

CUSTOMERS

Essentially, customers collect information on their suppliers in the same way their suppliers collect information on them. Let's go back to the car buying example, but now let's say that you represent the dealership. The potential buyer could do extensive research: read *Consumer Reports* and similar maga- zines to see how a particular car performed; use a variety of resources to learn your (the dealer's) invoice price; investigate the best time of the month to buy a car to get the best deal. The customer could also collect intelligence on the dealership, looking into the dealership sales record. Is business good or is the dealership going through a slow period? In addition, the customer could contact the local Better Business Bureau to see whether any complaints have been filed against the dealership, ask other customers about their experience with the dealer- ship, even shop around and compare prices with other dealers.

Customers are seldom left without options if they do their homework. Unless there is a situation in which a supplier has a monopoly, customers can usually gather information to improve their bargaining power. Even if the exercise only improves their deal by a few percentage points, it can easily be worth the effort. With the perception that the customer is competing for limited resources with the company, these few percentage points represent a huge loss to the company.

OTHER THREATS

Depending on the nature of your organization, you probably have many other threats to your information that you should be aware of.

The press, for example, is a major threat to a variety of organizations, especially the government. The job of the press is to reveal information that might be of interest to the public, and let's face it, they're always looking for a good story. Any company that employs a substantial number of people is likely to be a target of the press. What would happen if the press learned of your company's business plans? Would an early release of that information hamper your plans or cause your expenses to rise? If the press were to report that a company was looking to buy a plot of land to put up a factory, would the cost of the land magically rise? The press may report on major or minor setbacks that might be relatively unimportant but which, because they were revealed to the public, create a negative public image that inevitably hurts your business. Bad publicity has caused the ruination of many organizations. It is definitely in your best interest to limit your exposure to the press and protect your information from the prying eyes of reporters.

As a consequence of the 1996 presidential election, an immense amount of information about private corporations and individuals has been released to the public. Because of politics, a relatively small law firm in the middle of a very small state has found itself in the public spotlight. The Rose Law Firm and Whitewater Savings and Loan have become almost household words in this country. Neither organization is a large company or considered to be a major player, yet all of their private information is now on the public record. A special prosecutor would never have been appointed by Congress if not for the fact that these companies were associated with President Clinton. Information about every company that has donated to any presidential campaign is also likely to become a target of political adversaries on both sides.

The Watergate break-in is another example of political targeting of organizations and individuals. During that incident, doctors' offices were broken into and medical records were compromised. People not directly associated with politics in any way became targets because they were associated with people or organizations that were associated with politics.

These types of threats are not the result of easily recognized business competition but of intangible, often emotion-based political games. Unfortunately, it is these kinds of threats that could cause you the most harm. To understand how this often-hidden threat affects your organization, you must determine what information you possess that might be of political value to others.

HACKERS

I have left the discussion of hackers for the end because, contrary to popular belief, they do not represent a major threat to your organization. Oh, I know, most people hear the word "hacker" and envision a computer anti-Christ, wreaking havoc at will on unsuspecting companies. In reality, almost all hackers are little more than nuisances. The primary threat they present is that they sometimes mask and facilitate more serious crimes.

The term "hacker" was originally used to refer to the computer science students at the Massachusetts Institute of Technology (MIT) who had little hardware and software documentation and were forced to hack their way through primitive computer systems to circumvent problems. When personal computers began to proliferate during the 1980s, a new breed of hacker emerged. These new hackers used their PCs to connect to corporate and university mainframe computers through modems over telephone lines without permission, which was and is illegal. However, for young people who wanted to learn about computers, there were few other resources in those pre-Internet days.

Connecting to different computers around the world by telephone was an expensive proposition (no local calls to an Internet service provider in those days), and the new criminal hackers were compelled to hack the phone system, which is actually the world's largest computer network. Combining the words "phone" and "hack," they coined the term "phreakers" to describe their activities.

Although many computer professionals believe otherwise, I doubt that the intentions of these early hackers were criminal. They wanted to learn about computers, and this kind of experimentation was one of the few ways they could do it, even though it was criminal. There was really no point of reference for these hackers. Their parents never told them that hacking was wrong; they didn't even understand what it was. The movie *War Games* glorified the hacker community, attracting many teenagers. An underground ethic developed, which painted hackers as freedom fighters protecting the public's right to information access. This sure sounds good to a teenager.

Many people don't realize this, but there are major computer networks that have better capability than the Internet. These networks, with names like Tymnet and Telenet, were put together in the 1980s to connect businesses with each other. These businesses include the world's largest banks. Hackers were able to compromise many of these systems at will. Again, most hackers were not interested in money and just used the exercise as a means to learn and gather information. It was also a major ego boost to have such power.

By the end of the 1980s, many of the first hackers had grown up and were now selling information and services. Members of one of the most notorious hacker groups, the Masters of Deception, have been accused of modifying and selling credit reports, selling wiretaps to private investigators, and stealing phone services, among other crimes. Some of their members have pleaded guilty to several of these charges, and one of them admitted his guilt on *60 Minutes.* Hackers began referring to hackers that break into computer systems specifically for criminal purposes as "crackers."

Whether a person is called a hacker, a phreaker, or a cracker, his or her (mostly his) actions are considered criminal when they involve unauthorized use of a computer. The folks from MIT are offended by the use of the word "hacker" to describe anyone who illegally uses a computer. The teenagers are offended when people lump crackers in with hackers. With all due respect to the MIT group, I use the term "hacker" to identify anyone who breaks into a computer illegally. The supposed difference between a cracker and a hacker is only one of intention; the two groups are only separated by a few key strokes. Organizations must treat every intrusion as though it were committed with criminal intent.

As the Internet began taking shape in the early 1990s, the numbers of hackers wandering around in cyberspace began to increase. However, the skill and knowledge required to be a hacker decreased sharply. The original hackers had to develop their own techniques for exploiting computers; hackers today have only to look on the Internet to find a computer program that exploits the computer for them. They don't even have to know how it works to use it. The first hackers wanted to learn about computer systems; the new hackers just want to break into systems without the challenge of learning about them.

Hackers exploit computers through vulnerabilities that are unknowingly built into the operating systems or programs running on the machines. There are very few people walking around today capable of finding new vulnerabilities. Those few who can are the true computer geniuses (see Figure 4.1). There are probably less than 200 of them in the world. These geniuses are the ones who tell other hackers about the vulnerabilities. There are perhaps 1,000 hackers who can take that knowledge and develop a tool to exploit it. When that tool is posted on the Internet for the general hacker community, it becomes available to everyone. According to my estimates, there are between 35,000 and 50,000 hackers who fall into the "clueless" ranks. These people would be lost without the knowledge and the tools produced by their more competent brethren. As a matter of fact, there have been numerous cases—several of which I personally observed— involving hackers who broke into a computer system using a

Figure 4.1   *Hacker Community Diagram*

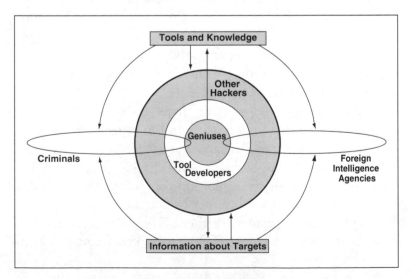

very sophisticated attack, then did not know basic commands to manipulate the system.

There is little rationale for how these hackers choose their targets. Sometimes they focus on a company that just sounds like a good target. The National Computer Security Association, the Computer Emergency Response Team, and other security organizations are popular targets of mischievous hackers. As the earlier AOL example illustrated, hackers may devote themselves fanatically to a particular victim. Often, they target companies randomly, using the passwords captured through password sniffers (programs that capture passwords as they are sent across a computer network). Some hackers keep lists of computer systems with which they've had experience; when a new vulnerability presents itself, they check their lists for likely victims. Frequently, hackers hear about other hackers' successes and try the break-ins for themselves.

The threat presented by unskilled hackers is twofold. First, unskilled hackers can cause a lot of damage, often simply because they can't think of anything else to do once they get inside a system. A hacker once wrote to *2600: The Hacker's Quarterly,* bragging that he had broken into a system and deleted all of its data. Although the editors berated him for his vandalism, his attitude represents the thinking of a significant portion of the hacker community. Even when hackers don't intentionally cause damage, they can ravage a system accidentally. Well-trained computer professionals cause major, but accidental, damage all the time; just think about what inept hackers—and there are tens of thousands of them—can do.

Second, most hackers divulge their information out of a desire to prove themselves and to publicize their successes. When a typical, immature hacker manages to break into a system, the main thing on his mind is bragging rights, and he's on the Internet and other bulletin board systems with his story almost immediately. His story is often challenged by his peers, and he must give out the details of his activities to prove himself. That's how the word gets out about system vulnerabilities.

Foreign intelligence agencies and criminals will sometimes dupe these naive hackers into finding vulnerable systems for them. Hackers so indiscriminately spread this information that they could be considered accomplices to many crimes.

Thus, the problem with typical hackers is not that they commit industrial espionage but that they facilitate and mask industrial espionage. They make the work of law enforcement and systems administrators much more difficult, allowing industrial espionage to flourish in places that it should not. Foreign intelligence agencies and criminal elements rely on the hacker community to hide many of their crimes. Probably less than 1 percent of computer hacking is actually perpetrated for criminal purposes. Just think of the effort required by law enforcement and system administrators to figure out if a computer break-in is caused by a hacker or a master criminal. If hackers were not committing so many break-ins, it would be much easier to track down the real bad guys. Criminals also use the knowledge and tools developed and publicized by hackers for their own purposes. Unfortunately, hackers don't seem to care who else uses their information.

CONCLUSION

If your organization is not susceptible to natural disasters, has no competition, doesn't compete with foreign companies, uses no computers, produces no information of value, has no enemies, and all your past and present employees are happy and loyal, then I congratulate you—you are threat-free (and how are things in Oz, anyway?). If, on the other hand, your business functions in the real world, then you must take the time to consider the elements that threaten to compromise your organization's information. Only then can you take reasonable steps to protect yourself.

5

Vulnerability

VULNERABILITIES—THE HOLES IN YOUR ORGANIZATION'S security—represent another essential set of considerations in your risk analysis. Although threats are always present, there is no *risk* without vulnerabilities. Attackers are looking for weaknesses to exploit, gaps in the fence, thin spots in your armor. They're looking for a way in, and they'll keep on looking until they find one. In my experience, they usually find more than one.

The best way to prevent attacks is to familiarize yourself with your organization's weaknesses; you want to know how they're going to come at you. Some security-minded people recommend focusing on the attacks themselves, emphasizing a strategy of second-guessing the attackers. Prevent the potential attack, the thinking goes, and you have no problems. However, to my mind, this approach cures the symptoms while ignoring the disease. For example, if you believe that you might be attacked by people calling up your employees and asking for their passwords, you could create an awareness program that tells people not to give out their passwords over the telephone. But what if an attacker calls up and gets your people to cooperate in other ways, by getting them to transfer

money to the attacker's account, for example? (Never underestimate the abilities of skilled people.) You must take care of
the root cause of the problem, which in this case is poor general security awareness. Chapter 14 provides a long list of
generally simple and highly effective countermeasures that
will plug up an awful lot of holes. You can't plug a hole,
though, if you don't know it's there.

Of course, some vulnerabilities are simply unavoidable.
Businesses must exchange information with other businesses,
companies must bring new people into the corporate fold, and
organizations of all kinds are using the Internet in myriad
ways. There is no such thing as perfect security. Your goal
should be to understand the vulnerabilities in your organization and to take reasonable steps to minimize your risk.

A word about technology in this context: When most
people consider information security, they think about technical issues. They believe that protecting information is all about
protecting computers. Please remember: *information is information*. This phrase should be your mantra. Information on a
computer can be quite valuable, but the same piece of information written on a crumbled up cocktail napkin is worth just
as much. It is therefore just as important to protect that napkin as it is to protect the computer. Focusing on computer-
based data can leave an organization extremely vulnerable to
tried-and-true espionage techniques.

I think it's useful to look at vulnerabilities in four broad
categories: operations, physical, personnel, and technical.
Some vulnerabilities don't fit perfectly into any single category, but, for clarity's sake, I've grouped the examples in this
chapter into the most appropriate of these subdivisions.

OPERATIONS VULNERABILITIES

Operations vulnerabilities refer to weaknesses that result from
the way your organization does business day to day. When a

company becomes a target, attackers look first to company operations for vulnerabilities. How does this company go about giving out information? What do this organization's actions reveal about its future plans?

This security concern is actually a military concept, but it is appropriate in the commercial environment. In a military campaign, you might want to surprise an enemy with a sneak attack at an unexpected location, and you have to get your army over there without giving away your plans. Spies notice when you're gassing up the tanks. They notice when you put refueling stations on the way to borders. They can observe service personnel calling their families and canceling appointments. Remember the example of the pizza deliveries to the Pentagon (Chapter 4)? When military strategists work late in Washington, they call out for food—and spies take notice. Many of your operational activities telegraph your secrets.

Companies also just give their secrets away. I can call up the mail room of hundreds of companies and ask them to send me the company business plan. And they'll do it, with a little creative lying on my part.

Operations security vulnerabilities are the most threatening and ominous weaknesses in any organization. They are also the most plentiful, because they result primarily from human error and weakness. By taking the time to learn about these weaknesses in your organization, you can prevent or minimize the exploitation of them.

Poor Awareness

In my experience performing penetration tests and investigating information-related crimes, poor awareness of security issues stands out as the most common operations vulnerability. Moderately skilled criminals can get well-meaning employees to hand over just about any piece of information they want. The damage from this lack of awareness of general security issues is compounded by a lack of understanding of the value of your company's information. This lack of understanding underlies the success of the attackers in most of the case studies presented in Part II of this book.

Professionals often complain that employees lack common sense when it comes to information security. What the security pros forget is that *there is no common sense without common knowledge.* The general public is not aware of the security implications of the "little things," such as passwords, secured telephone lines, and cleaned and locked desks. It's been my experience that many security professionals fail to realize the importance of some of these things themselves. Most people find it hard to believe when I tell them that I can walk up to employees and ask for their company's most sensitive secrets and they will give them to me. However, if I ask for information in the right way, those skeptics would probably give me the same sensitive data.

The basic principle to keep in mind here is that the most successful industrial espionage crimes result from many small successes—several seemingly unimportant incidents that add up to major losses.

The all-too-common attitude that "It will never happen to me" is a spy's best weapon. Victims who feel this way ignore basic security considerations and allow unusual incidents and requests to go unnoticed. They hand over information to anyone who asks for it in the right way. They leave valuable information out in the open, vulnerable to theft and compromise. Usually, they don't even notice that they've been attacked.

One infamous incident illustrates the potential for disaster from poor awareness. During the Gulf War, a U.S. military officer took home some classified plans. On the way, he stopped at a store. While he was in the store, someone broke into his car and stole his briefcase, which contained the plans.

In a lesser-known incident, a researcher in a high-tech company took some very sensitive research notebooks with him on a trip to New York. He, too, left his notebooks in his car. The car was broken into, and the notebooks were stolen. I cite this incident because such occurrences are startlingly common. My guess is that almost every security manager of a mid-sized to large firm reading this will believe that I'm referring to his or her company. These things happen because people don't realize the value of the documents they toss on the seat next to them. The fact that someone might want the information never occurs to them, nor do they realize the ultimate threat to the company's security that such behavior invites.

Poor awareness also means that employees don't know the proper way to react to potentially compromising situations. They don't know how to deliver quality customer service while maintaining security. Security and customer service are not mutually exclusive. In most cases, they can even enhance each other.

Many people believe that strong security is the same as martial law, and they end up—sometimes consciously, sometimes without knowing it—avoiding the issue altogether. They dismiss company protocol. Security warnings go in one ear and out the other. It isn't maliciousness that moves people to believe that company security measures are just procedural and unnecessarily restrictive; it is poor awareness.

I firmly believe that most people actually want to help protect their company's information—or they would if they understood the seriousness of the problem. Your employees do care, and they will cooperate, if you let them know what's at stake with an appropriate employee awareness program (see Chapter 14).

Most of the vulnerabilities that follow in this section grow out of poor awareness. In other words, your people would not do these things if they were aware of the problem. That's why I've listed this vulnerability first, and why I believe it is so important.

Social Engineering

Social engineering is not a vulnerability per se but a type of attack that exploits operations security vulnerabilities, specifically poor awareness. Hackers frequently use this method to get around technical security protection mechanisms. If a computer system has no generally exploitable technical vulnerabilities, a hacker might call up a company randomly and ask people for their user IDs and passwords. To get people to give them this information, they might imitate technical support personnel. Hackers also use social engineering—or *pretext phone calls*, as the police refer to this method—to get people to give them computer access points and other information about their computers and software. Chapter 6 presents a very successful use of this attack method to compromise an investment banking firm. Kevin Mitnick (see the Introduction) also used social engineering to get companies to set up accounts for him on their systems.

In a broader sense, social engineering can refer to any situation in which people are interacting with others to manipulate them. The Nazis originally coined the phrase to mean the manipulation of the general population; the Soviet Union adopted the term as well (the term remains offensive to many people because of its sinister roots). In the 1980s, hackers made the term popular in their community to describe strategies for getting information from people through nontechnical means. The term can also refer to basic criminal confidence scams.

Social engineering is an extremely widespread and common attack technique. At the 1996 DefCon convention (an annual conference for hackers), I surveyed the attendees for the methods they used to get into computer systems. Fully 20 percent of the activities they described involved social engineering methods. It was no surprise to learn that some hackers relied totally on social engineering.

During a penetration test I was once involved in, a colleague of mine was performing a technical penetration test against a large bank when he received a call from an irate bank employee. The employee was upset because he thought we were using social engineering techniques in the test, which we were not supposed do. We asked him why he thought we were using social engineering, and he told us that someone had called up a help desk at the bank and asked for the types of software specifically in use for a certain banking function. The telephone number that the would-be attacker gave was false, the bank employee said, so the call had to be illicit. The call was illicit, but it wasn't from us.

Social engineering is so effective that it has even been used by law enforcement agencies to capture criminals. In one example, the New York City Police Department sent letters to people with outstanding criminal warrants. The letters announced that the recipient had won a television set or sports tickets. All he or she had to do was come down to a rented hall and collect the prize. Once the room was full of eager "prize winners," the cops arrested them.

Reverse social engineering refers to an interesting variant on this attack method, in which the victim comes to the attacker, instead of the attacker approaching the victim. For example, a hacker once posted fliers on a company's bulletin boards announcing that the help desk telephone number had been changed. The number posted was to the hacker's home phone. Employees of the company called the number regularly, and the hacker secured passwords and just about anything else he wanted to know from employees wanting help.

Social engineering is a very powerful tool. It can bypass millions of dollars' worth of security mechanisms, it's very cheap to perform, and it doesn't take much technical expertise. All that's needed is someone to be a good liar.

Accidents and Carelessness

Accidents and carelessness are described in Chapter 4 as the cause of the largest losses to corporations. Lawyers refer to this as Errors and Omissions. Accidents take on many forms and are an unavoidable fact of life. Even when people mean well, they make mistakes. People accidentally leave documents in the wrong places at the wrong times. They give away floppy disks that inadvertently contain sensitive files. An innocent slip of the tongue can be extremely costly. Virtually everybody has caused the compromise of sensitive information at some time or other and will cause it in the future. Much of this is due to poor awareness.

Just because accidents happen doesn't mean you should stop trying to prevent them. In my experience, accidents are dealt with by organizations most often after the fact. The problem is, people often fail to report them because of ignorance. Some very destructive slips are covered up as a natural reaction to screwing up. You can't stop what you don't know about, so, as far as accidents are concerned, an ounce of prevention is worth a pound of cure.

Policies and Procedures

Sometimes, the policies and procedures of your organization can create security vulnerabilities. Although they can go far in reducing risk, many policies and procedures are developed without any consideration for security issues. Mandatory internal reporting of sensitive issues, for example, can generate sources of revealing information. Some policies simply require too much documentation and allow for distribution that is too widespread. Policies that require people to give their names and departments when they answer the phone give unknown callers essential information that social engineers can use against you.

Take a look at your policies and procedures, and ask yourself which policies force your people to give out information that might be useful to an attacker. Is it necessary to give out that information? In situations where an employee is required to give out that information, do they give out just the required data or do they go further than necessary? Obviously, some information must be given out from a business perspective, but can you limit that information from a security perspective?

Predictability

Criminals are always looking for the best times to commit their crimes. Bank robbers usually stake out a place to watch its operations patterns. They notice when the bank opens and closes. They keep track of when the bank is least crowded and when it has the most money. They study the guards to see if they are observant or lazy. Within a short period of time—a couple of days at most—they know more about the bank than most of its employees do. Terrorists watch their victims, observing when they leave for work, what routes they take, and who they meet during a typical day.

A hacker once told me a story about a young couple who approached him with a plan to steal from the company where the young woman worked. The company performed many computerized financial transactions, and they wanted the fellow to hack the system. They would let the hacker into the building after hours, they said, and then he could hack the system and extract five million dollars for the couple and take whatever he wanted for himself. When the hacker asked what made them think they would not be caught, they replied that they knew audits were performed only once a month. They would steal the money right after one audit and fly to the Caribbean, and it would be a month before anyone noticed.

Organizations and people are very predictable. Industrial spies know when people typically leave their offices, when buildings are left empty, when information is left unattended, and anything else that tells them the best time to strike. See Chapter 10 for a case study involving a German spy who used such information to his advantage.

Procedures in Practice

All companies have their rules and regulations, but often a wide gap exists between the procedures they put on paper and the procedures their employees follow. For example, many companies have a rule that employees are forbidden to write down their passwords; this rule is one of the most common among companies with computer systems—and it's one of the most violated rules in the world. People are not supposed to take work home, but they do. They're supposed to log out of the computer whenever they get up and leave their desk, but they don't.

Look around your organization and notice what is actually going on. Walk around the facility. Stay after everyone else has left for the day. How hard is it for you to get your hands on sensitive information? Often, there's a big difference between the way things are supposed to be and the way things are. It is more important that you understand the way your business really functions.

Sales and Marketing

The job of the sales and marketing departments is to get the word out about your products and/or services—and not just your current products. In this highly competitive marketplace, salespeople often leak information about upcoming offerings to potential customers. They give up key details, scheduling information, and product specifications, all in the service of making the sale. They don't do it to cause problems. For the most part, this is a matter of honest enthusiasm.

At trade shows, anyone expressing a sincere interest in a marketer's products can get just about any information he or she wants from that person. Salespeople are supposed to give out information, not protect it. On almost all occasions, if a sale is in jeopardy, sensitive information will be revealed. Trained industrial spies know how to pose as interested customers and drag out a purchase negotiation until they get the information they want.

In one case, a French firm invited companies from all over the world to bid on a contract job. As part of the bidding process, the companies were required to provide the French firm with a great deal of detailed information about their capabilities and production processes. In the end, the French company decided to hire none of the bidders. In effect, they had gotten the companies to spy on themselves and deliver the information for free.

Examine how your own sales and marketing people release information about your organization. Notice whether they seem to be ignoring the fact that some information is sensitive. They have a job to do, but you have to make sure that they're not undermining your security efforts when they do it.

Public Relations

To maintain a good corporate image and keep stock prices high, many companies keep up ongoing public relations campaigns, which are carefully crafted to minimize negative press. They release information about their people and anything else that might make the company look good. From a business perspective, this activity is very important; from a security perspective, any release of information is bad.

Your public relations (PR) department represents an unavoidable vulnerability. In large companies, the press releases gush out of the PR department month after month. Telling people about your organization is their job—they create publicity, and security is the last thing on their minds. You can reduce your vulnerability in this area by making sure that they don't tell the world more than it ought to know.

Help Wanted Ads

Now more than ever, good employees are hard to find, and companies use a variety of means to attract top people. Placing a help wanted ad is one of the most common methods. In an effort to glamorize the job and make it appealing, though, the ads might be saying more than they should.

Consider the following excerpt from a job advertisement run by Lockheed Martin in the October 21, 1996, edition of *ComputerWorld:*

Join the Elite Team at Lockheed Martin

F-22 Computer Resources Engineer
Performs change management activities for F-22 software products or develops and maintains Oracle databases. BSCS, BSE or equivalent and 5+ years experience in software development in a DoD environment required. Must have knowledge of CASE Tools, Ada, dataleaf, and Open VMS operating systems (Vax and Alpha).

What about this position required that Lockheed Martin mention the F-22? It does sound tempting to people who want to work on state-of-the-art technologies, but the fact that the work is being performed for the F-22 is irrelevant. The ad is for a computer professional to support software development. The fact that the work supports the F-22 does not impact the job qualifications. Besides attracting computer professionals who want to work on a major development effort, this ad also attracts a variety of spies. This is the place where I would apply if I had any intention of gathering sensitive information. The fact that this opening is for change management support is critical. All software for the F-22 will flow through the hands of the person who gets that job.

This is a glaring example, but I don't mean to single out Lockheed Martin. Most companies have given up sensitive information in want ads to attract top workers. I have read listings that describe a bank's entire computer environment, that explain how the bank supports billions of dollars of financial transactions daily, and that include detailed descriptions of hardware and software. That last piece of information tells me exactly how to attack the bank, as discussed later in this chapter. Besides making the job appealing to potential employees, these ads reveal vulnerabilities in your organization that criminals may use against you.

Internet Usage

The Internet can be a tremendous resource. It provides a wealth of information previously unimagined. However, the Internet can also expose major vulnerabilities within your company.

When people access the Internet, they leave tracks. Every time someone visits a Web site or reads a newsgroup message, a log of the activity is collected. A good spy will examine your Internet usage and use your activity to figure out what you are up to.

What your people say about your company and themselves on-line is also very important. While conducting research on an organization, I came upon a message posted to a technical newsgroup by an employee. He announced that he and everyone else in his department were just given new computers. He gave the model number, operating systems version, and applications he was using. He was putting out a call for software that might be useful, but he was really just asking for trouble. He had in effect made his company a prime target for hackers and criminals around the world. He had told the world exactly what type of computer he was using; all systems have known vulnerabilities that an attacker could exploit. From the message header, an attacker could easily figure out which company the poster worked for and even the exact Internet address of his computer. The fact that he also asked to be sent software left him particularly vulnerable; people could send him anything, including a virus-laden application that could damage his company's system.

In another case, an MIT student was browsing the Web and ended up at a neo-Nazi site. Several weeks later, the student began receiving recruitment literature from the group through the postal mail. The neo-Nazis were able to deduce his name and address just because he had stopped by the Web site.

Generally, any time people send information out over the Internet, they are giving away information about themselves and their company. Even an innocent visit to a Web site gives away some sensitive information. The repercussions for your company can be devastating.

Credit Cards and Other Travel Records

ABC's *Prime Time Live* aired a report on industrial espionage in 1996, in which a producer posed as a foreign businessman who wanted to collect information on a competitor. The producer contacted potential attackers (private investigators) and asked them how they would go about breaching the competitor's security. The first thing he would do, one investigator said unhesitatingly, is check the credit card records.

Credit card records can tell a savvy snoop almost everything about a person's life. They can also say a lot about what a company is doing. It's an electronic trail that stays around for a very long time.

Different types of travel records also reveal much about a company's plans and future actions. You can figure out who a company is negotiating with by finding out where its representatives travel. Find a copy of the rep's frequent flyer account report, and you'll be able to find out exactly which hotels he or she stayed in. Business travelers usually choose hotels that are close to the companies they're working with. If you get a copy of the hotel record, you might learn that the rep was given a special rate reserved for people working with and for a large company in a particular area. If the person involved works on mergers or new stock offerings, you have insider trading information.

Telephone Records and Conversations

No one can do business without using a telephone. It is probably the most essential device of the contemporary business environment, and it is easily the most ubiquitous. Consequently, telephone records—which are not that difficult to get—can reveal a lot about what you and your organization are doing. Think about it this way: If you were to access the telephone records of a young woman and find that she has placed numerous calls to caterers, bridal stores, and photographers, you might rightly conclude that she is getting married, even if you know nothing else about her. Think about your own telephone calls. What could a record of your calls tell a potential attacker about what you're up to? Like credit card records, telephone records stay around for a very long time.

Obviously the most sensitive information about a telephone conversation is the conversation itself, which can be compromised several ways. People can overhear what you're saying just by standing nearby or by sitting in the next cubicle. Telephones can be tapped in three ways: the telephone system can be compromised, the individual phone can be bugged, and a radio receiver can be used to pick up cellular and portable telephone conversations. Everyone knows about the first two, but many people don't realize that nonwire telephone communications are very easily intercepted.

In terms of potential operations vulnerabilities, what matters is what people talk about over the phone. If your employees are aware that there is a vulnerability, they can minimize your risk by watching what they say and whom they call, especially when using cellular and portable telephones.

Casual Conversations

People often talk about work in many inappropriate places without regard to who may be listening. I have already described casual conversations as a frequently overlooked form of information (Chapter 1). Such conversations can represent significant vulnerabilities, depending on where the conversations take place and who is involved. A good spy can enter a conversation in progress and turn the discussion towards more sensitive topics. These conversations can occur on the streets, at parties, on buses, and so on, and they involve just about every aspect of an individual's work.

Supplier Records

Even when you've gone to great lengths to make your own facility airtight, you still have to deal with other businesses, many of which are much less security-conscious than you. Your suppliers have a great deal of valuable information about you that they aren't necessarily taking steps to keep under wraps. They know what and how much your company orders, when it's delivered, when you ask for deliveries to be delayed, and when you cut back on your orders. Just knowing how much of a given item a company orders can tell a great deal about what it intends to produce. Depending on your relationship, your suppliers could know more about you than your own employees do.

Personal Aggrandizement

An individual's desire to impress others has caused some of the biggest security problems in history. People regularly compromise information for fame or the adoration of others. Some men do stupid things to impress women. Once, when I was once traveling for NSA with two coworkers, I found myself sitting in the international terminal of Charles de Gaulle Airport in Paris, waiting for a flight. One of the people I was traveling with began talking with a woman sitting next to him, and the conversation naturally turned to the reason for our trip. My coworker started talking about computers, and the woman seemed very interested. Although he didn't talk about anything sensitive, he did begin attracting attention from other people sitting nearby. Eventually, the woman asked a very natural question: "So, who do you work for?" At that point, my coworker realized that saying he worked for one of the world's most secretive spy agencies to a stranger in the middle of this airport was not a good idea, and he sat there dumbfounded for an uncomfortably long period of time. I replied for him, saying that we worked for the Department of Defense. If a terrorist had been among the interested listeners in that French airport, that conversation could have gotten us killed.

People want to be listened to, and they will say a great deal more than necessary when someone is giving them the attention we all crave. The case of Richard Morris, President Clinton's political adviser during the 1996 presidential campaign, illustrates this point very well. Never mind Morris's bad judgment in carrying on an affair with a call girl; the woman's accusations that he tried to impress her by letting her listen in on telephone conversations with President Clinton ruined his career.

I was recently traveling on an airplane that was rerouted from the original destination because of weather conditions.

Sitting several rows behind me was a salesperson who worked for a large defense contractor. He used the airphone to pick up his messages and to change appointments, and he carried on in such a loud voice that either he was trying to impress people or he was just plain stupid. I learned the name of his employer from four rows away (and I don't usually even learn anything about the person sitting next to me). I and at least thirty other people heard the names of the people he was meeting with and when and where they were meeting. We also heard about his plans for a sales trip to Hungary; he clearly raised his voice whenever he said the country's name. It seemed to me that this man was very insecure, just the type industrial spies look for. If I were a competitor, I could have written down everything that he said and handed it to my marketing department.

Technical professionals seem to be excessively vulnerable in this area. If a male technical professional meets a woman who appears to be interested in his work, he will tell her everything about his job. I don't say this to criticize; it's only human nature, especially in a field where so many people simply don't understand the person's work. However, this serious vulnerability affects many organizations, and as Chapter 9 shows, good spies know how to take advantage of this.

Taking Work Home

In such a competitive age, it's no surprise that so many people take work home with them from the office. They're working hard, filling every free moment, pursuing a work ethic that is the heart and soul of this country—and they're creating a serious vulnerability.

Look around the airplane the next time you fly. You'll see fellow passengers with open laptops and documents spread out and spilling onto the floor. Their bosses would be pleased, but the industrial spies reading company secrets over their shoulders are positively giddy. On a recent trip back from

Atlanta, Georgia, I was seated next to a young salesman from Diebold, one of the world's top manufacturers of automated teller machines (ATMs). He and several other people from his company were returning from a sales and marketing meeting. Throughout the flight, my fellow traveler reviewed his meeting notes, which were very detailed. They included an analysis of Diebold's present and future initiatives as well as other vital information on the company's products. How do I know all this? Sitting next to him, I could hardly miss a detail.

Whenever you work outside the office, you don't know who is watching. When you're out in public, you have little control over your environment, and it's impossible to implement even the most basic security measures. If your people are taking work home every night, you've got a vulnerability, and your organization might be creating security leaks in service of the short-term bottom line.

Poor Incident-Reporting Procedures

If an employee in your organization does detect a possible security breach, does he or she know what to do about it? When employees do take action—and remember, they usually don't—what they do most often is tell their supervisors. Unfortunately, most of the supervisors I've interviewed over the years don't know what to do, either.

Diligent employees are left helpless and frustrated when they don't get an adequate response to their concerns, which makes them even less likely to report similar incidents in the future. Remember: detecting espionage activity is the toughest part of combatting it, and you need all the help you can get.

Basic Human Weakness

Most employees are well-meaning and want to help their co-workers. They are used to cooperating, and management encourages them to be service-oriented. So it's only natural to find people within an organization who will gladly bypass those pesky company rules to be helpful to others they believe are coworkers.

Even poorly trained spies know how to take advantage of a person's goodwill and use it against his or her company. Sometimes attackers just confuse people into giving up information. When people feel overwhelmed with too much information, they often follow the lead of whoever appears to know what he or she is doing. No one wants to look stupid. Good industrial spies always look like they know what they're doing.

Perhaps the most dangerous human weakness is apathy. Many people want to avoid problems, and they tend to choose the path of least resistance. All a spy has to do with these people is persist, and they will eventually give in. Apathetic employees not only give up information more easily but are much less likely to report questionable situations. They just want to do their job and go home. If there is a choice between reporting a questionable incident, thereby attracting attention and scrutiny, or just letting it go, chances are they'll just let it go.

Giving Out Too Little Information

Although this seems counterintuitive, giving out too little information can be as much of a problem as giving out too much. Companies often hide information about threats or losses, fearing that publicizing a breach in security will make them more vulnerable. Employees are never told that they should be on the lookout for specific suspicious activity; consequently, they can't help. In the case cited in Chapter 8, Intel security had a suspected spy under surveillance while another group within the company was giving him access to additional, more sensitive information. With a little more intracompany communication, the company might have prevented a devastating loss.

You can provide too little information to outside parties as well. In a personal situation, two companies approached me to subcontract to them in performing a penetration test. Neither company was willing to tell me who the customer was because of various reasons. Comically, it turned out that both companies were bidding on the same contract. Since neither company was willing to tell me who the customer was, I didn't discover the problem until the last minute, causing problems for everyone involved.

When companies play their cards too close to the vest, so to speak, they often keep potentially valuable information from their own employees and others. Security that is so tight it strangles productive communication only helps the spies.

PHYSICAL VULNERABILITIES

When most people think about physical security, they imagine burly guards standing inside fenced-in compounds, iron doors with impenetrable time locks, and searchlights—lots of searchlights. Truth be told, if they had their way, many security managers would establish just such a prison camp environment so they could sleep better at night. Of course, the company wouldn't be much more secure. The fact is, successful industrial spies are the ones who exploit the small physical vulnerabilities. After all, if someone is already allowed inside the facility, say, as a temp or a janitor, what good are the searchlights? The greatest damage is done by people who are already on the inside.

Another often overlooked physical security issue is natural disasters. As I explain in Chapter 4, natural disasters cause more damage than malicious insiders ever have or will. A hard disk that crashes because of a power outage is just as great a loss as a hard disk that is stolen.

You should also remember that physical vulnerabilities often facilitate attacks against nonphysical vulnerabilities. An attacker might be able to technically exploit a computer system only if he or she can gain physical access to a terminal.

Apathetic or Poorly Informed Guards

Traditionally, security guards are trained merely to limit access to company facilities. They stand at the door, ask for your ID, and check their approved lists. In some cases, they're also called upon to search the belongings of exiting employees to make sure that people are not carrying out sensitive documents or property. But they are rarely trained to actually recognize sensitive material. Companies typically train their security guards to look for key markings or indicators on documents. In the defense community, guards are trained to look for documents with classification identifiers at the top and bottom of a page. In the private sector, guards are told to look out for green binder covers or something else just as obvious. This situation creates an enormous physical vulnerability. Smart attackers can just take their stolen documents out of the green binders and stuff them into red ones, or they can tear the classifications from the tops and bottoms of the pages and stroll out the door unhindered.

Let's face it, a security guard's job isn't always the most stimulating activity in the world. Guards can easily fall into a rut and lose their enthusiasm for the work—or maybe they never had any enthusiasm in the first place. The guards are there to spot the isolated security problem, but since there are typically very few of them, they become bored and apathetic.

This lack of devotion is particularly damaging when guards are supposed to validate access requests by checking people's ID badges. Hair styles change, people grow beards and mustaches, they gain or lose weight; badges frequently do not resemble the people carrying them. In addition, companies have "rush hours" when the traffic is heavy and the guards must look at dozens of badges per minute. Combine apathy, inaccurate ID photos, and overwhelming numbers, and you've got a recipe for a major physical vulnerability. There were stories at NSA about the Office of Security spot-checking the agency's guards by sending people through security with badges that did not resemble the people wearing them. In one case, a person is said to have walked in with a picture of a *dog* on a badge and was able to get through unchallenged.

Furthermore, employees are notoriously rude to guards, cursing the guards for making them wait or for checking their belongings—as the guards are supposed to do. To avoid offending people, many guards begin to back off; they've endured so many annoyed looks and out-and-out insults that they effectively loosen your security net.

No Physical Access Controls

Although poorly trained guards can be a problem, no guards—or locks—is a much bigger and more common problem. I can't tell you how many times I have personally walked into an office that was unattended, but it's something I do with great regularity in my penetration testing work. Once I'm in an unlocked office, I can get onto the computer systems or walk out with papers, even a computer. If spies can get through the doors and if they look like they know what they're doing, then very few people will challenge them.

Garbage

Your organization's trash can reveal a lot. Most of the time, garbage is garbage, but it can contain incredibly important information. A great deal of credit card fraud results from people throwing out their credit card receipts, which criminals pick out of the garbage. The Masters of Deception and Legion of Doom hacker groups were able to gain control of key telephone system assets by finding a list of passwords in the garbage of the New York Telephone Company. Companies throw away draft copies of many important documents that contain much or all of the information contained in the final draft.

Trash is valuable. The U.S. Army has a unit devoted to trash intelligence. I've even heard about a case in which a trash disposal company would pick up one company's trash and bring it over to a competitor.

Of course you have to be able to throw out your garbage, but you must recognize it as a potentially dangerous vulnerability. Tossed into large dumpsters outside your building, your trash is almost certainly a target of corporate spies. Although most of the information you throw away will be useless, there's almost always enough valuable information to make it worthwhile for attackers to dig through the dumpster.

Open Storage

When competitors want to see how well your factory is doing, all they have to do is watch what goes in and comes out of your facilities. Depending on the size and nature of your products, this could be a very easy task, especially if your products are stored out in the open. If a foreign intelligence agency wants to know how many tanks the U.S. is producing, all it has to do is count the tanks sitting outside the tank factory. One of the primary jobs of "spy satellites" is to photograph military equipment in open storage areas. In this post–Cold War era, satellites are used for more than just military observation; industrial spies use the same techniques. It's also likely that Aerobus, the European airplane manufacturer and Boeing's only real competitor for that market, monitors the production of Boeing airplanes to see whether it is behind or ahead on its orders. Aerobus uses this type of information to give its customers the impression that Boeing cannot deliver planes on schedule. The startling part of this story is that the photographs came from commercial, not military, satellites.

Of course, industrial spies don't need satellites to exploit your open storage vulnerabilities. They don't even need to break the law. A company in Virginia that specializes in the legal collection of business intelligence rents airplanes to fly over facilities and photograph storage yards. In one case, the intelligence collection company's photos revealed to its client that the client's competitor was not meeting its production schedule. The client company was able to go to its competitor's customers and use the production delays against the company, eventually capturing a very large share of the market.

Anyone who can watch what goes into or out of your company has a good indication of what your capabilities are. If you fail to take steps to mask your activity, you leave yourself vulnerable to anyone with a camera.

Information Storage

The way most companies store their documents makes it easy for spies to wander in, rifle through papers, and take whatever they want to the copy room. Banks go to great lengths to protect their cash; they all keep it in vaults. Retail stores monitor customers with video cameras and attach special tags to their stock to protect themselves from shoplifters. Yet companies with documents that are easily more valuable than a pair of jeans do virtually nothing to ensure the security of their hard-copy records.

In many cases, companies store documents in file cabinets in offices located throughout their buildings, leaving the responsibility for protecting those documents to the person who uses them. Rarely is a record kept of the locations of sensitive documents. Often, the file cabinets are left unlocked, leaving the information vulnerable to anyone who wanders through the area.

Some companies establish formal document storage areas. Often, these storerooms are little more than closets with a lock; how often the locks are used is another question. Frequently, the storage areas are left unlocked throughout the day and are locked only at night after everyone has left. These storage areas may or may not be attended, depending on corporate policy. Document storage rooms that are unattended are open to virtually anyone. Monitored storage areas are secured with varying degrees of effectiveness. In some cases, the attendant has an access list that specifies who can take out which documents, but such access lists are the exception. Typically, anyone in the company can walk in and ask for any document or browse freely through the files, picking up any document that looks interesting.

Copy Machines

"The copy machine," reads the message on a popular NSA awareness poster, "is a spy's best friend." The story in Chapter 8 is an excellent example of the sad truth of this statement. Copy machines allow people to steal information without removing it, reducing significantly the chances that they will be caught. Just about every major national espionage case has involved a massive document copying effort. In cases of industrial espionage, they are just as widely used.

Copy machines are usually accessible in many locations throughout an organization, twenty-four hours a day, and there are always at least a few located in discreet nooks where no one would notice a spy at work.

Unusual copy machine usage is one of the best ways to detect an industrial spy. Are your copy machines in your organization in visible locations? Is a video camera monitoring the areas? Does your copy machine use the available accounting features to track the number of copies different people in your organizations are making?

Although floppy disks might someday replace the copy machine as a spy's best friend, the copy machine will always be important to anyone trying to go unnoticed.

Your Neighbors

While you are surveying your operation for physical vulnerabilities, don't forget to check out your neighbors. This is probably one of the most overlooked physical vulnerabilities. The closer the competition—literally—the greater the danger that they will be able to monitor your activities to their advantage. Surprisingly, many people don't consider the dangers of physical proximity to a competitor.

Competitors can set up shop in the office across the hall. They can share electrical or computer wiring facilities. They might be so close that all they have to do is put a drinking glass to the wall to hear what's going on in your company. Proximity makes you more susceptible to technical attacks as well (see the discussion on TEMPEST, page 132). They can watch who visits your facilities and target them as potential clients.

If your neighbors actually have criminal intentions, they probably know very well what security measures you have in place, and they know how to get around them. Their workers could become very friendly with yours, due to proximity, creating more chances for information compromise.

Total Loss of Control Away from Main Facilities

Whenever you leave your corporate facilities, you are at the mercy of your environment. You should have no expectation of privacy beyond your home turf. If you leave anything in your hotel room, consider the information compromised, whether it's on a computer or on pieces of paper. As I point out in Chapter 4, in many foreign countries you can expect your facilities to be entered without your permission, bugged without legal repercussions, and infiltrated by local spies.

Even inside the U.S. you are vulnerable beyond the walls of your facilities. Hotel maids can leave doors open accidentally, making it easy for a spy claiming to be you to get inside, grab your papers, and run. Airports have become a favorite hunting ground of laptop thieves. One gambit has been particularly effective: the target puts his or her laptop on the conveyor belt, and one thief steps in front of the line, triggering the alarm and blocking the way while a guard searches for metal objects. Meanwhile, the laptop has gone on through the X-ray machine, and an accomplice on the other side snatches it up and takes off. I could go on for pages describing the attacks and dangers you face away from the security of your company facility, even in your own country.

Contributing to the problem is the fact that most people are not sufficiently aware of their surroundings when they are doing business away from the office. They don't recognize the many opportunities an adversary has to exploit them outside the cubicle.

Equipment Size

The fact that computer equipment is getting smaller all the time adds to your physical vulnerabilities. Simply put, smaller equipment is easier to steal—and so is the information it contains. Desktop computers used to weigh almost forty pounds; now we have laptops that weigh six pounds. We even have highly sophisticated palm-top computers with very large storage capacities that can be slipped into a coat pocket. All of this technology is very easy to conceal.

Data storage capacity is also increasing at the same time as the storage media get smaller. In the old days, the bulkiness of paper files made it difficult to steal very much information. Today, a floppy disk can hold more than a megabyte of data—

more information than is contained in this entire book. The disks for the new Zip drives can hold more than one hundred times the data of a normal floppy disk. Spies can walk out of your organization with billions of dollars' worth of data tucked unobtrusively behind their pocket protectors.

Poor Inventory Tracking

As equipment gets smaller, it also becomes harder to track. Computers, which were once rare, are now extremely common. In many companies, there are more computers than people. It's no longer odd to move a computer from one location to another. It is so common, in fact, that companies often fail to keep track of which machine is where. More important, they often fail to notice when people carry computers out of the building.

From an information perspective, it is almost impossible to track electronic documents. People can copy a document without creating a record. There is no system that can track disks or other information, so thefts can occur at the will of the spy or petty thief.

Messy Desks

Most industrial spies never have to break into filing cabinets, because they can find everything they need on people's desks. Many people tend to leave work out on their desks at the end of the day. It's only natural to leave out the components of the project you're right in the middle of. But when your employees leave sensitive documents unprotected on their desks, they make it easy for anyone walking by to see exactly what they're doing. Good industrial spies will recognize this bad habit and exploit it. They can visit the office when the employee is gone, snatch up sensitive documents, make copies, and return them to the pile on the desk. When the desk is really messy, a spy can just take a document, knowing that the employee will probably think it's lost somewhere in all the paper.

In-Boxes

Even among your neatest employees, in-boxes represent a major vulnerability. People routinely leave extremely sensitive information in these boxes. Even a very security-conscious worker can't stop someone else from dropping something very sensitive into his or her in-box. Papers lying in an in-box are vulnerable to the same exploitation as papers piled on a messy desk. Anyone can walk by and pick up the materials.

I have noticed that some people leaving sensitive material in an in-box will turn it facedown. I've even seen it taped to an office door this way. The assumption is that people will be less likely to read it as they walk by. However, this odd habit actually encourages the attention of good industrial spies. A document lying facedown is bound to get special attention.

Computers Not Logged Out

Even worse than messy desks and in-boxes are computers left logged on and unattended. An attacker can use such a machine to access everything that person is working on, or possibly, has ever worked on. More important, that person probably has access to other people's data as well. Computers that are left vulnerable in this way provide attackers with the foot in the door they're all after. Once an attacker establishes an initial access point, he or she can compromise your entire computer network.

Computers with No Password Protection

Many computer systems in use today require little more than the click of the "on" switch for instant access to information.

In this day and age, it's beyond understanding why any company would fail to establish tight password protocols for all the computers on their system. Without effective password protection, your company is vulnerable to the least-skilled attackers out there. Anyone can sit down at a computer in your organization and access almost every piece of information your company has to offer.

Lack of Locks and Their Use

Equally disheartening to me is the fact that offices, filing cabinets, and other storage containers in many corporate facilities have no locks. A desk you can't lock is like a birthday present to an industrial spy; an office you can't lock is like a personal piñata, except the spy is not blindfolded. Without locks, your people have no power to protect their information from physical attacks, even if they are actually trying to do it.

Unfortunately, even when locks are available, most people don't use them. Unless a company has a tough policy and its security guards check the desks at night, most employees will never lock up their materials. It seems like another aggravation to many people, and some actively resist lock-up policies. They don't want to carry around an extra key, which they might forget or lose. They just don't understand the risks involved, and they make the spy's job that much easier.

Electrical Systems

Although it's possible that an attacker might purposely cause your power supply to fail, it is much more likely that this physical vulnerability will manifest as an accident. The growth in computer usage in this country has resulted in overtaxed electrical circuits in buildings designed for a different age. Depending on your facilities, power failures might be commonplace. Such outages can cause serious damage to your computers, not to mention the loss of a great deal of work. Many PBX (corporate telephone) systems shut down when the power supply goes out, shutting off all communications. Additionally, frequent power outages can make you look incompetent or unreliable to your clients.

In some cases, poor electrical systems can create power spikes that can literally fry your computer circuitry. Lightning strikes can also cause power spikes that travel through the electrical lines. These power spikes travel through your power lines, ruining everything plugged into an electrical outlet. The reliability of your electrical circuits and sources is critical to the survival of your computers.

Your telephone system is also vulnerable to power spikes. If the telephone line itself suffers a power spike, the telephone system can be destroyed. People talking on the phone have reportedly been electrocuted when a particularly powerful spike hit.

Placement of Buildings and Equipment

The very location of your corporate facilities and its equipment creates vulnerabilities. For example, if you are located on the coast of California, you are very susceptible to earthquakes. If you are located in Florida, you might have a hurricane problem. There's not much you can do to prevent an earthquake, but these vulnerability issues should not be ignored. Your security planning should include some consideration of building and equipment placement. If your facility is located on a flood plain, you probably don't want to put your computer system in the basement (which many large companies do). When the sump pump in my home failed during a heavy rainstorm, my basement office was nearly flooded. Had I not noticed the problem in time, my computer would have been destroyed. Luckily—and it was luck—I'd set up my desk in an area of the basement that was slightly elevated. I did lose a VCR in that little flood.

If your facility catches fire, the damage could be compounded by your sprinkler systems, which would surely ruin your computers. If your computers are located in the basement, you can count on the water from the upper floors flooding the area. For this reason, many companies install Halon fire suppressers, which smother the fire without using water. Unfortunately, Halon systems are only used to protect large computer systems. Sprinkler systems are still widely used in companies with major investments in their computer systems.

PERSONNEL VULNERABILITIES

There is a fine line between personnel and operations vulnerabilities. Although operations vulnerabilities involve the way in which people and companies function, personnel vulnerabilities result from the ways in which companies hire and manage their employees. Weaknesses in this area greatly increase your risks, because they allow attackers to exploit all other vulnerabilities. The human resources (HR) department is usually the first and only line of defense against employees who would do your company harm. Once those with criminal intentions make it through the hiring process, they are free, at least for a while, from scrutiny; once they have all the rights and access of your other employees, they are extremely difficult to detect.

Failure to Validate Claimed Backgrounds

Although many companies do take the time to investigate the backgrounds of the people they hire, many more do not. Few organizations even take the time to check references, verify previous job histories, or confirm educational claims of job candidates. Hiring managers admit that the job interview is their key filtering tool. Basically, if candidates seem like they would be good workers, they get hired. When a company finds a candidate with rare skills that are much in demand, the HR people tend to streamline the hiring process even further. When a company faces a major worker shortage, it seems as though no one checks up on anybody.

This is a foolhardy practice fraught with danger. We read in the newspapers of child-care workers with child molestation convictions, programmers with malicious hacking backgrounds, janitors on parole for grand theft, and top execs with questionable qualifications. Bill Gaede's story in Chapter 8 illustrates what can happen when new hires are not carefully screened. The consequences can be truly disastrous. You could literally be giving the key to your company to criminals.

Employee Susceptibility to Crime

Even employees with clean work records can turn on you. According to former Russian intelligence operatives, many exemplary workers can be coaxed into giving up information about your company. The Russians use the acronym MICE (money, ideology, coercion, and ego) to describe areas of personnel susceptibility.

Money is easily the most widely employed device for recruiting people to commit espionage, both industrial and national. All of the most infamous espionage cases involve money, including Walker, Ames, Pollard, and others.

Ideology is another strong motivator. Some people become involved in espionage because they believe in what the attacker is doing, or they are against what the target organization is doing. Whistle-blowers are a good example of ideologically motivated spies. They are typically angry about a company's criminal practices or social actions. The tobacco industry has suffered at the hands of whistle-blowers in recent years (although people may agree with the motives, the theft of proprietary information is still espionage).

Coercion depends on a person's susceptibility to blackmail or manipulation. Blackmail usually involves sexual practices or indiscretions the blackmailing party threatens to expose. Sometimes people want to hide things from their past, such as criminal records. In some cases, people are coerced by love; in others, by threats of physical harm.

The human *ego* presents a juicy target for skilled spy masters. Many people believe they are underappreciated by their employers or that they have been somehow mistreated. These people would love to do something to get back at the company for perceived wrongs. Other people just want to play spy for the thrill of it. Some are mentally troubled for other reasons. Whatever the cause of their disaffection, observant spies find these people and manipulate them into cooperating in their criminal activities.

This is a difficult vulnerability to circumvent. It's very difficult to predict who will be susceptible to the influence of an attacker. You can't always tell when an employee is angry, disillusioned, or lonely. Even if you have suspicions, there's not much you can do about it until the employee in question takes some kind of action.

The Isolation of Human Resources

In most companies, the human resources department acts independently of all other areas. The primary reason for this isolation is possible legal implications of exposing a personnel issue. Basically, HR tends to be something of an island. It doesn't share information with other groups, and it doesn't tell people when their group members are involved in bad situations. This actually allows the bad situations to continue and ultimately increases the damage. It is fundamentally the same consequence of giving out too little information.

Even when personnel actions don't require confidentiality, human resources departments rarely inform other groups in a company that an action is pending. For example, when an employee resigns, HR typically does not inform many of the people who should know for security reasons. The information systems (IS) department is not made aware that it should be watching for any unusual activity and to deactivate the computer account after the employee leaves. Even if the employee does not come back to use the account, another attacker might use it as an unnoticed foot in the door. During my penetration tests, I have found thousands of unused accounts in some organizations.

Security staff should also be made aware of the plans of a departing employee. Many former employees have returned to company facilities to collect and gather information even after they have officially left. Since their faces look familiar, guards will be less likely to question their presence. This is a case where too much control of information can cause major problems.

Personal Hardships

Personal hardships can drive people to do things they wouldn't do under normal circumstances. Divorce, bankruptcy, medical problems, addictions—all can leave a troubled employee vulnerable to the influences of a generous and sympathetic spy master.

Company support programs can help employees with some personal troubles, but many workers simply won't avail themselves of such programs because they fear embarrassment or that their participation will become known and affect their jobs in some way. Managers should be on the lookout for changes in their employees' work habits or deportment. They could be signs of a potential vulnerability.

TECHNICAL VULNERABILITIES

Computer hackers, high technology, information warfare, cyberwars—these are the associations that come to mind when most people hear the words "industrial espionage." In truth, technical vulnerabilities are responsible for less than 20 percent of all losses or compromises of information. Of course, that still makes them a $20 billion annual problem.

Basically, technical vulnerabilities allow attackers to exploit an organization's computer systems. Although typical industrial spies take advantage of these vulnerabilities primarily to gather information, more malevolent intruders may use them to damage your computer systems and hurt your organization. As information resource management (IRM) principles imply (see Chapter 3), when you destroy an organization's information assets, you potentially destroy everything of value. It can be done with a bomb, but doing it with computers makes it more socially acceptable.

Technical vulnerabilities allow attackers to accomplish their goals without ever setting foot on your premises. As Scott Charney puts it, "Outsiders do outsider things: avoiding insiders and being detected." Make no mistake, technical attacks can be extremely successful within a reasonable time period, and give spies long-term access to your company. When attackers combine the exploitation of technical vulnerabilities with social engineering, they often end up knowing more about your organization than you know yourself.

Don't worry—the following discussion will not be heavily technical in nature. You don't have to be an engineer to understand this stuff, and you need not be technically adept in order to take steps to counter the weaknesses described in these sections. You do, however, have to be able to recognize them.

Known Vulnerabilities

When I surveyed the hackers at the DefCon convention, I asked them specifically what opened the doors for them most often when they set out to hack into a computer system. Virtually without exception, "known security vulnerabilities" was their answer. Known vulnerabilities are computer or network systems security problems that are very widely known.

Imagine you have discovered that a certain brand and model of dead bolt opens without a key if you twist the latch counterclockwise and give it a yank. That is a nontechnical example of a known vulnerability. Now, if you were a burglar, knowledge of this design flaw could be very useful. Every time you came across that particular brand and model, you could twist, yank, and open the door. In fact, you might spend your time looking for those kinds of locks and exploiting its vulnerability.

This is essentially what computer hackers do. They learn how to twist the lock and then they go looking for that brand. The technology behind the specific vulnerabilities is irrelevant, because there will always be new ones. The problem is that the bad guys are always searching for them and the good guys don't even know they exist.

Hackers and other people with criminal intentions regularly search the electronic world for news about security vulnerabilities. They go to Internet sites and newsgroups. They go to private bulletin board systems and computer chat areas. They watch a variety of security-related mailing lists. Those who know where to look are flooded with information about computer vulnerabilities. These people are also flooded with tools and instructions on how to use them to exploit those weaknesses; the tools are so good that many hackers will launch very advanced attacks without having a clue as to how to use the computer access once they get it. As Chapter 4 discusses, most hackers are not technically adept. It is no more reasonable to consider a hacker a computer genius than it is to call a teenager holding a gun a master criminal. Both demonstrate the ability to find the tools of their craft and the willingness to use them. This is hardly genius.

It doesn't matter whether the vulnerabilities are in a massive Cray supercomputer or a lowly desktop 486 PC, the Windows 95 operating system or UNIX; anyone with minimal training can learn about a vulnerability and find the tool to exploit it.

Computer systems administrators don't know nearly enough about so-called known vulnerabilities, let alone the fixes for them. The attackers almost always know more. When I administered systems myself, I was never trained to watch for new problem announcements. When the vendor released a new version of an operating system or a computer application, I and my colleagues would review the product primarily to determine whether its new functionality justified the effort and the system downtime required to install it. We never considered that there might be security problem fixes included in the release. We didn't even realize that anyone who could connect to our system could take control of it. Unfortunately, my previous lack of awareness is currently very common.

As I explain in Chapter 4, only a handful of people are actually talented enough to find *new* vulnerabilities. What they do with that information varies. People in intelligence agencies and crime rings might keep the knowledge to themselves, so that they can exploit the vulnerability with impunity. People in universities and research facilities work with manufacturers to develop fixes for the problems. Manufacturers then release the fixes on their Internet sites and alert the Computer Emergency Response Team (CERT), who in turn alerts the general population. These fixes are also incorporated in later releases of the software. When the hacker community starts exploiting a new vulnerability, it usually takes a short time for people to determine exactly what the specific vulnerability is and figure out a fix for it. In this case, CERT releases information on how to fix the problem.

Some people in the hacker community want to alert others about the vulnerability. They believe that if they do not release the way to exploit the vulnerability, the vulnerability will not be fixed. For that reason, they bypass CERT and the manufacturers and use Internet mailing lists to distribute the information. The best lists for this purpose are Bugtraq, Cypherpunks, and Best-of-Security.

As you can see, there are plenty of places to find out about these known vulnerabilities. The problem is that very few people actually know that the vulnerabilities exist or where to get the fixes. (By the way, did you know that security vulnerability fixes for Windows 95 are available on the Microsoft Internet site? Microsoft refers to them as "Service Packs.")

Remember, more than 99 percent of the problems that allow your adversaries to exploit your computers are problems you have not taken the time to fix.

Configuration Errors

To hackers, configuration errors are the same as known vulnerabilities; to vendors, they represent an entirely different legal subject. Known vulnerabilities are problems inherent in the operating system or computer program; configuration errors are problems created by the way in which the systems administrator sets things up.

Depending on the type of configuration problem, attackers might need a valid account to compromise the computer, or they might be able to compromise the system with network connection alone. Attackers can check manually for configuration problems, or they can use a scanner that finds potential problems for them. These tools are also readily available on the Internet.

Unless a configuration error is very common or widely exploited, no one is likely to bother posting an alert about it.

System administrators are expected to read their documentation and find these kinds of problems on their own. For a usually overworked and often undertrained person, this is a task with a low priority.

Another configuration issue is that many vendors have included security tools with their systems. Again, many administrators do not know that they have very powerful tools freely available to them. To use an analogy, these tools are like airbags and seat belts that have been hidden in the trunk of a car: if automobile owners want to use them, they first have to find them and then figure out how to install them. The problem is the lack of awareness.

Poor Passwords

Another of the more commonly exploited technical vulnerabilities are poor passwords. In many cases, users' passwords can be guessed easily by other individuals. A truism among members of the security community suggests that people's passwords are on their desks 70 percent of the time. Although attackers might not find the password itself, they're going to see a picture of someone or something from which the password was derived. If they spot a picture of a wife or girlfriend, they'll try the girlfriend's nickname or birthday. Sometimes the password is a pet's name. If a sports team banner is nearby, the attacker might try variations on the team's name. (I'll bet a lot of you readers are looking around your desks right now.) People also use the names of the projects they're working on as passwords. Companies can exacerbate this vulnerability by imposing predictable passwords, such as the user's employee number, or by using default passwords that never change.

Some attackers simply try every word in the dictionary as a password. The success rate of this strategy is between 20 and 50 percent, depending on the company. To employ this strategy, they must be attacking a poorly configured computer or already have access to the system. The attackers can either capture the password file from a computer system or just keep trying to log onto the system using a known or default user IDs.

Other attackers utilize what is called a password "sniffer." A sniffer is a computer program that grabs passwords as they are sent across a computer network. The attackers must have found a way onto the network in order to use this tool, but once there, they find the tool to be very effective. In a 1994 case, over 100,000 passwords were reportedly compromised by a sniffer running on the Internet. In a similar type of attack, hackers modify a computer's log-in program to automatically capture the users' password and save it for the attackers. Password sniffing is an incredibly valuable tool, as demonstrated in Chapters 12 and 13. Although these specific attacks are hard to prevent, there are specific countermeasures that minimize or negate their effects (see Chapter 14).

Difficult-to-Detect System Modifications

When knowledgeable attackers compromise computers or networks, the first thing they do is modify the system files and logs. Typically, they replace normal system programs with their own versions either to give them more information or to hide their actions. For example, they might modify a program that tells an administrator which processes are running on the system, so the program doesn't show their hacker processes. This kind of system modification is a major problem that often goes undetected, allowing crimes to continue unabated.

Modem Access

It seems as though everyone with computers in their organization is worried about their Internet connection. They're afraid that this one connection point will give hackers and criminals around the world direct access to their company networks. To combat this perceived threat, they buy firewalls, which in fact can do a good job of protecting the company from Internet intrusions. A firewall is a device that secures one network segment (usually the Internet) from another segment (usually a company's internal network). Unfortunately, in their rush to shield themselves from the Internet, they often neglect the company's thousands of modem connections and, in the process, overlook one of the biggest vulnerabilities companies face.

Modems have become standard features on most desktop machines sold in this country today. People use them to work from home. Software developers create applications that give people easy access to their computers from anywhere in the world. Password protection on these machines is the exception rather than the rule. Consequently, when telecommuters plug that telephone jack into the back of their machines, they're allowing anybody that dials the telephone number to connect to their computer. Due to the nature of computer networking, once someone connects to that one computer, he or she can connect to just about any computer in the company.

Even organization-sponsored modems can be extremely weak when they rely on poor passwords or are not configured properly. When organizations have thousands of these access points to monitor, they often lose track of them.

Data Storage

Any time information is stored on a computer, it is vulnerable to compromise, destruction, or modification. Although the information can be encrypted to prevent compromise and modification, it can still be destroyed by accident or through malicious actions. Even data on supposedly secure systems can be attacked (as the Shimomura/Mitnick case illustrates).

People leave very valuable information on computer systems that are directly connected to computer networks. When information is on a network, other people on that network can get to it, which means they can do anything with it. They can even modify it without anyone else noticing. Someone with access to a missile targeting system could instruct the missiles to attack the site that launched them.

Data Transmission

Information is never more vulnerable than when it is being sent across a computer network. Whenever you are connected to another computer, the information on your machine is exposed to all other computers on that network—and when computers talk to each other, they shout loud enough for everyone to hear. Most people expect the other computers to refrain from listening in, but that's not what happens when your organization becomes a target.

Sending information out over a computer network is like sending a postcard through the U.S. mail. Anyone at the post office who wants to read it, can. Not only can the data in transit be compromised, it can also be *modified*. People who know how can change its content in midflight. Someone could change a funds transfer from $1,000 to $10,000 or resend the same message over and over again so that the $1,000 transaction message is sent ten times. People can also block your message and substitute their own.

TEMPEST

You may not realize it, but others can read your computer monitor from hundreds of feet away with no visible access to your machine. They can even see the information as the chip in your computer processes it. All they need is a special receiver, available to anyone through a number of mail-order catalogs for under $800. With the right instructions, they can even modify their television sets to do the same thing.

Almost every electronic device gives off what is know as Van Eck radiation, which can be picked up and converted to readable signals. TEMPEST is the term associated with the control and exploitation of Van Eck radiation emanations. The technology was developed by the intelligence communities to pick up the signals. Equipment can be designed to contain the radiation.

Intelligence agencies recognize the threat presented by this phenomenon, and they pay almost twice the price for computer systems that are TEMPEST-protected. In some cases, it's cheaper to TEMPEST-shield an entire building complex than to buy protected computers. To protect a building from this kind of intrusion, the entire structure must be covered in copper. Because of the way Van Eck radiation travels, all pipes (like water and sewer feeds) coming into the building must be copper as well. It is a difficult and expensive process, but necessary, especially in high-security environments.

Unfortunately, the commercial sector does not typically TEMPEST-protect its computers or facilities. This leaves a great deal of information vulnerable to compromise by anyone with the initiative to buy a kit through the mail.

Electromagnetic Pulse

Electromagnetic pulses (EMPs) were accidentally discovered during the testing of atomic bombs. Scientists noticed that all transistor circuits within a given area were literally fried after the detonation of a nuclear device. They later discovered that the explosion was causing a high-energy pulse that had this effect on the transistors.

Military scientists eventually developed the ability to generate EMPs without a nuclear explosion. The U.S. supposedly used EMP bombs during Operation Desert Storm to knock out key Iraqi computer systems and radio transmitters. During the summer of 1996, the U.S. Customs Service was reportedly testing an EMP gun that could be aimed at cars trying to run border patrol roadblocks. The gun would destroy all of the computer chips in the car, stopping it dead in the road.

Unfortunately, this technology can also be used to destroy information, although it is useless as an information gathering tool. EMP technology can enable malicious attackers to ruin all your information.

Telephone Taps

The telephone systems have been compromised by hackers, criminals, and intelligence agencies for years. Some modern telephone taps are very advanced and almost undetectable; others are unsophisticated and easy to find. Either way, unless you specifically check for them, you will never know they are there. When you consider the amount and type of information you give away over the telephone on a regular basis, you can see how damaging this vulnerability can be if left unnoticed.

Bugs

Whenever there is a possibility of industrial espionage, there is a strong possibility that a spy has planted bugs. When I give presentations, I sometimes ask the people in my audiences how many of them have performed bug sweeps. I then ask those people how many of them have found anything. On average, 40 percent of the people claiming to perform bug sweeps find something. Organizations that specialize in performing bug sweeps tell me that they find bugs in about 15 percent of their cases.

In one case, a company that should have been very profitable went bankrupt. As a moving company crew was moving furniture out of the executive meeting room, it found a large transmitter behind a credenza. The company had no idea who put it there or how long it had gone unnoticed. Nevertheless, the damage was done. The sophistication of bugs varies greatly, but for the most part, the cheap ones work as well as the expensive ones. The more expensive ones are just harder to find. They are a standard part of industrial and economic espionage.

The case of the U.S. embassy in Moscow is a well-known example. The Soviet Union embedded bugs in the building materials throughout the entire complex.

CONCLUSION

No matter who is out to get you—your competitors, foreign governments, disgruntled employees, and so on—your attackers can only get to your organization through your vulnerabilities. It's up to you to learn what those vulnerabilities are so you can figure out what are the appropriate steps to take to reduce your risk. You should not become preoccupied with technical vulnerabilities, which is what most people do, especially since you're much more likely to be hit through operations, physical, or personnel exposures. It does you little good in the long run to focus on attacks. Instead, you must focus on your underlying problems. Then you can significantly reduce your risk by implementing countermeasures that address the root causes of your vulnerabilities.

PART II

CASE STUDIES

6

Crippling a Company by Telephone

|T TOOK ONLY THREE DAYS AND LITTLE MORE EFFORT THAN
you might expend making airline reservations. Using only a
telephone and a certain facility for prevarication, I was able
to infiltrate a large financial organization, secure computer
access to every significant computer system, and accumulate a
wealth of information about the company's employees and the
projects they were working on. I could have obtained additional personal information about employees, including credit
card numbers, home addresses, and the names of their next of
kin. If I had been a true spy, my activities would have been
devastating to the organization. I could have crippled the
company at will.

This first case study demonstrates what can be accomplished by a persistent attacker in a very short period of time
through nontechnical means. Specifically, this chapter looks at
a pure social engineering strategy, in which the telephone is
the only tool.

To protect my clients, the example described here is actually a compilation of several penetration test attacks launched
by myself and accomplices against very large financial institutions. The tests were part of a comprehensive vulnerability

assessment commissioned by the organizations. For the sake of clarity, I've assumed the lead role in the narrative. Every activity described here, although not always carried out by me personally, actually happened at several banks.

BACKGROUND

The goal of this penetration exercise was to identify holes in the company's operational procedures that could be exploited to compromise the bank. I was after not merely computer access but wide entry into the bank, which would provide ongoing opportunities to compromise the entire organization. Although the corporate officers of the bank were aware of the test, the remainder of the company's employees were not.

In this penetration test, I had no previous knowledge of the organizational structure, function, or personnel of the target company. Time constraints required that I utilize a bolder-than-normal approach; a true social engineering attack would likely have taken weeks, if not months. Also, an actual attack would probably have included several visits to the company's offices; an attacker might even have secured a job at the company. And, of course, a real attacker would have used the information gathered to further his or her criminal aims.

THE ATTACK

I began the attack, as I very often do, with a search of Internet-based library databases and resources, along with other open source information. In a local telephone directory, I found the telephone number of a company office in my area. A call to the local office furnished me with a copy of the company's annual report as well as the toll-free telephone number of company headquarters. From the annual report and the Internet searches, I found lists of names of numerous company employees and officials, their job responsibilities and the projects they worked on, a large number of news articles about senior company officials, problems with computers, strategic directions of the company, and more. All this would prove to be critical information.

To conduct an effective telephone attack, I needed to get my hands on a copy of the corporate telephone directory. I expected this document to contain a tremendous amount of information useful to a telephone-based attack, including all corporate locations, the names of all employees at those locations, important telephone numbers, lists of all departments, and a comprehensive view of the company's corporate structure.

The first thing to do to start any attack is to figure out how a company handles its internal charge-back procedures. Toward this end, I called the company's toll-free number and asked for the mail room, claiming to be a new employee needing information about how to ship packages both within the United States and abroad. I learned that generally two numbers were required to perform a transaction within the company: an employee number and a cost center number. A call to the corporate graphics department confirmed the importance of these numbers.

My team reviewed the list of people we had collected information on, and we chose an executive that we probably knew the most about. This executive's recent accomplishment had been noted in the annual report. I put in a call to his office through the company's toll-free telephone number and spoke with his secretary. Claiming to be from the company's public relations department, I told her that I would be highlighting her boss's recent success in an upcoming edition of the corporate newsletter and I therefore needed some information about him. I asked a series of basic and harmless questions about the executive's background. I then told the secretary that I might have more questions later and that if she gave me the executive's employee number I could probably look up the information myself. She gladly gave me the number. A later call to the secretary by an accomplice posing as an auditor secured the man's cost center number. My accomplice merely inquired about what department should be charged for the employee's computer usage.

I called the department responsible for distributing corporate telephone directories. Posing as the executive, I requested that a directory be sent to a "subcontractor" with a valid need for the book. After I gave the employee and cost center numbers, the department shipped the directory to me via overnight courier at the company's expense.

Once I had the telephone directory in my hands, I was able to contact dozens of employees, at all levels of management and in every department, to obtain general corporate information and their employee numbers. I usually obtained the numbers by impersonating a human resources employee who had accidentally contacted the wrong employee to pick up a travel package. The travel package ruse worked because it caught people off guard, and it was easy to joke about the "mix-up." I started each call by saying that I had a travel package to San Francisco ready for pickup. After the initial shock wore off, the person usually told me that he or she wasn't going to San Francisco. The quick joke, "Well, would you like to go?" put the person completely at ease. I then asked for his or her employee number and apologized for the confusion. To obtain corporate information, I pretended to be a new employee who needed to know something in order to do my job.

In this way—by simply lying over the telephone—I was able to accumulate a significant amount of sensitive information. This included information on sensitive projects throughout the firm and detailed information about its people and computer architecture. While it might not seem important, I had the specific knowledge required to know how to take down the most important systems in the firm, along with detailed information on the financial systems.

We were about two days into the attack, and the results were staggering to the target. Our contact inside the bank wanted us to be more aggressive and to actually obtain access to the computer systems. Selective computer access would make it possible to exploit much more information in a very short period of time and to get to the financial systems. To gain the access I needed, I would have to acquire user IDs and passwords to a variety of accounts on systems throughout the company and at least one point of entry on to their network. I decided that the most vulnerable targets for this level of attack were new company hires. Not only were new hires likely to be the most naive, they would also be scattered throughout the company.

To obtain the names of the company's newest employees, I called the new hire administration office. My plan was to pretend to be the assistant to a high-level executive who wanted to personally welcome new employees to the company. My boss was extremely upset, I would claim, because the list of new hires was overdue. (I found the executive's name in a variety of open sources. The company telephone directory and the annual report indicated that he was one of the most senior people in the firm. Scouring through the directory provided the name of the employee who could be his assistant.)

As luck would have it, my initial call to the new hire office was picked up by an answering machine. The message on the machine revealed that the office had moved, and it gave the new telephone number as well as the name of the person assigned to the telephone number. Learning the name of the person in the new hire office was critical, because knowledge of a specific name increases the credibility of any ruse.

It was late afternoon when I called the new number. I asked for the new hire administrator by name; the new hire administrator had left for the day. The person who took my call turned out to be a relatively new clerical worker with full computer access. I simply told the clerk that the absent administrator provided me with the information I wanted on a regular basis. Because the information was already overdue and my boss—one of the most senior people in the company—was upset (and because my pleading was so pathetic), the clerk told me everything I wanted to know. In short order, I'd obtained the names of all the employees who had started work in the past three weeks, along with most of the names of their departments. In total, I acquired the names of fifty-five employees in departments throughout the organization.

Impersonating an information systems employee, I contacted the new hires, supposedly to provide them with a "computer security awareness briefing." I had decided to avoid contacting any actual information systems employees, because they were more likely to be aware of the importance of protecting passwords; this criteria eliminated seven of the fifty-five employees. I used the security briefing ruse, because people are usually intimidated by any contact dealing with security and they usually provide all requested information without challenge. Additionally, people are unlikely to suspect that anyone would commit such a brazen impersonation.

I started my "awareness briefings" by first finding out about their hardware and software environments. I obtained information about the types of computers the employee used, the names of the systems, the types of software applications used, and the employee number of each person I spoke with, along with their user ID and password. If the person accessed the company via modem, I asked for the modem number and password. During one of the telephone interviews, an employee did not know the information I asked for, so she put her supervisor on the phone. Her boss gladly answered all my questions.

I did not start out the interviews by asking, "What's your password?" This type of question is extremely sensitive. It is a Red Flag question—if a person has even a basic understanding of security issues, he or she would stop the conversation in its tracks. Using basic intelligence elicitation techniques, I asked the innocuous questions first (I even tried to sound bored as I was asking them). After I asked a series of questions that anybody would answer, I started working in the sensitive questions. After I had the answers to those, I then asked some additional boring questions. This leaves the impression that no important questions have been asked. After the questioning ended, I made up some basic security guidelines to tell the employee as part of the official briefing.

From the telephone directory, I was able to identify all of the bank's telephone exchanges. One of my accomplices then used a war dialer (a computer tool that dials every telephone number in a specified range to search for possible modems) to find the computer access points. A call to the information systems help desk enabled me to locate some additional modem lines. The modem numbers provided me with computer access and the ability to exploit the compromised user accounts. Obtaining the modem information effectively circumvented a very sophisticated firewall system and rendered it useless. During a later attack, I used similar social engineering methods to establish my own computer account with the company. I also was able to convince company employees to send me communications software that accessed a "secure" modem connection.

CONCLUSIONS

Despite strong technical security countermeasures, the penetration activities described in this case study were extremely successful in a very short period of time. This attack bypassed millions of dollars of technical security mechanisms and put the company at my team's mercy. By the time I was finished, I had access to almost all significant systems.

Although the attack appears to have focused on computer access, I should point out that the company's computers were targeted only because of the information or services they could provide. Many of the early telephone attacks were exploratory in nature, designed to determine which departments and systems were critical to the organization. Certain individuals were targeted because of their access to information.

The attack might seem from my description to be very complicated and time consuming, but it was a relatively simple operation, accomplished in less than three days. It was also cheap: I used the company's toll-free telephone number and resources to pay for any costs incurred in telephone calls and overnight delivery expenses.

Even though my cumulative activities were unusually blatant, no reports were made to security about any strange or unusual incidents. This is understandable, since the assault was built from many small actions, which were, in themselves, innocuous.

VULNERABILITIES EXPLOITED

Many of the vulnerabilities exploited in this penetration exercise are common to most companies and definitely to investment banks. The following discussion of the specific weaknesses I took advantage of should provide insights that will help you protect yourself against social engineers.

Information As the Target

If the goal of the attackers in this case had been only to obtain computer access, they could have easily accomplished this by randomly telephoning people and asking them for their passwords. The parts of the organization attacked would also have been totally random. Little research would have been necessary, and the attack could have been accomplished in about an hour.

What I was after, however, was specific data that would allow me to significantly compromise a large cross section of the entire organization. I first conducted research to determine which information was valuable, and then I conducted further research to develop a plan of attack. The specific targets in this attack were carefully chosen for the information they could provide.

Computer access is important, because it can provide access to large volumes of data from remote locations with minimal effort. However, when financial organizations are involved, the potential volume of information obtained is irrelevant when compared to the potential value of a specific piece of information. I was very well aware that a single report containing insider information about a stock purchase or information about how to perform financial transactions was much more valuable than the combined value of millions of other random files. Using this knowledge, I chose specific parts of the company to attack. This allowed me to weed out a lot of garbage and focus on targets most likely to have extreme value.

Open Source Information

I began my attack by examining open source information. As I mention in Chapter 1, open source information is any piece of information that is publicly available, including newspapers, corporate annual reports, library computer search facilities, help wanted advertisements, and technical magazines. I acquired an incredible amount of "internal" knowledge by examining these kinds of materials, which are freely available to anyone.

This information provided accurate details on corporate budgets and major company projects. I also used it to learn about the individuals leading current projects, the names of major hardware and software vendors, and any significant problems in the organization. Through the publicly available annual report, my team learned about the company's high-level organizational structure and was therefore able to determine which groups within the organization were most likely to have the types of information we wanted. By accumulating information about the ongoing activities of the company, I was able to present myself as a company employee. Armed with this information, I was able to talk and act like a true insider.

Desire to Help

Most of the people I contacted during the attack were genuinely interested in helping out a fellow employee. This is an extremely desirable attribute, but one that is easily exploitable. Although some employees did attempt to verify my identity, once I offered a valid employee number, they handed over great chunks of information. More important, even if I had been the person I was claiming to be, I really had no need of the information I was asking for. Whenever I connected with a very helpful person, I "played dumb," which inspired my targets to fill in many gaps in my knowledge and give me much more information than anyone would have needed.

Anonymity within Large Corporations

Every phase of this attack was enabled by the immense size of the target organization. Most employees only know a small percentage of their fellow employees personally, greatly reducing my chances of impersonating a friend or colleague.

Additionally, most employees know very little about the jobs of other employees. For example, even though an employee might work for the information systems department, there is no way for another employee to know whether that person is actually responsible for providing a "security awareness briefing."

Reliance upon Common Internal Identifiers

During the early phases of the attack, it became clear that the employee number was a critical identifier used throughout the organization. This number was used when requesting capital assets and when requesting help desk support. Unfortunately, the employee number was used much too frequently (it appeared on all personnel forms), making it natural to disclose the identifier to just about anyone within the organization that seems to have any need for the number. To an employee, it is a tool for getting things accomplished and not a piece of information that needs to be protected. Even employees who were reluctant to disclose information to me during my attacks were willing to hand over their employee numbers with minimal coaxing.

This situation is common in every large organization in this country. When numbers are so widely distributed, they cannot be considered valid identifiers. In organizations using Social Security numbers, this problem is even more serious. A criminal who obtains an individual's Social Security number can impersonate that person in all aspects of his or her life. Numerous cases have involved a criminal using a Social Security number alone to retrieve a credit report, which contains all information about credit cards and bank accounts. The information was then used to reroute checkbooks and credit card statements, while the criminal ran up balances on the credit card and withdrew all funds from the bank accounts.

Organizations must differentiate between personnel identifiers and personal validation codes.

Assumption of Common Sense

Security professionals, especially information systems security professionals, tend to believe that individuals understand basic security principles, such as protecting computer passwords and locking up sensitive information at the end of the day. They believe that everyone is aware of the threat to information and the importance of the controls in place. In the organizations penetrated in this case, an incredible amount of effort had been put into implementing very strong technical security mechanisms; unfortunately, minimal (if any) effort was put into security awareness.

Common sense cannot exist without common knowledge. People were not made aware of which data was important or how to protect important information. In this case, even the technical people were compromised. Remember, this attack was 100 percent successful.

No Verification of Callers' Identities

Again, this case study is actually a compilation of penetration tests against several financial institutions. In every one of those institutions, I found no procedures for verifying callers' identities or their need for the information they requested. All the financial institutions in this case relied solely on employee numbers, which were very easy to come by and did not hinder the effort at all.

No Procedures in Place

Early in the attack, it became obvious that even if people had thought I was up to something, they could have done very little about it. There was no obvious place for them to report strange occurrences.

The problem here is threefold. First, the employees did not understand exactly what a possible "security-related problem" was. Second, there were no means for reporting unusual incidents to the right people (i.e., the security department). Third, assuming the incident was reported to the appropriate people, there was no way for those people to spread the word throughout the organization. In the absence of any one of these procedures, the attacks could continue with minimal modifications. Future attacks would only be improved by this detection, because it tells the attackers how to avoid getting caught.

7

Anatomy of an Industrial Espionage Attack

OR HOW TO STEAL $1 BILLION
IN A DAY AND A HALF

O N A COLD WINTER'S DAY IN 1995, I WALKED INTO NATIONAL Chemical Corporation for the first time in my life and reported for work. I had been hired as a temp and would be there for three days. I knew only as much about the company as anyone else could have learned from publicly available sources. I carried with me no high-tech devices, no special codes, and no inside information of any kind. Yet, within a day and a half, I had compromised twenty-eight of the company's twenty-nine top development projects and collected over a billion dollars' worth of sensitive information. And no one even noticed me.

The company name and the projects compromised have been changed, but the story is real, and it's not particularly unusual. Like many other firms within its market sector, the company I will call NCC was being hit by several cases of insider theft a year. Usually these thefts were "crimes of opportunity" involving employees attempting to sell information about the company's products to third-party buyers. NCC's employees felt helpless to prevent this kind of family thievery, because not only did insiders need access to the stolen information to do their jobs, they might have been the ones who created it. Consequently, even after a devastating theft, little was done to improve the security posture of the organization—until the NCC security manager decided that something had to change.

To demonstrate exactly how easily a temporary employee with criminal intentions could steal critical information from NCC, the security chief hired me to perform a penetration test against the company. I was given the temp job and permission to do whatever was necessary to obtain information, including using accomplices, as long as it did not cause harm to individuals or NCC. Financial considerations limited the scope of the test to three days. Of course, we agreed that I would not be arrested for my actions; however, if I were "caught," then the test would be considered a failure.

BACKGROUND

At the time of the penetration test, NCC was pursuing a number of potentially valuable research and development projects. The most notable among these was a synthetic-fat food substitute. Once perfected, sales of the chemical were expected to generate billions of dollars in revenue for the company annually. Some of the other NCC development efforts included a new type of fiber-optic cable and a new chemical substrate for computer processors. Although not as potentially profitable as the fat substitute, each of these latter projects was considered quite valuable.

NCC had developed a relatively strong technical security infrastructure. Unfortunately, the research mentality of the organization provided for a very open exchange of information and a weak operational security posture. NCC had over 1,000 temporary employees on-site at any given time. From previous experiences, the security manager knew that this population—many of whom had significant levels of access—presented a major security threat.

THE ATTACK

I wanted my attack to be as realistic as possible, so I decided to launch a full-scale industrial espionage campaign against NCC. For the security manager's purposes, it was important that the attack utilize both technical intrusion methods (i.e., computer hacking) and nontechnical methods (i.e., social engineering). If only nontechnical attacks were used, the non-technical organizations within the company would feel un-fairly targeted, and the results would leave the technical groups overconfident and uninspired to take action. If only technical attacks were used, the results would be of little rele-vance to nontechnical employees. Any real attack by an orga-nized group would utilize a holistic approach; any penetration test that failed to use a similar approach would be incomplete and of limited value.

Since I had been given no inside knowledge of the company, it was difficult to predict exactly which attack strategies would be the most effective. However, I knew that there were several cate-gories of attacks I wanted to attempt, including the following:

- Open source research
- Abuse of responsibilities and access
- Internal network scans and hacking of company com-puter systems
- Insider coordination of external accomplices
- Outsider hacking

The different types of attacks would be necessary to reveal the true extent of the company's vulnerabilities.

Because of the time constraints of the test, I would also have to be bolder than a typical spy. Before launching my campaign, I chose a team of individuals with the skills required to adjust to a rapidly changing environment. The key to our success would be coordination and discipline.

Espionage in all of its forms is primarily a matter of employing basic and proven techniques in a coordinated strategy. In this test, different types of attack were used simultaneously, when feasible, to optimize the time available and in some cases to mask other activities.

Open Source Research

Prior to beginning any intrusions, I wanted to develop an overall picture of NCC. Learning about the general organizational structure and working environment of a company is important to the success of any penetration effort. I also wanted to identify a "hit list" of NCC development projects, along with the names of NCC employees working on them. I began my research by tapping open source information resources, such as the Internet and on-line library resources. I also acquired a number of NCC press releases, a corporate newsletter, an annual report, and a company telephone directory. All of these sources are freely available to any insider. The directory was not marked as company confidential or sensitive in any way. The newsletter included several articles about emerging products and also highlighted many individuals associated with those products. It also included lists of all new employees and their assigned departments.

The annual report provided detailed information about NCC's corporate philosophy of openness "to facilitate innovation." It also provided facts about all NCC products currently on the market, financial data, the names of corporate executives, and plans for company expansion. The press releases highlighted recent company successes and the people who had worked on them. The telephone directory provided comprehensive information about company facilities, including maps of all the buildings, the names of corporate executives and their official positions, the names of emergency personnel (including the security manager who hired me), a detailed list of all international locations, and a complete list of company departments. Obviously, the telephone directory included the names, departments, and locations of all NCC employees. It did not, however include any information about employee job titles.

Internet resources helped me identify NCC's key development efforts. I found several news and television stories about three of NCC's highest priority projects, including the synthetic fat. Many of the stories highlighted the leading researchers working on that particular project.

I also read several news articles about previous incidents of insider theft at NCC. These articles indicated what data was stolen, the amount of money offered for the information, how access to the information was obtained, and, most important, what factors led to the criminals' arrest. This information taught me quite a bit about what tactics were unsuccessful at NCC and what information was worth stealing.

Internet newsgroups and information services provided a great deal of information about NCC's employees. A search for the text string "NCC" identified a large number of employees that accessed certain newsgroups. The NCC Internet domain name (NCC.COM) was on all the employees' messages. People generally post messages that are relevant to their jobs or their interests. By searching the Internet, I was able to learn about specific employees' personal interests and job responsibilities. If I had had more time, I could have used this information to develop personal relationships with NCC employees, who might have provided access to sensitive information. The employee messages that were posted to computer-related newsgroups talked about the hardware and software used throughout NCC.

From this preliminary research, I created a list of NCC's top six development projects. I also learned the names of several employees involved with the synthetic fat and the fiber optic projects. Using the telephone directory, I identified the office locations of the employees, which I targeted for physical intrusion. I also had a good idea about their technical vulnerabilities. I now had a firm foundation for the active phases of the attack.

Abuse of Responsibilities and Access

Any NCC employee, given sufficient time, could probably have obtained sensitive information on the synthetic fat development effort. However, I had only three days to accomplish all on-site activities. I was therefore required to abuse my position as a temporary employee to get information very quickly.

Misrepresentation After reviewing the information gathered through the open source research, I decided that the best method for gathering information on-site was to pose as a supervisor for information security. Most people assume that security personnel require access to sensitive data; plus, the implied authority in the title would give me extra leverage. I did realize that researchers are generally reluctant to cooperate with security personnel, because they believe security is a threat to an open environment. Still, I reasoned that it was a good cover for most situations.

NCC business cards of all kinds were readily available from a variety of sources, including restaurants, located near the company, offering free-meal drawings for people depositing their cards in a jar. I took the card to my local print shop and paid a small fee to create authentic-looking cards with my name on it and the title of Supervisor of Information Security. No one at the print shop questioned the print order, despite the fact that NCC's address was clearly 1,000 miles away.

Upon arriving at the company, I was asked to fill out the paperwork required to obtain a building pass. I made it a point to provide an incorrect Social Security number, address, and automobile license plate number. Nobody at NCC bothered to check the veracity of my form, which was typical when a temporary employee was involved. I was given a magnetic building pass that indicated my temp status.

I was then shown my office, which had a telephone line and a PC. I was also given e-mail and Schedule+ accounts. Schedule+ is a scheduling software application that allows company employees to see everyone's schedule. The program makes it much easier for people to arrange meetings without conflicts. My computer system was configured the same way as all other basic NCC computer systems. It had the ability to perform remote log-ins to other computer systems, to access shared computer directories and files, and to access the on-line corporate telephone directory. Prior to my arrival, NCC had added me to its on-line directory and caller ID systems. All of these facilities and accesses were standard for all temporary employees.

After spending a short time familiarizing myself with the PC and the operation of the on-line personnel directory program, I began my attack. I started with a phone call to the senior researcher on the synthetic fat project, whose name I got from news articles. I identified myself as the newly hired supervisor of information security and explained that I had been given the broad task of protecting all critical development efforts. I told her that I needed some general information about her project, and in particular, I hoped she would help me identify which aspects of her work were considered sensitive. More important, I was trying to find out where she stored her information. I also asked for suggestions on ways to improve the protection of that information. After a lengthy conversation, she recommended that I call her team leader, who could best provide the information I was seeking.

I telephoned the team leader and again, claiming to be the information security supervisor, told him that the researcher recommended that I talk with him. I asked to meet with him to discuss the issues I'd brought up with the researcher. During that telephone conversation, I learned that a series of management meetings was going on throughout the week at an off-site location. The team leader told me that he was only available for another hour before he had to leave to attend the meetings.

I rushed over to his building and slipped through the door with another employee, so there was no record that I entered the building. I put my temp ID badge into my pocket and found the team leader's office. I introduced myself and handed him one of my forged business cards. I'd been hired, I told him, because of the insider thefts that had occurred during the previous year. Apparently, the team leader believed that no one outside a select group of individuals would know the details of the incidents, which I purposely worked into the conversation. My knowledge of the thefts—which I acquired from the newspapers—lent me the credibility I needed. The team leader believed my fabrication and provided me with numerous details about the thefts.

After I sensed that I had established a rapport with him, I began to ask some sensitive questions. I specifically asked about which types of information could be considered sensitive to the synthetic fat development effort. The team leader told me that the most sensitive information concerned the manufacturing process. Although the research information about the product was considered sensitive, it was apparently more important to know *how* to make it than to understand the processes used to get to that point. I also learned about development schedules, problem reports, statistical data, and a variety of general information that could give a competitor an edge or compromise the entire effort.

I then focused my questions on where the information was stored. The team leader explained that the synthetic fat project team, like all other project teams at NCC, comprised people from all over the company. Everyone on the team was responsible for protecting his or her own information. Apparently, no standards for protecting or backing up data existed, and the quality of protection varied greatly with the individual.

After some additional probing, I learned that the researchers' information was generally unintelligible; the people responsible for producing the manufacturing and development information had the most valuable data. I said that I found it difficult to believe that no single individual in the company knew everything about particular projects. The team leader then told me that every NCC development project had a business manager responsible for general oversight of the project and for reporting project status to senior management. He also told me that the government affairs (GA) department was responsible for putting together the documents required by various foreign and U.S. government agencies for product licensing and patenting. Because synthetic fat is a food additive, the U.S. Food and Drug Administration required NCC to file extensive documentation on its manufacturing and handling processes.

Since I was "responsible for protecting the information," it seemed only reasonable to get the names of all the people working on the synthetic fat project. Without hesitation, the team leader showed me a typed list, which he had his secretary copy for me. When I asked to see what type of information these people would normally get, he produced a large binder containing the minutes of all the synthetic fat team meetings. I asked to copy the contents of the binder, ostensibly so that I could study "the potential threat posed by a compromise of the meeting minutes." My request to be added to the distribution list was also approved.

My initial review of the meeting minutes showed that they contained an incredible amount of sensitive data, which I expected. While copying the minutes, I noticed a shred container in the copy room, which was very secure, but next to it was a paper recycling container, which was not. A quick search through the recycling container produced some additional sensitive data that had been placed into the wrong bin.

When I returned to my office, I telephoned the company's GA representative for the synthetic fat development team. Using the same security ruse, I made an appointment with the representative for later in the day. Again, I went over to the person's building and followed another employee through the door. I slipped my temp access badge into my pocket and greeted my target with one of the false business cards.

During that meeting, the GA officer explained the licensing and testing process to me. He also told me about product documentation required by various governments, which included manufacturing information. It was clear that these documents would provide me with all the information I needed. I asked where the documents were stored and how they were protected, and he showed me some file systems on his computer. Claiming that I wanted to know exactly where the files were located, I had him log off the computer file systems and log back on. Although I was unable to see the password he used, as I'd hoped, I did notice the specific names and locations of the computer directories that contained the targeted documents. I also asked for and got the name of the person responsible for maintaining the GA department's computer systems.

I decided that my best approach to securing these documents would be to try to obtain a backup copy. I began asking the GA representative about his disaster recovery procedures, which I knew did not exist. The GA rep was clearly not a computer expert and would never have thought much about such issues. Although he wouldn't admit anything, it quickly became obvious that there were no backups of the files. He didn't like the idea of backing them up for me on the spot, so I suggested that the information security department might be able to back up the files remotely. Using that tactic, I walked him through the process of "sharing" his files, "just to see if it was possible." If the network were configured in the right way, this process could have given me direct access to the critical files.

After my meeting with the GA representative, I returned to my office and arranged two more meetings for the following day. The first meeting was with the business manager of the fiber optic development project (as recommended by the synthetic fat team leader); the other meeting was with the systems administrator for the GA department computer systems.

I also obtained an application for a corporate pager and forged the security manager's signature in the approval block. I walked the application over to the appropriate office and explained that I was on the security emergency call-in list and needed the application to be processed within twenty-four hours. The pager would play a prominent role in other phases of my attack.

Using the knowledge I had obtained from the GA representative, I located and accessed directories in the GA department computer that were not password-protected. I copied all potentially sensitive directories and files onto my own computer system and took some time to review the synthetic fat meeting minutes in detail.

The meeting minutes contained a lot of information that could be used by competitors to reduce the time and cost of their own development efforts. The information in those minutes could help a competitor beat NCC through the patent procedure. The most interesting tidbit in those minutes was the location of the critical document, currently in final draft form, being produced by the GA department. The minutes included the user ID and password needed to access the document.

The significance of this is incredible. Within five hours, I had the capability to access the manufacturing plans for a multibillion-dollar product.

The user ID and password worked like a charm, and as I'd expected, the document provided all of the information required to manufacture synthetic fat. Besides the manufacturing data, there was an immense amount of other information that would give any competitor a significant advantage. The document literally contained critical information on every important aspect of the synthetic fat effort.

As luck would have it, the same computer access provided me with the corresponding documents for the computer chip substrate and a third project. In one fell swoop, I had severely compromised three extremely valuable projects to the point that I could produce all of them myself. The same user ID and password also gave me access to several other directories that contained a large amount of sensitive information about several other projects in development.

The next day, I picked up my new pager and hurried to my meeting with the business manager of the fiber optic development project. I told the same story I'd told before and asked for information about her department's most sensitive data.

The business manager told me about management summary reports, which were prepared using input from the meeting minutes and other sensitive documents. These management reports summarized all critical aspects of the research, development, and manufacturing efforts of the company. If those reports fell into a competitor's hands, she told me, the competitor could beat NCC to market with the new fiber-optic technology. She was also very helpful in providing me with a list of NCC's primary competitors. During the conversation, it became clear that she had misgivings about security personnel getting involved in the development side. She believed, she said, that security would interfere with the open nature of the research process.

I wanted to get copies of the management summary reports, but she was reluctant to give them to me. She suggested instead that I get them from the security manager, to whom she had previously given copies. I told her that he was away at the management meetings that were going on this week, and I requested that she just show me one of the reports so that I could understand the issues we were talking about. She showed me the computer directories where the reports were stored and tried to access other directories where extremely sensitive information was stored. Again, I was unable to catch the password, but I did get her user ID. I also noted that her office door had no lock and that on her desk was a box of floppy disks marked "Management Reports."

When I arrived back at my office, I immediately tried to log on to the business manager's account. Within a few seconds, I'd guessed her password (it was the same as her user ID) and tapped into extremely sensitive files covering the research, development, and manufacturing issues of NCC's fiber optic development effort. From the other files in her directory, I learned that the business manager held a similar position on several development projects. I now had access to incredibly valuable data on several more projects.

I was amazed when I saw that the same directory was used by all of NCC's business managers. I had obtained incredibly sensitive and valuable information on about twenty-eight of NCC's twenty-nine most critical projects. I had detailed information on manufacturing procedures, schedules, problems, status, and so forth—on just about everything NCC believed was critical to its success.

If I'd been a real spy, I could have sold the information I had collected for hundreds of millions. And I'd found it all before lunch of my second day on the job.

Because I was flying blind, I was using a capture-first-analyze-later approach to data collection. Basically, I was scanning the files and directories and grabbing anything that looked possibly sensitive. I copied all available files and directories back to my computer system. Throughout the penetration test, I captured over 125 megabytes of data on my own computer and another 125 megabytes on another computer in an empty office. This roughly translates into about 250,000 pages of data. It is worth noting that I didn't copy another 1,000 megabytes of potentially useful data because I ran out of storage space. A real criminal would have copied all the data to a mass storage device, such as a storage tape, or shipped it to outside accomplices with larger storage devices.

During this attack, I talked to the security manager about how much data I should collect. By this time, it was obvious that I'd captured more than enough information to prove the point he wanted to make. Anyone could see how vulnerable the company was to anyone with inside access. We agreed that I would continue to use the misrepresentation strategy to capture only extremely critical data.

At this point, a real intruder would have packed up and not returned from lunch. I had a day and a half left on the test, however, so I toned down my attacks and avoided contact with most people. Despite what I'd accomplished, if I were caught now, the whole test would be invalidated.

I had already made one other appointment, which I decided I had to keep. After lunch, I met with the systems administrator of the GA department's computer systems, posing again as the supervisor of information security. When I originally called the administrator, he had heartily welcomed any involvement from security and was enthusiastic about talking to me. When I arrived at his office, the receptionist mistook me for someone else and handed me a book marked "Laboratory Notes." I couldn't pass up such an opportunity, so I took the book to a copy machine and ran off a few sample pages. I then returned it to the receptionist, telling her that there must have been a mistake. She took the book back without a blink and introduced me to the administrator.

I learned that his department was responsible for the company archives, which contained both hard copy and soft copy documents. He walked me through the vault containing all hard copies of NCC documents that had ever been filed with the government. He showed me one of the most sensitive documents, and he invited me back to look through some more when I had more time.

I then turned the conversation towards the subject of soft copy documents, and he introduced me to a young woman responsible for maintaining the company's electronic documents. I learned the format of the documents and some other information about the computer systems, and it was obvious that the files were fairly well protected. However, the woman was primarily responsible for document storage and not for technical issues. I then started asking if they had thought about performing remote backups of the documents. I gave her instructions on how to do it. The procedure, as I described it, was purposely very complicated, and the young archivist welcomed my offer to do the procedure myself. I was able to manipulate the security of the archives at will, which allowed me to electronically steal the information later.

In less than two days I had secured access to billions of dollars of sensitive information using totally nontechnical means. The information I'd gathered was priceless and would facilitate all other types of attacks.

After-Hours Walk-Throughs   After dinner on the first day of my attack, I returned to NCC to try physically stealing information. Using the knowledge I'd obtained from the team leader and the GA representative, I targeted two specific locations: the areas of the product licensing and legal departments, and the area where the development organization was located.

My access badge allowed me into all but a few specific locations throughout NCC, at all hours of the day. It is important to note that my temp access badge actually unlocked the doors, which would have allowed me to bring in a large number of accomplices undetected.

I went to the product licensing area first. The only other person in the building at that time of night was a cleaning person, who simply ignored me and carried on with his work. Once I located a copy machine, I began looking at all the desks and papers I could find.

In an open in-box that was in no way protected, I found a set of documents about several products NCC was planning to acquire. Taped to someone's door was a document marked "Sensitive." The person had tried to protect the document by taping it with the text facing the wall. The door to that office was open, so I went in and looked around. I turned on the computer and searched for sensitive data files. I also looked through any file cabinets that were unlocked. I collected a variety of documents that detailed potential licensing scenarios for a new type of plastic that NCC was developing. The documents revealed potential licensees, their strengths and weaknesses, and negotiating positions.

I then moved on to the legal department. There were over a half dozen offices for that department, none of which were locked. I found a wide variety of documents, most containing information about patent filings and pending lawsuits. The patent files contained specific details about many development efforts. All but one of the files concerned patents that were already available to the general public. However, one file contained a completed patent application that was going to be filed in the upcoming weeks. I could have stolen it and filed it with the patent office myself.

I also obtained a significant amount of information about pending lawsuits. NCC, like most other multibillion-dollar companies, is always in the midst of dozens of multimillion-dollar lawsuits. I obtained the NCC negotiating positions and instructions on how to answer questions about most of the cases. Because this was just a test and I didn't want to interfere with company operations, I simply copied the first pages of the most sensitive documents, to show what I could have taken. Obviously, all of this information was worth millions and could have compromised the long-term viability of the company.

With the licensing and legal departments significantly compromised, I moved on to the development area. This time, I walked past a security guard and several other people working late. To make it look like I knew where I was going, I walked rapidly to the back of the building. While contact with another individual would not necessarily have compromised my activities, I knew it was safer to avoid others. During the next few hours, I played a game of cat and mouse with the other employees. If anyone caught me going through someone else's desk, I'd probably be in trouble.

I didn't know what I was looking for; I was just wandering around in an area that was likely to contain sensitive stuff. By chance, I eventually found a number of problem reports concerning the testing of several priority products. These reports were extremely sensitive because they could have helped a competitor improve its own products. The problem reports could also have been used by competitors to challenge the safety of the food additives NCC was developing, causing big problems for the company in its patent filings, both foreign and domestic.

At this time, I learned that many of the company's PCs used a security tool that locked up the computers whenever they were inactive for a period of time or when they were first booted up. They were essentially secure screen saver programs. The computer would only unlock after a valid password was entered. This tool prevented me from compromising most computer systems during my nighttime visit.

I then wandered into an area that contained a cluster of secretarial spaces, which usually indicates that an executive's office is in the vicinity. On the secretaries' desks, I found a large number of documents that were marked "Sensitive." The documents contained a variety of information. I also found many unlocked filing cabinets, which were organized by product names. Many held copies of the important documents that were filed with the government, which contained complete manufacturing details of the company's products. I found detailed manufacturing instructions for five of NCC's most profitable products.

Further down the hallway, I found an open office with a very large number of papers strewn about. It was too tempting to pass up. I found most of the papers to be of modest value. Then I noticed that the computer was on. The monitor had been shut down, but the CPU was running. I turned on the monitor and discovered that the security tool had not been loaded onto this machine, so I could access everything on the computer. I was very pleased to learn that the person was still logged on to his e-mail account. Not only did I have access to the data files, I also had access to his mail messages, which dated back several months. This person was a real pack rat.

From the files on this system, I could tell that the person was probably responsible for developing a variety of mathematical models, including manufacturing models, sales forecasting, and problem prediction. He was therefore required to have a wide variety of sensitive information on a number of projects. The models would be of enormous value to any competitor. They could be used to determine expected successes, failure rates, sales and market forecasts, and other essential projections. Of extreme value was a master research and development schedule that listed "all" NCC development efforts and critical dates. Some of the projects listed were known only to a handful of people inside NCC.

After copying or printing the most sensitive files from the desk and computer, I left the area and headed for the exit. Along the way, I noticed the office of a person whom I'd previously learned was extremely important to one of the company's most vital projects. The door to the office was open, so I walked in. The computer was locked, but a quick look at the open file cabinets and desk produced the detailed test plans for the fiber optic effort. The test plans were considered to be critical to the effort and very sensitive.

The night was getting long, and I had already worked a full day. When I left the area, I had hundreds of millions of dollars' worth of information in my hands.

By the second day, I had gathered enough information and I decided to keep a low profile. However, I did go back on the second night to steal the box of disks marked "Management Reports" that I'd seen in the business manager's office. I walked to the office, snatched the box, and walked out. I then copied the disks onto my computer system and returned them to their proper place. While I had already compromised most of the documents on the disks, some of them turned out to be new.

With that final theft, I had completed the physical intrusion phase of the attack. No one reported anything unusual in the days and weeks that followed, leaving these thefts totally undetected or at least unreported to anyone who could do anything about them.

Internal Network Scans and Hacking of Computer Systems

Before I reported for my first day of work at NCC, I acquired a portable UNIX computer workstation. (UNIX is the computer operating system widely considered to be the backbone of the Internet.) I had learned from my Internet research that NCC utilized a large number of UNIX workstations, and I wanted to be prepared to fully exploit them. I also acquired a commercial software package, the Internet Security Scanner (ISS), which performs a search for all known vulnerabilities on UNIX computers. Since NCC also depends on a large PC network, I also acquired a software package that finds PC security holes. Using both security tools, I would have the ability to find and exploit almost any vulnerable system on the NCC network.

I began my technical attack by unplugging the network connection from my office PC and connecting the portable UNIX workstation to NCC's internal network. The Internet Security Scanner software quickly identified more than 9,000 computers on the company network.

Since most employees of NCC used PCs, I decided to start my first attacks against the desktop machines. I plugged my PC back into the network, loaded a PC vulnerability scanner on it, and then scanned the PCs on the most sensitive NCC network segments. I focused on the segments that were most likely to contain high-value information, such as the development and government affairs segments. The scanning software identified numerous PCs that permitted anyone to access any of their files.

Once I had found the vulnerable PCs, I reattached the UNIX computer to the network and scanned the high-potential UNIX systems. The scanning software not only identified system vulnerabilities but also identified user accounts with easily guessed passwords. It also checked for shared directories. These shared directories allowed any user to access all data not given additional security protection. One of the vulnerable UNIX directories was used by PC users for the storage of extremely sensitive data.

Since the directories were set up for sharing, I configured my portable systems to get the files. In a few minutes, the process was complete. I then tried to copy all of the files over to my computer. I got most of the files; however, the ones I did not get had extra protection, and their names indicated that they could be extremely valuable. They were not only a critical target, but also a challenge that I could not pass up.

ISS told me the type of operating system the computer used. (As Chapter 5 discusses, knowing the type of operating system tells you what potential vulnerabilities could be on the system.) For this type of system, I first needed to have a valid account on the system to exploit it. ISS had guessed the passwords of four user accounts, which provided me with the foot in the door that I needed. I logged on to the targeted computer using one of the accounts. I had equipped my computer with several dozen hacking tools that could exploit the known vulnerabilities of all types of computer systems in use at NCC. I copied over the tool to exploit the vulnerability that was specific to the targeted computer.

Within seconds, I had complete control of the system. I identified all sensitive directories and transferred them back to my computer. Most of the holes in my database were now filled.

I had spent a lot of time on the system and was becoming concerned that a system administrator might notice my attacks and close the holes. To make sure I could get back in later, I created a "back door." I did this by adding another computer account to the system. Of course, the account had superuser privileges. I also transferred the hacker tool to another compromised account, just in case the system administrator spotted the first back door.

From the one fully compromised UNIX system, I could have obtained superuser status on almost all of the other UNIX systems, but I left the performance of this task to my outside accomplices. It should be noted that my attempts to compromise NCC's firewall system failed.

Now I turned my attention to the PC systems. I plugged the PC back into the network and used it to share many of the unprotected directories I had previously identified. I found and captured a wide variety of information. NCC uses a maintenance tool that allows a remote systems administrator to control and correct problems with any PC on the network. It was designed to make administration more responsive and convenient. I used it to fully exploit the vulnerable computers on the network.

I had completed my internal network scans entirely on my third day on the job. My computer work had yielded data that was as sensitive, if not more so, than the data I'd captured with social engineering tactics. And there was lots of it—thousands of megabytes of data, equivalent to millions of pages. I had compromised virtually all of NCC's most valuable data.

Insider Coordination of External Accomplices

Since a real industrial espionage attack would involve the use of accomplices, I used others to help exploit the internal networks. Mike and Bob both had experience in UNIX and PC computers and the right backgrounds to take advantage of any circumstances that might arise. Throughout this phase of the process, my accomplices stayed in contact with me through the pager I had acquired on the first day of the attack, which they called whenever they needed more information or needed me to commit an action on their behalf. Our close contact allowed me to proceed confidently on other aspects of the penetration.

I set up the outside attack by asking for an account on a UNIX computer system. Without questioning my need for it, the administration staff provided me with an account. After I asked whether I could check my e-mail from home, I was shown how I could log on to the system from home. I then called Mike and gave him my user ID and password, as well as the telephone number of the company's modem connections.

My accomplices used the access to fish around the system. Their first target was the UNIX password file. They captured the file, then proceeded to run a program against the file that guesses user passwords. Approximately 10 percent of the passwords were guessed by the program, which gave us access to over 800 user accounts. Mike then faxed me the list of compromised user accounts, and I used NCC's on-line telephone directory to look up the departments of the employees whose accounts had been compromised. After I identified the departments, I prioritized the accounts, based upon the departments, and faxed the list back to Mike and Bob.

It turned out that a large number of the compromised UNIX accounts were unused or still assigned to employees who had left the company. However, they provided us with important access points to the network. Many of the accounts did produce very valuable information. Mike and Bob secured superuser status on several UNIX computers by exploiting known vulnerabilities.

Accessing the PC systems was a little more complicated. NCC did have a modem number specifically for remote PC connections, but the modem access required a Smart Card, which is a one-time password mechanism. This access was very secure; however, once access was obtained, it allowed the computer that dialed in to appear to be right on the network, just like any in-house machine. I obtained a Smart Card application form through e-mail, then I forged my supervisor's signature on the form as well as the signature of an NCC vice president. I also forged a letter from the vice president requesting that the delivery of the card be expedited. Within twenty-four hours, I had the card and the software specifically required for the modem connection. I then sent the whole package to my off-site friends via overnight courier.

With Smart Card access, Mike and Bob were then able to search all vulnerable PCs at NCC from 1,000 miles away, using a toll-free telephone number. Bob also ran a password guesser against several critical PCs and was able to compromise a very large amount of information. By the time this phase of the test was completed, my accomplices were able to exploit all of the information I had previously captured.

Mike and Bob helped me obtain significantly more information than I could have gotten myself. They performed the technical attacks against the internal network, while I attended to other aspects of the attack. Working together, we optimized the time available. I was able to tell them exactly what to look for (such as types of documents, names of projects, and so on), significantly speeding up the process and reducing the chances that we would be caught. Without an insider, the outside attackers could have been fishing around for weeks.

Outsider Hacking

To complete the exercise, the security manager requested that we try to hack into the NCC system without insider help. His specific concerns were about Internet exposure and the threat posed by NCC's modem lines. For this phase, we agreed to forgo the social engineering attacks hackers would normally employ and just attempt to break into the system technically.

During the internal network hacking, I performed an internal scan of the company firewall for vulnerabilities but found no exploitable holes. My attempts to hack the firewall through other means also failed. We scanned the firewall via the Internet, again, with no success. The firewall proved to be invulnerable to outside attacks—for now. In the future, as NCC provides its people with greater connectivity and new technical vulnerabilities are discovered, holes could appear in the system.

From the company telephone directory, I identified all company telephone exchanges. Using a war dialer, we scanned the telephone exchanges for modems. We found hundreds of potential modems. Bob sampled many of the lines and determined that not all of the modems belonged to NCC. Most of the NCC modems were fairly secure; they did not identify the name of the company, and they did require a log-in procedure. None of the default user identifiers were enabled, and the modems we dialed did disconnect the telephone call after three failed log-in attempts. The modems, too, seemed to be secure against a haphazard, random attack.

However, the company employed no authentication procedure beyond a valid log-in identifier and password. User accounts are easily compromised through social engineering techniques. While a sampling of the modem connections indicated a relatively high level of security, there was a strong reliance on perimeter security—in other words, once you got through the front line, there was nothing else to stop you. And some of the modem connections were bound to have some problems.

CONCLUSIONS

The level of success we achieved at NCC in just three days was phenomenal. The security manager expected the exercise to expose vulnerabilities from an operational perspective, but nobody expected me to compromise twenty-eight of the company's top programs through misrepresentations and walk-throughs alone. The officers of the company were shocked at our success, especially at the seeming ease with which I collected everything a competitor could want to know about the synthetic fat project. The fact that that project was compromised within only a few hours was horrifying. Using only *basic* tools of the trade, I could have dealt a deadly blow to the company.

How important was luck to my success? Some may claim that finding small pieces of information, such as the location and password of the manufacturing documentation, was an obvious piece of luck. Performing the attack during a week when many managers were out of their offices could also have been a factor in my success.

But clearly, when senior people from multiple departments disclosed extremely sensitive information to me, I wasn't lucky. I was a convincing liar, I was well prepared, and I exploited a loose system. No one ever bothered to confirm my identity or verify my need for the information I asked for. The organization's innate environment of openness made it incredibly vulnerable. An environment of openness is common to many organizations, especially research and development firms. Unfortunately, research and development firms have the most to lose.

Furthermore, two weeks after the penetration test, the security manager had yet to receive a report of any unusual happenings. I appeared and disappeared without comment from the people I exploited. None of my team's technical scans were detected by the information systems department. The systems administrators did not detect our modifications to key computer system files or report unusual superuser activity. Nobody detected our massive download of data from a variety of key systems throughout the company. Nobody reported any disturbances to their offices or computer systems. Failed attempts of computer access were not reported to security.

The manufacturing information for synthetic fat was obtained within one day, indicating that it was possible for anyone with minimal access and a little knowledge to acquire the data. The implications were grave when you consider what could have been accomplished by an insider with a great deal of knowledge.

Remember: billions were compromised during this test without the use of any advanced techniques. Even the computer hacking was relatively unsophisticated. This is the real face of corporate espionage.

VULNERABILITIES EXPLOITED

The penetration test succeeded because it was a focused attack. I targeted sensitive information on specific development projects. I identified who could best provide me with the information, and I aggressively approached those people to learn where the best information was located. Without that kind of focus, I might not have achieved the same level of success. I could have gathered millions of pages of documents and never acquired the most valuable information.

Throughout the exercise, the security manager and I considered when an actual attacker might have taken everything and left the country. Initially, I would have been tempted to leave after obtaining the meeting minutes within three hours of my arrival. We believed that an attacker would certainly have left after obtaining the manufacturing data for synthetic fat and two other projects. However, as my attack progressed, I was able to capture equally sensitive information for twenty-five other programs by the end of the following day. Think of the extensive damage a protracted attack by a trusted insider could do. Once a person is familiar with the information that can be gathered on one project, then that person knows the type of information and where to look for it with other projects. This predictability makes the life of a spy very easy.

Failure to Use Available Security Features

Throughout the penetration, I exploited many vulnerabilities that should not have existed. The company's first line of defense was the access badge. If any of the people I manipulated had asked to see my access badge, they would have seen that I was only a temporary employee and not a supervisor for information security. My cover would have been blown. Although it's possible I could have talked my way around the issue, at least a few more red lights would have gone off.

A lot of the material I collected was picked up during the physical walk-throughs. No sensitive information would have been captured with this activity if people had simply locked their doors, put away sensitive papers, and locked their file cabinets. Everyone at NCC has some form of locked storage space; failure to use it was almost universal. Some very senior executives did lock their doors at night. However, they obviously did not enforce that policy on their subordinates.

PC security was better. More people used the software tool that locked up their PCs and required a password to unlock it.

Ironically, it seems that the people with the most valuable information were the least likely to use the security software. Although the program is not infallible, it can make an intruder's work much more difficult so that the intruder moves on to a more vulnerable target or is more easily detected.

The information systems department is not without blame, either. Many technical protection mechanisms could have been in place. Software is available that forces users to enter passwords that cannot be guessed, even by the most sophisticated password guessers. The systems administrators could also have implemented a more secure access control system. The fact that Mike and Bob were able to grab the password file demonstrated how vulnerable the network was.

Additionally, inactive computer accounts can be locked. We were able to access many computer accounts that were apparently not used for at least one year. Although these accounts might not have any valuable information, they do provide an attacker with an access point that can be further exploited to compromise the entire network.

The administrators should have been able to review log files to see whether their systems were being scanned. When the Internet Security Scanner determined what systems were on the network, it located several "sniffers" that were there to identify unusual activity. Apparently, nobody at NCC was looking at the sniffer logs on a frequent and regular basis.

Many mechanisms were in place that could have minimized the success of the attack or at least detected the attacks. Unfortunately, these mechanisms were not used properly. This situation is not unique to NCC. The company has a wide variety of protection mechanisms that many other companies do not.

Intellectual Openness

Throughout the exercise, I was told about the openness that "made the company what it is today." Many NCC employees feel that the free exchange of information is the only way a research and development firm can succeed. The development team leader and business manager I spoke to were very familiar with the previous thefts and the effects they could have had on NCC. But ironically, both individuals seemed to be more concerned about security interfering with the development process than about the previous incidents of insider thefts.

I agree that intellectual openness is important to development efforts. However, openness without any consideration of the principle of valid access is not only ridiculous, but also dangerous to the long-term viability of a company. If I had been working for a competitor that was able to beat NCC to market because of the information I had stolen, then the results would have been lost profits and probably large-scale layoffs.

Anonymity within Large Corporations

Employees working in large organizations often do not know all the other employees. It's a situation that allows outsiders to claim to be insiders. This case study demonstrates that large companies are very vulnerable to insider misrepresentations of authority and responsibility.

At NCC, mechanisms are in place that actually facilitate misrepresentations. The caller ID system, for example, gives a false sense of security that the caller is legitimate. The truth is, anyone could walk into someone else's office and impersonate that person from the telephone. Organizations must ensure that their people understand that all identifiers are not equally valid.

Reliance on Perimeter Security

From a technical standpoint, NCC proved to be relatively secure against outside attacks. However, once an attacker got inside the perimeter, the security significantly weakened. Several critical computer systems were apparently not regularly updated for known vulnerabilities. Additionally, a more secure version of the network operating system could have been used to provide additional network security.

The use of the Smart Card and secure modem configurations indicates that the NCC organization was taking proactive measures to prevent unauthorized computer access. However, the company's focus on preventing unauthorized access took resources away from internal security measures. These measures are necessary to prevent further abuse by outsiders who are able to break through the firewall or modem security. They also ensure that other insiders don't abuse the system.

The perimeter security mind-set is also pervasive among nontechnical employees. People generally believe that since physical access is restricted to employees, they do not have to lock their offices and file cabinets. Reliance on perimeter defenses gives a false sense of security to people who do not know about or acknowledge the insider threat.

Failure to Monitor for Known Vulnerabilities

New vulnerabilities in computer systems are identified almost weekly. My team was able to obtain superuser status on several computer systems at NCC by exploiting known vulnerabilities. The fixes for such vulnerabilities are easily available to the systems administrators, yet NCC's administrators either did not know about them or failed to take the time to implement them.

Another measure that could have prevented the exploitation of the company's vulnerabilities is the use of a vulnerability scanning tool, such as the Internet Security Scanner. Most scanning tools are developed for administrators to allow them to identify weaknesses before they can be compromised by an attacker. Unfortunately, attackers themselves seem to use the scanning tools more frequently than administrators do.

Other Tactics Not Attempted

Due to the success of our early efforts, I did not use many tactics that could have increased the success of the attack. Using a desktop publishing software tool, I could have produced a new front for my access badge to make myself look like a regular employee. I was also prepared to produce forged letters from the CEO on the company's letterhead, telling people to give me unlimited access. I obtained the CEO's signature from NCC's annual report and scanned it into a computer file. Such a "signed" letter could have given me additional access. I was also ready to write a letter from the CEO stating that I was operating under his authority, in case I was caught.

If this was an actual case of industrial espionage, I might have performed other more intrusive attacks as well. Specifically, I could have planted bugs in the offices of many critical employees. Bugging devices could have been planted in computer systems to transmit data to waiting receivers. Telephones could have been tapped, and fax transmissions could have been captured. The likelihood of such an attack is high when the stakes involve billions of dollars.

What Else Might Have Happened?

Despite the sensitivity of the captured information, none of the attacks were ever reported to security. The security manager who hired me couldn't help wondering how many other attacks have gone unnoticed.

A penetration test only identifies the vulnerabilities that were actually encountered during the test. Although I would like to believe that I identified all possible vulnerabilities, that is unlikely.

Due to the value of the products it develops and the previous cases of espionage that it experienced, NCC is being targeted by foreign and domestic competitors and even foreign countries. These organizations have extensive financial resources and highly skilled people who could launch a very effective penetration effort. The threat is real, and it is impossible to know if, or to what extent, NCC's information has already been compromised.

8

Chips and Dips

ILL GAEDE ALWAYS MADE A GREAT IMPRESSION ON THE
people around him. He seemed like a fine, light-hearted
person with a great sense of humor. He was the kind of
guy who was probably good at any job he tried. Everyone
found him to be extremely well-spoken and intelligent. He
was very personable, a pal to everyone; yet he was a close
friend to few. Because of his fair skin, blue eyes, and generic
American accent, most people had no idea he was originally
from Argentina. He could be your neighbor.

Or he could be a spy. He could even be the greatest semiconductor thief of all time.

Guillermo Gaede (a.k.a. William or Bill Gaede) used corporate espionage tactics that were even simpler than the ones
I employed at NCC (described in Chapter 7). Yet the value of
the information he stole from American high-tech companies
over a thirteen-year period easily exceeded $1 billion.

Some people at the FBI, Intel Corporation, and Advanced
Micro Devices (AMD) might challenge the motives Mr. Gaede
claims, and they might quibble about the sequence of certain
events. But no one will argue about the extent of his crimes. I
visited Mr. Gaede in prison to get his story.

BACKGROUND

An engineer by training, Mr. Gaede entered the computer chip industry back when it was still in its infancy. In 1979, he went to work for Advanced Micro Devices, a chip manufacturer based in Silicon Valley in California. He was employed by AMD until September 6, 1992, when he went into hiding to avoid possible arrest by the FBI on charges related to the theft of proprietary AMD information and for selling it to the Cubans.

Eight months later, in May 1993, he was hired by CDI, a technical employment agency, as a temporary employee for Intel Corporation, the world's leading computer chip manufacturer. He so impressed his bosses at Intel that he was given a permanent job on September 20 of that same year. On April 29, 1994, Intel security personnel confronted him about his past and warned him that he would suffer serious consequences if he tried anything there. On May 1 and 2, Mr. Gaede completed his theft of the Intel Pentium chip design plans, and then he left the country. Upon his later return, he was arrested and accepted a plea-bargained sentence of thirty-three months at a minimum-security facility.

Gaede's story represents industrial espionage at its most typical: a gentle, sustained attack by a patient, single-minded insider; and a comedy of errors committed by the thief's victims when looked at in hindsight. At both AMD and Intel, Gaede was given pivotal positions that provided him with all the information and access an industrial spy could ever want. His activities went almost completely unnoticed despite some clearly questionable behavior. While he was under investigation, his bosses gave him even more critical access than he already had at the time.

The Pre-Espionage Years

Guillermo Gaede applied for work at AMD in 1979 as William Gaede. He was hired and was asked to provide the standard proof of citizenship documentation, which for him included a fake birth certificate and driver's license. This established him as a U.S. citizen in the eyes of the company and exempted him from scrutiny by the U.S. Immigration and Naturalization Service (INS). Gaede is convinced that the INS would have been a constant source of aggravation had he not faked his citizenship.

From all indications, Gaede was an ideal worker. He performed well in all his jobs, put in late hours, and helped out other people in different areas of the company. He was very friendly to people, and other engineers came to him for help. He was well established, and his face was known to many people in different areas of AMD. To this day, AMD officially describes his performance as "exemplary."

Becoming a Spy

Gaede claims that throughout his life he has admired Fidel Castro. He said that as a child in Argentina he was taught that Castro was a freedom fighter. He had no loyalty to AMD and appeared to have no misgivings about stealing sensitive information from his employer. Gaede intended to help advance Cuba's semiconductor capabilities.

In the semiconductor industry, the chips themselves do not have value to competitors; rather, the specific sequence of assembly gives a competitor the capability to manufacture the chips. In other words, one can buy a chip and dissect it to discover what it's made of, but to actually make it, one has to know exactly how it was assembled. Approximately 100 individual steps are required in the chip manufacturing process; each step must be performed in sequence to produce a specific chip. If the manufacturing process performs one step out of sequence, the resulting chips are worthless.

The manufacturing information comprises three physical forms. *Run cards* instruct an engineer to perform a specific task on a given wafer. A *wafer* is actually a ceramic sheet containing multiple chips. At any given point in the manufacturing process, a detailed inspection of a wafer indicates an intermediate step in the process. If the competition can get one wafer from each phase of the process and can sequence it, then it can deduce the entire process. *Design specifications* provide step-by-step instructions on how to manufacture a chip. Specifications, which are actually documents, have all the information on how to produce a chip in a single document. With any of these forms of information, all a competitor needs is the manufacturing equipment to produce the chip.

Gaede first approached the Cuban government during a trip to Mexico City with his wife in 1982 with an offer to provide high-tech information. He simply walked into the Cuban embassy and asked to meet with a consul. Gaede provided the consul with some run cards, wafers, and design specifications to show him the types of information he could provide. According to Gaede, his only purpose in providing this information was ideological. Castro was a larger-than-life hero to him, and he wanted to help the country. He claims that he wanted no money. Law enforcement authorities and his victims claim otherwise.

That meeting seems to have led nowhere. Gaede claims that the Cuban diplomat expressed tremendous interest in his information but never followed up. When Gaede tried to contact the diplomat by telephone, the embassy hung up on him. This initial rejection did not discourage Mr. Gaede.

THE ATTACK

Gaede began his corporate espionage activities in earnest after the Mexico City meeting (I believe he was expecting the Cubans to get back to him). He started at AMD by gathering information that was readily available. For the most part, the information was taken for granted by people inside the company; but to a third-world country like Cuba, even the most basic information, such as clean room handling procedures, were of critical importance. In many cases, documents widely available to everyone inside the American semiconductor industry are prohibited by law from being shipped to Cuba. Everything was of potential value to a country that had nothing.

Getting Started

Gaede became a regular at the copy machines. He simply walked around company offices and facilities, picking up documents of potential value and dashing off copies. He knew where all the copy machines were. He carried a map in his mind of the machines' locations. He knew which were closest at all times. The security guards frequently saw him in many different locations, but they never recorded any unusual activities. Guards would occasionally question him, he would show his badge, and they would walk away content.

Making Gaede's task easier was the fact that nobody inside AMD seemed to understand the value of their information to people outside of the company. Employees often don't realize that the documents they work with on a daily basis contain information that has a very limited distribution. There is also the prevalent it-won't-happen-here attitude, which leaves information widely unprotected. Gaede flourished in this environment.

He quickly discovered that outdated documents were often more valuable to a third-world country than state-of-the-art ones. New manufacturing equipment was simply not available to Cuba, so the latest designs were useless. But black market U.S. rejects were available, and that kind of equipment usually came without documentation. The documents that Gaede provided gave the Cubans the capability to use and repair the equipment they had but which they knew little about.

Gaede collected a wide range of information for his potential Cuban clients, including equipment specifications, repair documents, installation manuals, building plans, clean room procedures, and clean room design specifications. The clean room information was critical because of the sanitary conditions required to manufacture computer chips. To avoid contamination of the chips themselves, they are kept in environments free of any contamination—even dust. It is simply impossible to manufacture semiconductors with substandard clean room facilities. Knowledge of the acceptable pollution limits and how to control them was taken for granted in the U.S. technology companies, but the information had not made its way to Cuba. Thanks to Gaede, Cuba was able to gain—in just minutes and at almost no cost—information that U.S. companies had struggled for years to compile.

Gaede got most of this information from an unlocked document room at AMD headquarters. This room held a wide range of unused documents and was conveniently located near a copy machine. There were no controls at all on the materials. He regularly walked into the room, picked out a document of interest, and made a copy of it. He then replaced it, and nobody knew it had been touched. Occasionally, he would notice a repairman working on a complex piece of high-tech equipment. When the repairman broke for lunch, Gaede would grab his diagrams and manuals, make copies of them, and then quietly return them before the repairman finished eating.

Gaede also became an expert in copy machine repair and maintenance. He never wanted to attract any undue attention to his activities, so he learned to fix the machines himself. He also took precautions to avoid leaving behind any traces of his activities. He always took any damaged copies or paper misfeeds with him. When he got home, he would burn them or otherwise destroy them.

Since Gaede was gathering these materials over time, he was careful not to attract attention by taking too much out the door in a single batch. He never took out more than 100 pages at a time. If he had to, he would make several trips throughout the day, stashing the documents in his car.

Getting the information out of the door was easy. Although the guards were expected to be diligent, they were instructed to watch primarily for green- and blue-colored binders, which were used to store extremely sensitive information. There was nothing to prevent people from taking the papers out of the binders and carrying them out the door in paper bags or briefcases. The guards also watched for equipment, floppy disks, and other storage media—but floppy disks could, of course, be carried out in a pocket.

According to Gaede, the security guards simply didn't know what was valuable. They could look at the specifications for building the Pentium chip and not understand the potential value it represented. Basically, the guards prevented law-abiding people from making innocent mistakes.

After Gaede got his materials outside the company, he stashed them in a rented storage locker. He used a fake name to get the locker, probably using another forged ID. He is somewhat vague on the details here, due to some charges still pending against him. However, one thing is certain: his locker protected him against sudden unexpected searches of his home and served as a holding bin for billions of dollars' worth of information. Overall, it was a simple, almost innocuous, attack strategy.

A Friend to All

In his early days at AMD, Gaede used his charisma as his best weapon. His job, the document rooms, and bookshelves provided him with a tremendous amount of basic yet valuable information. However, his access to the newer technologies resulted from establishing friendships with people all over the company. He hung out at the coffee machines, he volunteered for committees, and he offered to do favors for everyone. He became widely known around the company and was well liked. Most important, he established plenty of reasons to visit people in parts of AMD to which he normally had no access.

In this way, he was able to map out which areas had which types of information and learn where it was stored. People knew him, so it did not strike them as odd when he stopped by for no apparent reason. Through various working groups, he also acquired access to many projects other than his own. His popularity and technical competence as an engineer led others to call him when some projects were having problems. This not only gave him access to new developments but taught him how his company was fixing the problems, which could also be helpful to the Cubans.

He became known for putting in twelve-hour days. He was an "exempt" employee, which meant that he was paid a salary and not by the hour. He also drew limited supervision. As long as he continued to perform, no one was going to bother him about how he spent his time.

Gaede spent most of his late afternoons going through other people's areas and belongings. By five o'clock, many people had gone home for the day. Few were left to see him checking office doors to see if they were locked.

Not that companies like AMD had many office doors. The employee cubicle, a mainstay of modern high-tech company interior design, provided Gaede with easy access to cabinets and drawers. Much of the information that he sought was lying on top of coworkers' desks or piled in their in-boxes. Chip wiring charts made attractive wall decorations to chip designers and other people in the semiconductor industry—of course, they also showed others how the chips were wired.

In 1986, AMD downsized its Sunnyvale, California, operation. There was a recession in the computer industry, and people were more concerned about having a job than doing a job. Many people were leaving the company, and it was hard to keep track of equipment. Gaede's wanderings throughout the company allowed him to identify expensive equipment that would not be missed. He would go into areas to which he'd managed to gain access late in the afternoon and carry out the targeted equipment. He did not want to attract the attention of the guards in any way, so he went to great lengths to sneak the equipment out. When possible, he would take the equipment to fenced-in areas that he could get to without going through guard posts. He would then force the pieces under the fence and pick them up later. He would sometimes sneak equipment out under his clothing (much of the high-tech diagnostic equipment was very small and could easily be hidden in a pocket).

The Cubans Call Back

In 1985, Gaede decided to contact the Cubans again. This time, he visited the Czechoslovakian embassy in Washington, D.C., which maintained a Cuban interests desk staffed by a Cuban diplomat. He brought along more sample materials. The Cuban representative said he would get back to him.

Gaede returned to California, and he was later contacted by the Cubans and told to go to Mexico City in May 1986. There, he met with a Cuban intelligence officer at the Cuban embassy. Gaede provided him with a variety of information, including design specifications, machinery manuals, and chip schematics. He would have provided more, but he was limited by what he could carry with him on an airplane.

At the end of this meeting, he was provided with contacts and a "shopping list" of technologies desired by the Cuban government. At last he was doing something to support his hero. It's worth remembering that Cuba's allies included the Soviet Union and East Germany; they were likely served by Gaede's efforts as well.

During the ensuing years, Gaede traveled frequently to Mexico to pass information to his Cuban friends. When the Sunnyvale location was downsized, Gaede was transferred to Austin, Texas, which is very close to the Mexican border. During this period, he would take his family to Mexican border towns, where he would meet his Cuban spy master. He always brought along carloads of documents and equipment. He took special precautions to make sure the U.S. Customs police did not mistake him for a non-U.S. citizen. His non-Hispanic appearance was very helpful. He would also feign ignorance of customs policies and would tell the officials that he was bringing beer into the country. This changed the issue from an immigration issue to a customs one. He continued to leave no tracks.

In 1989, Gaede and his wife were invited to Cuba. They met their Cuban contact at a Mexico City subway station, where they were provided with fake passports. They were flown to Spain and given another set of passports, and then on to Austria to receive another set of passports. From there, they were flown to Cuba. During their stay in Havana, Gaede and his wife were treated like heroes, and he received some basic training on industrial espionage collection techniques. He also received some simple and very basic "spy toys." He was given a micro camera, a jacket with Velcro linings that allowed him to sneak things in and out of AMD inside his coat, a wallet with a secret compartment, and instructions written on rice paper that he could eat if he were ever caught.

Now he was a real spy.

Transferred to Austin

When AMD downsized the Sunnyvale facility in 1986, the company tried to find jobs for anyone willing to relocate to another AMD facility. Gaede was a popular employee, and they readily found him a job as a process engineer at an Austin, Texas, facility. This fabrication facility produced many chip families, including the 286, 386, and 486 chips.

Gaede's new job was not considered to be a critical one. He was in charge of aluminum and gold processes. More important to his spying activities, he was responsible for the backgrind process. The silicon wafers, on which computer chips are created, are left thick during the early stages of manufacture to reduce the risk of cracking; after the manufacturing process is finished, the thickness of the wafers are reduced through another process called backgrinding. Since backgrinding was common to all chips, Gaede had almost unlimited access to all of the company's semiconductors, and he was privy to most of what went on in the development and manufacturing of those products at the AMD Austin facility.

Gaede's position gave him access to almost all chip manufacturing facilities, including the clean rooms where the chips where assembled. Consequently, he was able to take wafers at various stages of the assembly process, which revealed the assembly sequence.

Production personnel were supposed to account for all wafers going through the manufacturing process. Occasionally, however, wafers disappeared, and to prevent "problems," operators logged them as broken (broken wafers were tossed in a recycling bin and were not accounted for).

The broken classification was very useful, because nobody asked questions about busted chips. Some breakage was expected, and as long as it was not excessive, management was not concerned. Management seemed not to understand the value of the information contained in a broken chip. Wafers were typically small enough that they could be put in someone's pocket—a fact Gaede abused regularly.

Gaede also developed a long-term collection strategy for gathering step-by-step designs. He started by going to the company library. Unlike the Sunnyvale facility, the document library in Austin was attended by staff most of the time. At first, Gaede requested specific documents he knew about. The library staff knew that he was an engineer and assumed that if he asked for it, he needed it. Access to documents was not logged, so he left no tracks. After a while, library staff just allowed him to look for himself and find whatever documents he wanted. Through this method, he was able to get his hands on the design specifications of most of the semiconductors produced in Austin.

Now that he had the design specs, he knew which items to request from the chip fabrication groups. Naturally, he was also able to secure documents and manuals on all machinery in use at the facility. The Austin facility had much more manufacturing equipment than the Sunnyvale facility did, and he was able to get that much more documentation.

With the chip specifications in hand, he wrote up requests for the wafers at specific phases of manufacturing. He used his status as a backgrinder to call for "tests of wafer resilience at different phases of production." Through a drawn-out series of requests, he was able to piece together the entire process. He used AMD's own wafer shipment containers to take the wafers out of the buildings.

Gaede's wife also worked at AMD during this period. She worked on a project to which Gaede did not have access. He used her access to secure the specifications for the 486 chips, which he then used to request wafers at specific phases of the manufacturing process. He also took wafers out of the broken wafer bins. The camera his Cuban friends had given him became very useful as Gaede walked around the design areas. These areas had chip wiring diagrams hanging on almost every cubicle. He was able to photograph the designs for many chips that were then in development.

Gaede and his wife did not limit their collection activities to information. Highly sanitary conditions are required for the manufacture of computer chips, and that process requires

workers to wear special clothing. American clean room workers discarded their clothing after a single use. Gaede and his
wife went around collecting discarded gloves and clothing for
shipment to Cuba. Without this clothing, Cuba would have
been unable to make the chips.

The mail rooms in high-tech manufacturing operations
store many documents that are supposed to be tightly controlled. At AMD, the mail room was a repository for documents reserved for companies authorized to purchase AMD
products. The documents contained many details about the
installation and repair of many AMD products, and they were
used by engineers who installed the chips in other products.
Gaede was able to walk into the mail room and request any
document he wanted. He had no legitimate need for the
information, but nobody questioned his requests. The mail
clerks did not understand the reason for the controls (export
restrictions) and did not bother to enforce them.

Nothing Is More Valuable Than Friendship

As he did in Sunnyvale, Gaede made it a point to befriend as
many people at the Austin facility as possible. He focused on
the design engineers and the product engineers. The design
engineers allowed him to track new developments and the
technologies being used in them. He also heard about any
emerging problems and their solutions. The product engineers
provided him with information about manufacturing problems as well as their solutions. Gaede claimed these engineers
would spill their guts when anyone expressed the slightest
interest in their work.

Gaede's access to production reports (through his backgrinder status) helped him to strike up conversations with other
employees. Whenever he spotted a report about specific problems, he would go to the engineer most likely to be responsible
for fixing it and find out how it was done. Gaede's awareness of

these problems and his apparent technical ability led to his appointment to many working groups. These working groups gave him access to a tremendous amount of information while providing him with contacts all over the company. Again, he used his tried-and-true techniques to gather information and equipment of all types.

He also knew to befriend secretaries. Although the secretaries did not generally have valuable information, they could tell him when people would be in and out of their offices, so he would know when he could safely go through them.

In his thirteen years at AMD, Gaede made it a point to learn everything he could about the company's security strengths and weaknesses. He has said that the company's greatest weakness was its tendency to look for symptoms and not problems. For example, the security guards had been trained to look for specific items, but they were never taught which things might be valuable to the company and its adversaries.

Other Assistance

Cuba is banned from purchasing or acquiring a great deal of American semiconductor manufacturing equipment. Even though Gaede was able to tell the Cubans how to manufacture chips, they did not have a great deal of the equipment required to manufacture them. Gaede used his expertise to help Cuba bypass export restrictions. Over the years he worked in the semiconductor industry, he learned how high-tech companies disposed of outdated equipment, which the Cubans could later purchase.

To get rid of spare equipment and recover some maintenance costs, chip manufacturers often sell their old equipment to refurbishers. The refurbishers take the equipment, perform basic repairs, and then resell it. Gaede helped the Cuban government locate these resellers and facilitated its acquisition of the equipment through intermediaries in Spain. This allowed

Cuba to get relatively sophisticated equipment at low cost. Additionally, the resold equipment was not tracked by the U.S. government, so these activities went unnoticed. Gaede significantly enhanced Cuba's high-tech capability and probably the capabilities of many other Soviet-aligned countries.

Things Did Not Always Go Smoothly

Gaede was always extremely careful. He did his best to leave no trails of evidence. However, on three separate occasions he was nearly caught. Once he was searching an office and the occupant returned unexpectedly from lunch. On the spot, Gaede made up a story about looking for a book he'd seen on her bookshelf. The person was very upset to find Gaede in her office, and she admonished him never to do such a thing again, *but she reported the incident to no one.* On another occasion, a security guard caught him in a storage closet that contained many sensitive documents and challenged him about his presence there. Gaede responded aggressively that he belonged there. He showed the guard his badge, and the guard left him alone. During one attempted theft of equipment, he carried the item into a storage yard and the door locked behind him. If he had been caught there with the equipment, some serious questions would have been asked. But he kept his head and shoved the equipment far under the fence. He then started banging on the door and yelling for help. When a guard appeared, Gaede pretended to be angry, yelling that his access card wouldn't let him back in. The guard apologized for the situation and told him to go to the security office for a replacement card the next day.

Any one of these incidents, if at least logged, should have attracted attention to Gaede. When combined with his frequent copier use and library access, it could have compromised his whole operation. But the company had no system for keeping track of unusual incidents.

Fleeing the Country

On September 6, 1992, Gaede and his family fled the United States. Gaede claims that he approached the FBI and CIA several months earlier because some of his Cuban handlers wanted to provide information to the U.S., and Gaede was to be the intermediary. In his interrogation, he had to admit how he had become involved with the Cubans. During his contact with the FBI, he became concerned that they would arrest him on espionage charges. So he drove his family into Mexico and flew from there to Colombia, where he and his wife left their children with her family.

Several months later, Gaede returned to the U.S. without his family by going to Mexico and then hitching a ride with an American tourist in Tijuana, Mexico. Gaede claimed to be an American tourist, and he showed Customs a fake driver's license at the border.

Gaede and his wife set up a cleaning service called Mary Poppins in the Phoenix, Arizona, area. This small business provided a good cover to explain a period of unemployment. During this time, Gaede contacted the FBI to try to arrange some sort of deal. Although the truth of his bargaining with the FBI may never be known, he felt comfortable enough staying in the country. He even used an FBI agent as a reference on his later job applications.

The Attack on Intel

In May 1993, Gaede was hired by CDI, a temp agency that provided temporary workers to Intel Corporation in Chandler, Arizona. Intel had a strong need for someone familiar with a software package called Work Stream. This application helps companies manage work flows and processes, such as the chip manufacturing process, and Gaede was familiar with it from his days at AMD. Gaede's application included not only an FBI agent as a reference but also his AMD work experience. For this application, he even used his correct green card number and admitted to being a foreign citizen. To cover his period of unemployment between leaving AMD and his application, he claimed that he left AMD to start the Mary Poppins cleaning service. He said the business was not doing well, so he needed a new job. Gaede claims that Pete Costner, the AMD security manager, created a wanted poster with Gaede's picture on it, and, ironically, it had been distributed throughout the semiconductor industry several months before he was hired by Intel. (Pete Costner denies ever doing this.)

Because Gaede had experience with Work Stream, his application was quickly approved by Intel. He was brought in as a systems specialist. His job included managing the Work Stream database, which contained the product specifications for all chips produced at the Chandler facility. He also provided help desk–type support, and people throughout the company came to him when they had problems. Intel had given him the keys to their kingdom.

His first collection of Intel information was the software that he was responsible for maintaining. He made copies of the Work Stream software, along with the underlying database programs. The database programs themselves could be used for a variety of applications beyond chip manufacturing. He provided Cuba with the software for both VAX- and PC-type computers. The Work Stream software greatly improved Cuba's chip production capabilities as well as other manufacturing operations.

Gaede established himself as a problem solver throughout the Chandler facility. People came to him with a variety of computer and manufacturing problems, and he developed a reputation as a valuable employee. On September 29, 1993, Intel hired him as a permanent employee and increased his responsibilities.

Gaede says that, during this period, he was no longer providing information to the Cubans. He claims that he was just slowly gathering information over a period of time for an undetermined purpose. His collection methods remained the same, though they were not as targeted and intense in scope.

He began collecting information using the same methods that he had used at AMD. He again struck up friendships with key engineers and managers. At this time, he began to schedule regular meetings with the managers. He would talk to them about regular issues and then take the conversation off on a tangent. Conversations about computer usage would turn into conversations about future products that Intel was producing as well as other valuable targets. Gaede also took these opportunities to scan people's desks and offices. Whenever he spotted something of potential value, he was sure to return later that day.

Sensitive documents were stored in documentation rooms. These rooms were kept locked at all times, unless somebody went in to get a document. Gaede would wait for a person with a key to open the door, then he would follow the person into the room. People assumed that he was allowed in the room and never questioned him. Almost all of the document rooms were near a copy machine, providing Gaede the opportunity to quickly make a copy and return the documents before the person with the key left the room.

As with AMD, Gaede regularly wandered through the building looking for information. Gaede says that the facility at Intel was almost a fire hazard. Many people left stacks of papers on their desks. He was overwhelmed with valuable information. The mail room at Intel also stocked a variety of documents that were supposed to be controlled. During his short tenure at Intel, he stole product design specifications, wiring diagrams, production reports, high-tech equipment, equipment manuals, product manuals, and a wide variety of other documents.

An Unusual Request?

Gaede claims that in October 1993, an FBI agent he was working with asked him to steal something valuable for him. He claims he does not know why the FBI wanted it, but he obliged. He decided to give them a production report, referred to as a 629.5. This report contained the production details for a specific family of microprocessors. It had the manufacturing instructions for the family, the current quantity of wafers at each phase in the production process, and a variety of other production-related details. This report would significantly help anyone who wanted to produce a similar type of chip.

How did Gaede acquire this document? He made it a point to regularly meet with the manager in charge of production for this specific chip. Gaede was very familiar with his office and would regularly go through it. On one occasion, he found the production report sitting in his in-box, and he made a copy.

Telespying

Intel, as most other companies had begun to do in the 1990s, started a telecommuting program while Gaede was working there. Besides his main responsibility as computer systems administrator, he was regularly called at odd hours of the day and night to fix problems with the computer. He became a prime candidate for telecommuter status. In November 1993, Intel provided him with a computer terminal and telephone line for his home, as well as a beeper. Intel was security-conscious as far as the telecommuting effort went and gave him a Smart Card that created a new password for each time he logged on to the computer. He could now access almost any computer at Intel from his home.

Although this did not give him any more access than he already had, it allowed him to perform his activities away from the prying eyes of others and in the comfort of his home. This setup also allowed Gaede to gain his notoriety of videotaping his computer screen. He did not want to copy the data from the work computer to his home computer, because he thought it would leave a trail. Instead, he set up a video camera to focus on the computer screen. He would scroll through screens containing valuable documents, such as chip specifications. A single tape could hold thousands of pages of documents, and it was easily transported.

A sequence of events that occurred during the months of April and May 1994 allowed Gaede to steal the much-coveted design specifications for the then-emerging Pentium computer chip while simultaneously evading capture. The chip was being manufactured at the Intel Rio Rancho facility near Albuquerque, New Mexico. Gaede's boss wanted him to study the Pentium manufacturing process to see if any new processes or procedures could be implemented to improve the Chandler facility. His boss filled out a form, requesting that Gaede have access to the Pentium technology, and sent it to Rio Rancho. His boss had provided him with access to one of the few technologies he had yet to steal.

Sometime during Gaede's employment at Intel, the security department learned of his past. Gaede believes that one of the Intel security people saw the wanted poster produced by AMD and reported him. (Again, AMD denies ever creating the wanted posters.) He also thinks that Intel had him under surveillance for several months before confronting him. He was getting access to the Pentium chip even while this surveillance was ongoing.

On April 27, 1994, Gaede was officially given access to the Pentium technology. The Rio Rancho systems administrators gave him a user ID and password for their computer system. On April 29, Gaede was confronted by the security manager and told that his background had been uncovered. Rather than firing him on the spot or turning him over to the authorities, they just issued a stern warning, giving him the impression that he was going to be fired, and let him go about his business.

As Gaede tells it, "I thought they would fire me, so I wanted some *insurance*." Over the following weekend (May 1 and May 2), Gaede used the terminal in his house, provided by Intel, to log on to his computer at work. He then logged on to the Rio Rancho computer and accessed the Pentium information. Throughout the weekend, he videotaped thousands of screens of information related to the Pentium chip. He intended to leave the country and then sell the information.

Gaede traveled to Colombia and was negotiating the sale of the Pentium technology with Iran, China, North Korea, and Russia throughout the summer of 1994; Iran and China were the only countries that expressed continued interest. For some reason, Gaede returned to the U.S., and was soon arrested. He accepted a plea bargain and was sentenced to a thirty-three month prison term for his crimes. He states that his plea bargain protected him from being deported; however, as of this writing, deportation proceedings are underway.

CONCLUSIONS

This case caused a great deal of finger-pointing among Gaede, AMD, Intel, and the FBI. The FBI claims that it warned Intel about Gaede's background. Intel denies that the FBI said anything about him. AMD claims that the FBI knew about Gaede's activities long before alerting the company to the problems. Gaede contends that the FBI wanted him to gather information for the Cubans so that the FBI could gather information on Cuban intelligence activities. He also says that he performed many of his actions at the request of the FBI, a charge the agency vehemently denies. Gaede does have some tapes that challenge the FBI position. In the end, why he did it is really not as important to us here as how he did it.

Clearly, Gaede fit both the characteristics of a spy and of a star performer. He was always working late hours. He was always interested in what everyone else was doing. He also volunteered for extra assignments. If he was not a spy, he might have risen to senior management levels.

VULNERABILITIES EXPLOITED

Gaede's crimes were immense in their scope, but taking each action separately, the crimes were simplistic. No super high-tech gadgets were in use, despite the involvement of foreign intelligence agencies. Nobody crawled through the air-conditioning ducts like they do in the movies. Gaede was just extremely patient, taking years to gather his information. This case clearly demonstrates the importance of basic security measures. Companies do not have to declare martial law and impose draconian standards and procedures on employees. They just have to enforce policies that are probably already in place.

Poor Security Awareness

Many vulnerabilities were exploited by Gaede, and one of the most notable was poor security awareness. Workers at both companies saw Gaede at strange times, in strange places. Nobody felt comfortable challenging him as to why he was in areas where he did not belong. This is just a single example of how poor security awareness allowed him to exploit a very wide variety of operations vulnerabilities. He basically exploited security holes in the day-to-day operations of the companies. Some technical, physical, and personnel vulnerabilities were exploited, but they just facilitated the exploitation of the operational issues. As with the previous case studies, the scariest part of the story is that it could have happened in almost any company.

No Understanding of Real Value

Even Gaede recognizes that one of the factors that allowed him to be so successful was that people did not understand the real value of the material they handled on a regular basis. The best example is the broken wafers. Although it is true that the wafers could not be sold, they could still be used by competitors to determine how to make the wafers themselves. This means that a stolen broken wafer is worth more than the production cost of the wafer itself.

The clean room gloves and clothing were another example of hidden value. Countries and companies that cannot afford their own equipment scavenge for it in the garbage of others. Although no direct financial loss was suffered in this kind of theft, the secondhand gloves and clothing facilitated the production of black market clones. This in the long run cost the companies millions of dollars in lost revenue.

Gaede also took a number of documents that helped Cuba. Documents on equipment repair and maintenance also facilitated the cloning of chips. The employees of both companies failed to consider the potential value of information and equipment to competitors.

Poor Inventory Procedures

Gaede relied heavily on the fact that people did not keep track of many valuable items at both Intel and AMD. The wafers, as valuable as they were to AMD, were poorly controlled. The broad category of "broken" left an easy way for thieves to cover their tracks. Apparently many workers had discovered that wafers were missing, but to avoid any unpleasant investigations or responsibility for the loss, they always classified the missing wafers as broken. It was the perfect cover. The wafer tracking process was only useful for tracking production problems and not potential security problems.

Since real broken wafers were not tracked, they could also be stolen. The wafers that Gaede requested for "testing purposes" were also not accounted for after they were given to him. He had hundreds of these wafers made. All of these holes allowed the entire production process to be compromised.

Documents at both companies were also poorly controlled. No one knew who was looking at which document or whether a person should be looking at it in the first place. Gaede probably looked at every document in the company libraries. The lack of inventory control systems not only gave him access but also allowed him to go undetected.

Gaede's theft of equipment was also a problem that went undetected. Apparently nobody tracked the equipment, or if someone did, he or she did not make the losses widely known. Hiding this problem kept important information from the employees and eliminated the opportunity for employees to recognize that they may have seen something worth reporting.

Poor Physical Security

Gaede collected an immense amount of information by just taking things off people's desks. Employees left some of their company's most critical information available to anyone that walked by with sticky fingers. Few workers bothered to lock their desks or filing cabinets.

Many chip designers had decorated the walls of their cubicles with chip schematics. These schematics represented the future of the company, yet they were hung up for display. The wiring of circuits is possibly the most critical aspect of the design of new generations of chips, and the design engineers left their work out for the taking.

Poorly Trained Guards

At Intel and AMD, the security guards were apparently trained only to look for clearly marked materials. For example, the guards at AMD looked for green- or blue-colored binders. Walk out with useless information in a green binder, and the guards would treat it as a major offense; on the other hand, walk out with chip schematics in an orange binder, and nobody would bother looking at it. As Gaede said, the guards were trained to look for the symptoms of problems and not the problems themselves.

Guards also walked by Gaede while he was in areas where he was not supposed to be. He sat at other people's desks while guards made their rounds. On almost no occasion did they even try to find out who he was or what he was doing. Almost anyone could have walked through most of the facilities of both chip manufacturers, assuming that they were able to get through the front door.

No Logging of Unusual Activity

On three separate occasions, Bill Gaede was caught in the act; two of those occasions involved guards. Yet no official report was ever made of his activities. Although a single report would not be an indication of a major problem, multiple reports could be. A report of a security-related incident should not usually result in a firing, but when security receives several reports about a single individual, it should conduct an investigation.

No Copy Machine Control

The copy machine is a regular, and critical, part of the office environment. Gaede was a regular at the copy machines all around both companies. He would be at a machine for up to an hour at a time; during his many hours of copy machine use, he probably made hundreds of thousands of copies. Neither company had a system to audit machine usage or log large volumes of copies. According to Gaede himself, his copy machine usage would have been the best way to discover his activities.

No Background Checks

Gaede started out at AMD by lying on his job application about his citizenship. It is likely that he at least exaggerated about other things as well. Even a minimal background check could have spotted his lies, which should have prevented him from being hired. Although there was no indication that he intended to be a spy, lying on a job application indicates a potential problem.

His applications to CDI and Intel clearly should have been rejected. His green card should have been flagged somewhere, since he was wanted for stealing information from AMD. If either company had performed a reasonable background check, his entire story would have been uncovered. Looking into the Mary Poppins business would have also shed light on this man. Especially when you consider that Gaede had pivotal roles in both companies, he should have definitely been the subject of a background check.

Pivotal Jobs Treated As Unimportant

Gaede's position as a backgrinder was considered low-tech and therefore not prestigious at AMD. However, he had access to almost all chips going out of the Austin facility. He could request that chips be made, and he could freely access all production facilities. He also received very little scrutiny in that position.

At Intel, he was only a systems administrator in a company that relied on the work of electronic engineers. Even though he did not have the prestigious job of designing or producing the chips, he had access to all production information. Despite this access, it does not appear that he was checked out in any way before being hired.

Technical Vulnerabilities

Although Gaede rarely exploited computer systems, his unusual patterns of computer activity could have been noticed. He did not hack into computers—he never had to—but he did use computers at very odd hours of the day and night. If audit logs were reviewed, they might have noticed that the files he was looking at were well beyond the scope of his job. Unfortunately, unless Intel specifically had a security administrator that examined remote access audit logs, it was up to Gaede himself to detect his unusual behavior, which would obviously not happen.

Security Acting in a Vacuum

Although security at AMD did not detect his actions, the Intel staff was definitely on to him. Security was monitoring him, while other areas of the company were giving him more access and more responsibility. The fact that he was given access to Pentium technology—while security believed that he was one of the worst semiconductor thieves in the business— shows that security policies of acting covertly only added to the problem. Assuming that Gaede's sequence of events is correct, Intel security management not only allowed Gaede to get Pentium access, they failed to limit his access even after he was confronted with the situation. The likely scenario is that security was investigating his previous actions without examining his current potential to cause damage. As discussed in Chapter 5, a security staff wants to limit the exposure of its investigation by keeping investigations under wraps. Although this does limit potential exposure of the investigation, it allows criminals to continue, and in Gaede's case expand, their crimes.

Vulnerabilities Beyond the Companies' Control

The weaknesses in the Customs and Immigration services allowed Gaede to freely move in and out of the country without being noticed. Normally, this would indicate a problem, but Gaede was good at exploiting the human weaknesses of the border guards. Since Gaede had no close friends, nobody could have known that he traveled into Mexico on a regular basis. Frequent foreign travel is one of the stereotypic signs of a spy.

There are also limits to the extent that a company can monitor its employees. The companies couldn't have found out that Gaede maintained a rented storage facility to store stolen goods. Not every vulnerability could have been accounted for by AMD or Intel, but clearly there is much room for improvement.

9

Russian Roulette

CUBA IS NOT ALONE IN ITS EFFORTS TO STEAL U.S. TECH-nology (Chapter 8). As I explain in Chapter 4, Russia has stepped up its corporate espionage activities directed at American commercial technologies. Russian intelligence agencies are able to utilize extensive spy networks that are already in place; the Russians freely use all of their traditional military intelligence assets for economic espionage purposes ("economic espionage" is what we call industrial espionage when it's conducted by a foreign country). In this case study, we see how the GRU, Russia's military intelligence agency, used a network of moles to further the interests of the country's defense-related companies.

This case details the efforts initiated by the Krunichev Institute to acquire a navigational system developed under the Strategic Defense Initiative (a.k.a. Star Wars), later renamed the Anti-Ballistic Missile system, by the Boeing Company under a subcontract to Martin Marietta (now Lockheed Martin). Probably the most troubling aspect of this case is that Boeing has contracts with the Krunichev Institute for support on the U.S. portion of Space Station Alpha project as well as other space-related efforts. (Alpha is an international effort that replaced the space station Freedom, which was canceled when Congress cut the program's funding.) Other aerospace firms around the country and the world also have contracts with Krunichev. Too many U.S. aerospace firms assume that the Krunichev Institute is a part of the civilian Russian Space Agency.

The source for the following case study is a very senior Russian defector, whom I confirmed to be very reliable with sources in U.S. counterintelligence. This person does not remember the exact name of the Star Wars project compromised. Accordingly, it will be referred to only as the Star Wars project.

BACKGROUND

Approximately two dozen separate civilian research facilities make up the Russian Space Agency. These facilities develop technology for the Russian space program and are strongly encouraged to enter joint ventures with foreign companies. The Krunichev Institute is one of the most elite research centers in Russia, and it attracts the best talent from the former Soviet Union. It has also been extremely successful at attracting foreign contracts from companies such as Boeing. What these companies don't know or acknowledge is that the Krunichev Institute is part of the Ministry of Defense Industry and not the Russian Space Agency. This means that foreign companies are funding Russian military research and development and that the technology they share with the Krunichev Institute goes straight to the Russian military.

As a member of the Ministry of Defense Industry, the Krunichev Institute provides intelligence gathering requirements. A representative from the institute attends monthly meetings of the ministry and can request that the Russian intelligence agencies acquire specific technologies to further its efforts. The Krunichev Institute provides an approximate value of the technology to Russia and volunteers funding for the effort. On many occasions, the Krunichev Institute gets other members of the ministry to help fund the collection project.

After the meetings, representatives from the SVR (the bulk of the former KGB), other KGB successors, and the GRU send the new requirements to their organizations. There is a strong financial incentive to be the first to collect the information, so each group scrambles to get the best leads. Whoever secures the best leads is approved to go after the information; the other agencies are not supposed to interfere. Upon successful collection of the information, senior people in the organization are financially rewarded.

In this case, which took place from 1991 to 1992, the Krunichev Institute learned of a new navigational system being developed by a team led by Martin Marietta under the Star Wars effort. Many projects comprise the Star Wars program. The target of this collection effort was the navigational system of one of those projects. The institute asked for the collection of the navigational system design instructions, and the request was approved. This project was given extremely high priority, and all Russian intelligence assets were mobilized.

The overall sequence of events described here is accurate; however, since these espionage operations are extremely sensitive and the people involved only know about the pieces in which they have direct involvement, some details were not available. I have filled in the gaps with common GRU tactics provided to me by the GRU defector. Also, some of the information presented here has been altered to mislead would-be spies.

THE ATTACK

At the start of the operation, the Russians knew only that the development of this Star Wars effort was being led by Martin Marietta, which is headquartered in Maryland. But Russian intelligence agencies are constantly collecting information. They are known to save even the most trivial bits of data from open source information. They also search transcripts of telephone calls intercepted by specially configured Aeroflot flights, the Lourdes signals intelligence collection facility in Cuba, Russian embassies and consulates scattered throughout the world (especially in Washington, D.C.), and satellites. The intelligence agencies scoured their databases for more information. Russian spy masters put out calls to their moles inside Martin Marietta as well as to other moles inside government agencies and Martin Marietta's competitors.

Within two days, the GRU came up with the first and most promising lead: an article in *Aviation Weekly,* an aerospace trade journal, which referred to Congressional funding for the Star Wars system. According to the article, the navigational system was actually being developed by Boeing at its Seattle area facilities. The GRU searched its databases and found that it had a mole inside Boeing.

Within two days, the GRU was able to identify Boeing as the actual source of the information it sought and developed a plan of attack. The SVR and lesser intelligence agencies did not have a better plan, so the Ministry of Defense Industry authorized the GRU to proceed.

Exploiting a Friendship

"Peter" was originally recruited by the GRU while he was working for another aerospace industry contractor in Washington, D.C. At the time, he was going through a messy divorce, and he made regular stops at a bar near the company offices. "Alex," a GRU operative, frequented such places near the vicinity of important targets. He had noticed Peter and the fact that he was alone and often depressed. In the Washington area, many people have access to sensitive information, and Alex approached Peter with the hope that this sad man might have something useful to offer. Peter knew that Alex was Russian, but he didn't report that first meeting, as government regulations required, or the many subsequent "accidental" encounters with the man. Alex ran into Peter with increasing frequency, becoming a sympathetic friend and learning about his problems.

Over a two-month period, Alex cultivated his relationship with Peter to the point where he felt comfortable asking for information. Alex began asking Peter for people's telephone numbers, and he gave him some money for the information. The telephone numbers Alex wanted were corporate numbers found only in a classified telephone directory. Peter welcomed the cash—his legal bills were killing him. The Russian eventually asked him for a classified telephone directory. As the months passed, Peter provided Alex with information of increasing sensitivity. Eventually, Peter would give Alex anything he asked for.

When Peter's divorce was final and he was given limited custody of his children, Alex convinced him to begin a new life. He suggested that he apply for a job at Boeing in Seattle, where he could start over. Boeing has always been a prime target for foreign intelligence agencies, but because their movements were restricted to twenty-five miles from their diplomatic facilities, the Russians had found it especially difficult to penetrate the company. Peter provided the GRU with a prerecruited operative in a hard-to-target company. Alex provided Peter with money to "compensate" him for the move. The GRU allowed Peter to settle into his new job as a senior accountant at Boeing with an undetermined amount of access. Even within the GRU, Alex was one of the few people who knew Peter's identify.

When the GRU officer in charge of U.S. operations received the authorization from GRU headquarters to proceed on the Star Wars project, he decided to use Peter to collect the information. Alex was well-known to U.S. counterintelligence, so he could not travel to Seattle without being heavily monitored. His presence would almost certainly compromise the operation. Alex would have to pass the lead off to a GRU agent in deep cover. Although the SVR had more operatives in place, the GRU was unwilling to share the glory with a competing agency.

One day, when Alex was sure he was not being followed, he stopped at a pay phone and left a message on Peter's answering machine. He would call, he told the machine, at a specific time later that day. He placed the second call from another pay phone and told Peter that the GRU once again needed his help. He was sure to have mentioned that there was a fairly large payoff involved. However, Alex would not be his contact on this operation. Alex gave Peter some pass phrases to confirm the identity of the GRU operative he would be working with. He was told to expect a call.

"Mike" was working in the U.S. under deep cover. He had entered the country illegally through Canada, using a fake passport. Upon his arrival in the Buffalo, New York, area, he searched the obituary sections of local papers and found the name of a deceased person approximately his age, who was originally from the New York City area. *That* Mike had died in an automobile crash. The agent assumed his identity, getting copies of his college transcripts, birth certificates, Social Security card, and other relevant documents. Then he moved to Seattle.

Mike and Peter met at a park near the Seattle waterfront. There, Mike told Peter about Star Wars and asked him for his help. Peter said that he wanted more money than Alex originally offered ($75,000), and Peter negotiated the price up to $85,000. This was still well below the money offered by the Ministry of Defense Industry for this information. Mike told Peter to make a chalk mark on a particular mailbox when he had secured the information or when he needed to contact him. Mike reminded Peter not to act suspiciously or to be too aggressive in his collection activities. He also reminded him never to use his own computer accounts during his search.

The Search for Star Wars

When Peter arrived at work the next day, he began going through the files in the contracting office where he worked. He was responsible for assisting with the pricing of proposals on contract bids. Peter found the initial cost section of the proposal for Boeing's portion of the Star Wars project. Although this document included some basic information, it contained nothing about the navigational system itself.

Peter decided to try to get a copy of the Star Wars proposal by pretending to need more information to help price the project he was currently working on. He managed to get permission to look at the plans, but he was warned that they were classified. His access was logged into the record. He copied pages that looked important and hid them among his other belongings. The Star Wars proposal had some initial plans and specifications but nothing that would give the Russians the capability to produce this system themselves.

Peter smuggled the information out of the Boeing facility in his briefcase, which was never checked by security. He left a mark on the mailbox, as instructed, and met with Mike at a designated park. Peter told his contact that he would never be able to get a look at the design specifications for the navigational system. Mike assured him that although the hard copy specifications would be kept under lock and key in a document control room, the plans would also be available on the computer systems of the Star Wars engineers. Mike left Peter with instructions to try accessing those engineering files from his own computer.

Peter stayed in the office late the next evening. After everyone else had left the area, he went to the desk of one of his coworkers, a fellow who always turned off his monitor but often left the computer itself turned on; this coworker believed that it was bad for the machines to be turned on and off every day. Peter wasn't sure where to start, so he opened an on-line directory and looked for the e-mail address of one of the lead engineers (he knew the name of the engineer because he'd seen it on the proposal). When he found that it was not possible to e-mail that engineer, he telephoned the Boeing user help desk. The help desk people told Peter that the engineer was on a different network that was physically separate from the company's main intranet.

Mike instructed Peter to find the wiring closets for the company networks. Wiring closets are rooms in which all the cables connecting computer systems come together. The cables are plugged into boxed hubs that allow many computers to connect to each other. Mike also recommended that Peter try to find out whether the wires and their corresponding outlets were labeled.

Peter did find a number written on each computer cable wall outlet in his office. He also found a wiring closet near a staircase, and it was unlocked. It contained many slim, metal boxes stacked on top of each other, with lights flashing and a lot of cables. Each of the cables in the closet had a piece of tape wrapped around it with a number that looked very similar to the numbers on the cable outlets in the offices. However, Peter had no idea how his network could be connected to the engineers' network.

He decided to unplug one of the cables connected to his office. He'd found the outlet numbers of everyone around him, so he was able to select the cable of an office mate who used his computer more than the rest. The next day, as expected, his coworker's computer wouldn't work, so the coworker put in a trouble call to the help desk. The help desk people determined that the problem was probably physical and called in a technician. A technician showed up a day later, took out a bunch of testing equipment, and quickly determined that the line was dead.

Peter followed the technician as he left for the wiring closet and struck up a casual conversation. He expressed innocent interest in the repairman's work, asking seemingly innocuous questions about the purpose of all of the wires and the different boxes. He eventually got around to asking about the separation of the different computer networks. The repairman showed him that his computer was plugged into one set of hubs and the engineers were plugged into the other set. The separate hubs, he explained, were established for security reasons. The technician noticed that the cable to the coworker's computer had fallen out of its socket. He plugged it back in, and the problem was solved.

Peter contacted Mike and told him about what he had learned about the wiring closet and the separate networks. It was clear he needed technical help, and Mike agreed to provide it. But Peter needed to find out what types of computers the engineers used, especially the one on which the navigational system plans would be stored.

Now Peter had to make up an excuse to meet with one of the Star Wars engineers. He looked through some of the recent cost proposal documents in his office and found the name of an engineer who had worked on Star Wars but had recently been assigned to another project. He contacted the engineer to ostensibly meet with him about a proposal Peter was currently working on. He needed the engineer's help, he said, and would be glad to meet in his cubicle in the company's engineering area.

Peter and the engineer talked about Peter's current proposal for a while, and then, as the conversation wound down, Peter asked the engineer a seemingly casual question. He wondered whether the pricing information they had just discussed was similar to that of other projects on which the engineer had worked. The engineer responded that the only other project he'd been associated with was Star Wars. They talked a little about the project, and then Peter asked the engineer if he knew anything about computers. Peter told him he wanted to buy a computer for his home, and he wondered about the one on the engineer's desk. It was a Silicon Graphics machine, the engineer told him, not the kind of computer Peter would want for home use. Was that the same machine he'd used when he worked on Star Wars? Peter asked. Yes, said the engineer, same one.

Following Mike's instructions, Peter told the unsuspecting engineer that he wanted to use his computer to help his church computerize their membership database. He asked what type of database they used in the engineering department. The engineer was helpful. He told Peter that the type of database Boeing used for its design specifications was definitely not appropriate for home use. Peter played dumb, and the engineer showed him how hard the system could be to use. Peter watched closely and noticed the name of the computer system as it flickered on the screen. It also seemed to be a Silicon Graphics system.

With the engineer's help, Peter learned the type of computer, the version of the operating system, and the type of database.

Technical Help

Mike and Peter met to discuss the technical details Peter had uncovered. The Russian operative then contacted his GRU support people and put in a request for technical assistance. Although Mike's superiors were hesitant to share their operation—and the potential reward—with other branches of the GRU, they really had no choice but to ask for technical assistance from other GRU groups.

The GRU identified a technical specialist, "Vasya," within their Signals Intelligence Directorate, who was ideal for the job. The Signals Intelligence Directorate is responsible for collecting and processing foreign and domestic communications, such as telephone calls, and satellites and computer communications. Due to the highly technical nature of its work, Signals Intelligence is known for its outstanding computer expertise. Once he was briefed on the operation, Vasya put together a computer system and some cables for the project. He scanned the Internet for postings about the latest attacks against Silicon Graphics computers. He also checked with other people in his group to see if any of them had developed any new attacks against Silicon Graphics machines.

With a fake German passport and a ticket to Seattle, Vasya left Moscow via Frankfurt, Germany, posing as a German tourist. From the Seattle airport, he went directly to his hotel, where an envelope was waiting for him. Inside the envelope was a map to a "safe house," a condominium in Seattle. The condo was located on the first floor of a corner apartment building. The layout was such that people could enter the building and go straight to the apartment with little risk of running into anyone. From inside, you could see down the street for blocks. The condo was chosen by the GRU to be the residence of a local communist sympathizer.

The sympathizer was a stereotypical sixties hippie who had never really found his place in American society. He was first identified by the GRU at anti–Vietnam War rallies. The GRU considered him to be very loyal to their efforts, but had, when the Soviet Union collapsed, converted his ideological support to more of a monetary relationship.

A note on the map told Vasya to be at the house at eight o'clock that evening. Peter had received a similar map from Mike. The resident had left the condo; he was never allowed to see anyone who might be involved in espionage activity so that he could never compromise an operation. When Vasya arrived, Mike was waiting for him. Vasya performed a quick bug sweep just before Peter arrived.

Vasya gave Peter a hollowed-out book that held a cassette tape drive, a cassette, a floppy disk, and some cables. He explained to Peter, step by step, what he would be doing, and he told him what to do if he encountered any problems. Peter was to use the cassette to store the acquired information. Vasya provided a cassette that had about ten minutes of "an audio postcard" at the beginning. The fake message from home would play in case anyone tried to examine the tape. Vasya and Mike insisted that Peter repeat his instructions several times until they were satisfied that he understood them.

A Successful Operation

Peter took the book with the secret compartments with him to work hidden in his briefcase. He waited for his coworkers to clear out at the end of the day, and then he went to work. First he headed for the wiring closet. He took a cable that ran to one of his coworker's computers, unplugged it from its normal hub, then plugged it into one of the hubs for the engineering network. He put one of the cables that Vasya gave him into the now open socket on the normal hub, basically as a marker until the proper cable was put back. A computer in his office was now connected to the engineering network.

Back in his office, he put the floppy disk into his coworker's computer that was now connected to the engineering network. He was carefully instructed to do "real work" while he was there, so that if anybody checked, they would find him being productive.

Peter then started a program that was on the floppy disk. This program was specially designed by Vasya to quickly attack the document database. Periodically, he had to enter a command or two to confirm some actions, but it was basically automated. The first attempt at breaching the system, which exploited widely known vulnerabilities, was successful. Vasya did have some lesser-known attacks ready as backups, but they were unnecessary. The Russian computer expert had designed the attacks to be as simplistic as possible so that the company would think it had been hacked by a teenager and not a Russian intelligence service. The system asked Peter to connect the cassette drive to the computer, and a few minutes later, the theft was complete. The system then instructed Peter to start the "clean up" menu option, which took steps to erase any possible logging of the theft.

When the cleanup operation was finished, Peter unplugged the tape drive and packed everything back into the carved out book. He went to the wiring closet and put everything back into its proper place. Then, as instructed, he went back to his desk to finish up the work he had been doing. He put the book back into his briefcase and went home. He waited for one hour and left for the safe house.

This time only Vasya was there waiting for him. The Russian looked at the captured files and found that they not only had collected the specifications for the Star Wars navigational system but also had captured information on several other programs as well.

The Russian kept all of the equipment from the carved out book, and Peter went home. Vasya met with Mike later that evening and gave him the cassette and the equipment. Mike made a copy of the tape and disposed of the computer gear. He kept one copy and gave the original to another American working for the GRU, who took it to San Francisco. There, the American put the cassette into a converted soda can with a screw-off lid. He left the can at a particular spot, where it was picked up by a Russian assigned to the San Francisco consulate. When Mike received confirmation that the original had been received, he destroyed his copy. The Russian consulate sent the tape back home in a diplomatic pouch.

Over the next three months, Peter received five separate envelopes containing $17,000 each. The Ministry of Defense Industry had authorized approximately $500,000 for this information. Mike, Alex, and Vasya's superiors split a bonus for coming in under budget. Vasya returned to Russia. Mike and Alex continued with business as usual. All three operatives received some minor bonuses. Peter continues to work at Boeing—and to wait for additional tasking.

The entire operation, from the time it was first proposed by the Krunichev Institute to Vasya's return flight home, lasted only three months.

CONCLUSIONS

Unfortunately, it is very likely that the GRU and other Russian intelligence agencies have at least one mole inside most, if not all, companies of Boeing's stature. With these moles in place, they believe they can get their hands on any information they want, whenever they want it.

Although it's true that Boeing's system had a few exploitable holes, the company did have significant countermeasures in place. Two in particular prevented Peter from just walking in and taking the information the Russians wanted. First, all of the company's printed materials were tightly controlled, and access to the documents was restricted and logged. Peter's own access was carefully restricted to the pricing information that related to his legitimate work.

Second, the engineering network was a closed one. No one was allowed access to the network outside the engineering areas. This prevented Peter from simply hacking into the system from anywhere inside Boeing, or for that matter, the world. Closed networks eliminate a tremendous amount of risk.

VULNERABILITIES EXPLOITED

Even though this attack was extremely sophisticated in many ways, it still relied on the exploitation of very simple vulnerabilities. Although a portion of the attack depended on a highly automated computer attack system, it would not have been successful without the exploitation of basic weaknesses.

Unlocked Wiring Closets

The fact that the wiring closets were not locked allowed Peter to enter and manipulate the computer cables. This allowed him to work around the problem of the closed engineering network. Also, the network hubs were co-located; once somebody did get into the wiring closet, he or she could easily connect the networks. This could have been intentional—the company might have wanted the option of connecting the two networks in the future. It could have also been the case that the networks were originally set up as a single network and then broken apart later.

Even if the network hubs had been separated, the fact that the door to the wiring closet was unlocked allowed an intruder to go into the room and attack the system. Peter could have entered the room and plugged a laptop computer directly into the network hub. The only reason he collected the information from his desk was to eliminate the risk of being caught. Any time a wiring closet is accessible, whether it's a computer or telephone facility, someone can manipulate it.

Human Pride

When Peter spoke to the technician who "fixed" the problem in the wiring closet, he asked a few seemingly innocent questions that gave the technician a chance to talk about his work. The same was true for the engineer who told him about the engineering computer systems. People generally enjoy talking about their work. I've found this to be especially true of technical professionals. They do not typically find people who appreciate, or at least understand, their work. When they do, they savor the moment and try to make it last as long as possible. Even a mediocre mole can get technical types to talk about their work and lead the conversation in the desired direction.

Not Knowing When to Stop Giving Out Information

This is basically an awareness issue that is very closely related to the vulnerability of human pride. In any work-related conversation, people have to recognize when the talk is weaving into inappropriate areas. The technician should never have told Peter about the network separation at Boeing. The engineer should never have given Peter the details of the engineering database. No one wants to be rude, but people should not discuss security countermeasures with anyone. Even a little knowledge can help attackers avoid detection and capture. Without the chatty technician or engineer, Peter's attack might not have been successful.

No Auditing of Facility Access Logs

Access logs are very useful counterespionage measures—if they are ever reviewed. Peter's activities went unnoticed, despite the fact that Boeing logs everything. He was in the facility after hours. He entered the engineering area. He looked at the Star Wars proposal. None of this activity rang any bells.

Supervisors should review their activity logs on a regular basis to look for strange employee behavior.

Failure to Follow Security Procedures

When Alex first approached him, Peter should have reported the contact to his supervisor. Anyone with a security clearance is supposed to tell *somebody* when a Russian national starts buying him drinks. Foreign operatives recruit moles through "coincidental" social meetings, and people with clearances are warned about this. There are bound to be violations of security procedures due to ignorance, but when a citizen of a well-known restricted country, like Russia, starts buddying up at the local watering hole, there's trouble waiting down the road.

Lack of Post-Activity Detection

Once Peter began his espionage activities, there was no way for the Boeing people to learn about them unless they caught him red-handed. And there was no deterrent or fear of later capture after the espionage acts were finished.

Failure to Account for Known Vulnerabilities

Peter conducted his attack on the Boeing database server through the exploitation of known vulnerabilities—let me emphasize *known*. These vulnerabilities represented problems that could have been prevented before they were exploited. Critical data was widely available to any insider with criminal intentions. Vasya likely configured his attack system with tools that were optimized to rapidly compromise that specific system, but even a less-skilled attacker could have been successful in similar attempts.

No Intrusion Detection Capability

Since Boeing trusted its employees (primarily because they had security clearances), the company made very little effort to detect intrusions or review audit logs.

Yet, internal attacks are definitely the most common. Boeing, as a major target of aerospace competitors, foreign companies, and foreign intelligence agencies, should have expected such an attack. Instead, the company relied on perimeter security, which does nothing about malicious insiders. It left itself open to the biggest industrial espionage problem of them all.

10

The Liaison

EW INDUSTRIAL SPIES ARE AS ACCOMPLISHED OR SOPHIS-
ticated as Karl Heinrich Stohlze. An operative in the German intelligence organization, Bundesnachrichtendienst
(BND), Stohlze has been infiltrating American and European
firms, especially in the U.S., France, and Switzerland, for over
a decade, apparently specializing in acquiring biotechnology
secrets. His personal social engineering techniques are a bit
slimy, but a look at one of his successful corporate espionage
attacks should be quite illuminating.

BACKGROUND

Stohlze never breaks into companies himself. He prefers to
recruit people who already work at the targeted firms to provide him with information. When beginning an assignment,

---

Some material in this chapter was drawn from the book *Friendly Spies* by
Peter Schweizer (Atlantic Monthly Press, 1993), with permission of the
author.

he avoids contact with anyone at a company. Like his Eastern Bloc counterparts, he may take several months to prepare his attack. He begins by observing the target company and its workings. He notices when employees come and go. He notes the name on delivery trucks to see who the company uses for supplies. He watches when lights go out in corner offices. Going through newspapers, company reports, legal documents, and other records, he learns who the company officials are, and then he finds out where they live. He studies their habits and looks for any hints of susceptibility to recruitment.

He also focuses on other workers. He looks for German citizens working at the company. Going to bars is a critical part of his job. He looks for anyone who regularly drinks alone. These people are the dissatisfied loners, often alcoholics, who hate their lot in life. Also, people with older, dented cars are more likely to need and want money. Stohlze looks for subtle clues to identify the people with access to sensitive information who might be willing to deliver it with the proper coaxing. And he is not above tapping telephone lines or eavesdropping on cellular or cordless telephone calls.

THE ATTACK

In the fall of 1989, Stohlze came to the U.S. to collect information on biochips, probably for the benefit of Siemens, one of the largest science and technology firms in Germany. This field of research involves applying genetic engineering techniques to the development of computer chips; American companies are pioneering the entire field. The BND provided Stohlze with money and a list of companies that were developing biochip technology. His assigned targets were located in the Boston area and North Carolina. Stohlze chose to begin his work in Boston.

Upon arriving in Boston, Stohlze rented a hotel room near the target companies' facilities. He drove around the facilities and the surrounding neighborhoods to familiarize himself with the local terrain. He quickly identified the local hangouts near the companies and began hanging out there himself.

Stohlze knew the value of a company telephone directory, and he made getting one a priority. He called up a company receptionist and claimed to be having a party for his brother, who worked at the company. He asked, "Could you possibly send me a copy of the company's phone directory so I can invite his friends?" The receptionist agreed without asking for any other information, even the name of the employee. Continuing with the ruse, he asked, "Could you suggest where I could hold the party?" The receptionist told him about a local club where the company was going to have a party for a departing employee. She recommended the place highly and invited him to stop by the party to take a look. With a five-minute telephone conversation, Stohlze not only had secured a telephone directory but had gotten himself invited to a company function.

A few weeks later, Stohlze showed up at the party. He is a charming man, and he easily struck up conversations with several people. He eventually noticed a reserved woman sitting by herself. She wore no wedding ring, and her body language indicated that she was shy and insecure. To a trained intelligence operative, one who considers himself a ladies' man, this was a clear opportunity. Stohlze approached the woman and asked if he could sit down.

Stohlze skillfully focused the conversation on the woman, giving her the impression that he was interested in her as a person, and she provided the spy with information about her job and responsibilities. Stohlze's seeming attentiveness also helped to hide his own personal details. When she asked about him, Stohlze described himself as a researcher for a similar company, but he kept his answers vague. He soon learned that the woman was a midlevel administrator at the company—an ideal position that usually has access to a wide variety of information. Stohlze turned up his charm. He appeared totally sympathetic and supportive as she told him of all her frustrations and disappointments with life and her job. Stohlze learned that she had access to most of the company's biochip research. This administrator was Stohlze's ideal patsy; meanwhile, this woman thought that she had found the man of her dreams.

The relationship quickly became romantic. The woman had never been married and seemed starved for affection. Stohlze encouraged the romance and contacted the BND to inform his superiors that he would be devoting most of his efforts to her. They approved wholeheartedly of the situation and told him to forgo the North Carolina operations.

Manipulating the Insider

During the early part of the relationship, Stohlze learned a great deal about the company and their operations from the woman. He also learned about progress on the biochip research, but he wasn't getting the process details he needed. Essentially, he was learning a lot about how the cookies tasted but little about how to bake them. This situation proved frustrating to Stohlze and especially to the BND, so after a month he became more aggressive in his work.

Although the woman was obviously frustrated with her job and the company, she seemed basically honest and loyal. She would never steal something for money or just to hurt the company. However, Stohlze was fairly certain that she would steal something for him, especially if she thought it would prevent him from leaving her.

In the first week of December, Stohlze met with the woman and told her he was having some significant problems with his research. He said that the company was becoming dissatisfied with his work. His bosses were very upset with him. Unless he came up with something to overcome his problems, he told her, he would likely be transferred, probably back to Germany.

The thought of losing a man who had made her happier than she had been in years was almost overwhelming to the woman. "I wish there was something that I could do," she told him. "Actually, there is," Stohlze told her. His supposed problems were in the biotech field, which must be similar to the kinds of things her company's biochip researchers were working on. He knew it was a difficult thing to ask, he said, but he needed her to bring him whatever information she could on the biochip research.

Her initial response was shock, and she told him she could never do such a thing. Stohlze apologized "for even asking such a thing," but added that he was desperate to stay with her. He quickly told her to forget that he ever asked, and he changed the subject.

In a calculated move, he waited two days to talk to her again. He called her at work to let her know that he was on his way to Washington, D.C., to talk to his superiors about their plans to reassign him. He told her that he didn't know when he would return, and that he loved her. He apologized again for asking her to steal information for him, and then he gave her a telephone number in Washington where she could reach him.

Stohlze actually traveled to Washington, where he took some time to research other possible targets, and waited for a call. Two days later, the phone rang. It was his lady love. He told her that he loved her and missed her—and he turned on a tape recorder. When she asked about his transfer, he told her that things looked bad and that he might be transferred to the West Coast, but most likely he was headed back to Germany. The next time he saw her, he said, would be when he returned to Boston to pack his bags.

"Remember what you asked me to do for you?" the woman asked, hopefully. "You know, get some information from work? Well, I've thought it over, and I'm willing to do it for you."

Stohlze was very excited. He told her that he would fly back to Boston the next day and meet her for dinner. He asked if she could have information for him that quickly. Time was an important factor, he said, because his boss would make a decision about transferring him in the very near future. He needed the information to help persuade his employer to let him stay. She promised to go back to work late that night and get something for him by the next day.

Stohlze flew back to Boston the next day and met the woman in a restaurant. She had a package for him, and Stohlze treated her like royalty. He was pleased with the information but told her he still needed more. She agreed to go back to her office later that night. Stohlze was relieved that he would not have to have sex with her that evening. He was anxious to shift their relationship to the blackmail phase, which he thought would prove to be more fruitful than the romance in the long run.

The first package she had given him contained some DNA research methods and some general information about the status of company projects. It was basic, but it was a start—certainly enough to hold against her.

The next night, they met again. She had more information for him, but she was scared. She was afraid she might be caught and lose her job or go to jail. Stohlze was surprised at her reluctance so soon after the first theft. He was uncertain whether romance or blackmail would bolster his patsy, so he used both. The information she had given him was good, he said, but not enough to keep him in Boston. He needed more. He talked about how unfortunate it would be for her to have done this thing and accomplished nothing for their relationship. Then he put on a worried expression. "I may have made a mistake," he said. "I told one of my associates in Washington what you are doing for me. I had to tell him. His job is on the line too, and I thought he should know. The trouble is that Hans is crazy. He does not want to be reassigned; his family is settled here. I fear if the information stops coming, he just might contact your company and show them the documents, just to get even with you."

This ploy worked beautifully. The woman was stunned and helpless. Stohlze was blackmailing her without being the source of the blackmail. He told her that he would try to keep Hans calm, but to help the situation, she should keep the information coming for a little while longer. He also told her that after the whole situation was worked out, they could continue their relationship.

Stohlze flew back to Washington the next day. When he arrived at Dulles airport, he wrapped up the information the woman had given him and took it to the Lufthansa air freight service. By insider accounts, he had about two thousand pages of documents and four computer disks. He addressed the package to a BND front company in Hamburg, Germany, for forwarding to the BND analysis division.

Completing the Operation

Later that day, he found a message on his answering machine from the woman. People at the company had been asking her questions, she said. She was frightened and didn't know what to do. Stohlze was careful not to expose himself with a return phone call; she might already have told the authorities everything. But he had to return to Boston. The previous night, she told him that she would get him some very important documents, and he couldn't pass up a chance that she was still under his control. He planned to fly back that day to meet her.

To avoid possible surveillance, he did not return to his leased hotel room; instead, he rented a room at a local Sheraton. He arrived at the scheduled meeting place an hour and a half early to watch for a possible setup. After three hours passed, the woman hadn't appeared.

He decided to see if the documents might be at her home, so he left the restaurant and drove to her place. The lights of the woman's townhouse were out, but he kept his distance when he noticed that her car was not in its usual spot. He knew that she kept a key hidden in her bushes, but he chose to play it safe.

He drove to the company parking lot, where he spotted the woman's car parked next to several others. From his previous surveillance, he knew that there should have been no other cars in the lot at that time of night. He searched the woman's car but found nothing.

He spotted some lights on in the building that were usually out. Was his victim being interrogated? Was she admitting to everything? Did she have the documents on her, or had she stashed them at the house? He decided to back go to the townhouse and look around. Before he left, he let the air out of the tires of all cars in the parking lot.

Stohlze drove through the neighborhood, looking for anything unusual. When he found nothing amiss, he went to the front door and used the hidden key to open it. He found nothing on the first floor, but on a desk in a second-floor study, he found a set of manila envelopes and several floppy disks. The envelopes contained the documents that she promised. They appeared to be numbered as though they were under some sort of document control. He checked the street from the window of the study, then slipped out to his car.

On the night Stohlze broke into the woman's apartment, company officials approached her about her unusual late-night visits to the facility. Some documents were missing, they said. Did she know anything about it? They questioned her late into the night. After several hours, her interrogators allowed her to go to the bathroom. While Stohlze was letting the air out of the tires of the cars out in the parking lot, his lover swallowed half of a bottle's worth of pills. After ten minutes, the security staff forced open the door to the women's room and found her on the floor. They induced vomiting, called a doctor, and took her to the company infirmary.

The next morning, she told company officials everything she knew about Stohlze. She told them who she thought Stohlze worked for and what she gave him. Company officials decided to call in the FBI. It was then that they learned of Stohlze's true identity.

According to the company, the woman was fired, but no charges were filed against her. The company is continuing its efforts in the biotechnology field with the hopes of reaping the benefits that hundreds of millions of dollars of research should produce. However, company officials know that some of their most valuable information has probably fallen into the hands of the BND and Siemens. Karl Stohlze was last seen in western Europe working on other assignments.

CONCLUSIONS

This case study is an excellent example of the simplicity of an actual espionage operation. In his attack on this company, Stohlze never resorted to particularly sophisticated methods. He performed an initial surveillance on the company, but even that was a very low-technology operation.

Although Stohlze did "seduce" a lonely woman, he is no Sean Connery. He is described as middle-aged and stout. He does have a certain air of confidence about him, but nobody would picture him as a super spy. He is systematic in his methods, and he knows how to take advantage of promising situations. He used a single insider with the right access to gather very significant information.

From a security standpoint, company officials appear to have detected the incident before it went too far. They caught Stohlze's source within three days of her initial thefts of information. Despite the fact that they were dealing with a well-trained operative from a well-financed and professional foreign intelligence agency, they identified the mole and prevented future losses.

The company had its facilities monitored carefully for people coming and going at unusual times. Security personnel had noticed the woman carrying envelopes out of the company at night, so it knew whom to question when documents were determined to be missing. The documents were also well accounted for and logged, so people could easily recognize that the documents were missing in the first place.

However, the woman's own mistakes—primarily that she stole the documents rather than copied them—were more central to her discovery than any of the company's security measures. If she had placed the stolen documents in something other than the manila envelopes, she might not have attracted any attention. Also, the fact that Stohlze rushed her made her sloppy. Actually, a better spy would have coached his moles more thoroughly, as the Russians did in Chapter 9.

VULNERABILITIES EXPLOITED

The company did do a lot of things right. However, there is still significant room for improvement. The problems are typical for most companies, which is what makes them such an easy mark for Stohlze and his peers.

Common Information Has Value

The first obvious mistake made by the company was the receptionist giving Stohlze the telephone directory and the information about the party with no questions asked. The woman did not understand the value of a telephone directory to an attacker. If she had realized this, she would never have given out the directory and the information about the party. The lack of awareness in this regard is probably rampant throughout the company.

Poor Awareness of Threat

The woman who was Stohlze's victim trusted the man far too readily. This is not to say that people should be afraid of all foreigners, but a German researcher within the same industry should have been suspect. Many companies, both foreign and domestic, target their competitors. Whenever someone is talking to a potential competitor, he or she must be aware not to share sensitive information.

In this case, a person who claimed to work for a competing firm was able to sit at a company function and get a great deal of information without anyone in the room being concerned. This is not unusual for most firms, nor should it be. However, there must be some basic employee awareness about what and what not to talk about to outsiders.

Failure to Secure Sensitive Documents

Although the company was able to detect when documents were missing, the woman was still able to access those sensitive research documents late in the night. She was able to go to unlocked file cabinets and take the information. The only reason she was caught is because she did not copy the information or try to hide it when she left company facilities. Apparently the information was watched by people during the day, but it was left unprotected in the evenings.

Leaving a Key behind the Bushes

Although this is a minor aspect of the case, a single woman should not be leaving a key to her house in a place where anybody can get to it. In this case, it did allow for the final theft of very sensitive information that was tightly controlled by the company. On other occasions, the woman could have been robbed, or worse.

Lack of Surveillance of Facilities

When Stohlze approached the company on the night that his source was being interrogated, he let the air out of the tires of several cars. This should have been observed by company security personnel. There were few cars in the parking lot to begin with, and Stohlze took fifteen minutes to vandalize them without being observed.

11

Smile, You're on Candid Camera

ALL THE CASE STUDIES WE'VE LOOKED AT UP TO NOW HAVE involved actions that were clearly illegal or that would have been illegal had they not been part of approved penetration tests. Although the vast majority of industrial espionage cases do involve illegal activities, some attacks are actually perpetrated through totally *legal* methods of intelligence collection. The following is one such case. The incident is real, and though it might seem almost comical, dozens of American biotech firms aren't laughing.

Biotechnology is a hot industry, and the U.S. leads the way in this field, so it's hardly surprising that so many American biotechnology operations are the targets of industrial espionage. Dozens of other firms were targeted in this case, but only this company agreed to talk with me about the attack with the condition that I don't mention its name. The company's security manager provided the details of his company's story. He has a counterintelligence background and is acutely aware of the issues involved. More important, he knew what the Japanese were after, and he knew how to prevent a significant compromise of information. This case study focuses on one company's experience; approximately thirty other biotech companies and U.S. government research facilities went through the same experience within a month of the incident described here, however, most of them were not as diligent in their security practices.

(The Japanese film crew and the Japanese External Trade Relations Office [JETRO] would not speak with me about this case, for reasons that will become obvious.)

BACKGROUND

One sunny morning in 1994, the public relations (PR) officer at one of America's top biotechnology companies received a telephone call from a Japanese-owned translation firm based in New York City. The firm specialized in providing services to Japanese enterprises doing business with American firms. The company was acting, the caller explained, as a representative of NHK (the Japanese PBS equivalent), which was planning to film a documentary on the U.S. biotechnology industry. The translation firm had heard that this company was trying to break into the Japanese market, the caller said, and thought the company might be interested in participating in the documentary project. The company would receive "very favorable treatment" in exchange for its participation, and it would be the focus of the film.

The public relations officer was excited about the documentary project. It seemed like the perfect medium for generating name recognition in the Pacific Rim. She took the request to corporate management, which approved the idea immediately; she then scheduled the NHK film crew's first visit.

As the day of filming approached, the translation firm called back to let the PR officer know which company employees and executives NHK wanted to interview. The list was substantial and included the vice president of manufacturing, the vice president of research, a manufacturing plant manager, the vice president of sales and marketing, and several researchers.

What the PR officer didn't know was that dozens of American biotechnology companies had been contacted about the documentary project and were given the same promises. It wasn't until the company's security manager checked with the FBI that he learned what the Japanese film crew was really after.

THE ATTACK

The day before the NHK film crew was scheduled to arrive at the company's facilities, the public relations officer contacted the security manager and explained the project. It was the security manager's practice to keep track of all foreign and media visitors coming into the company's facility. Calling him was a matter of procedure. This film crew business came at rather short notice for his taste; he would have preferred to have the time to do his job thoroughly. After he received the call from PR, he contacted the local FBI Development of Espionage, Counterintelligence and Counterterrorism Awareness (DECA) office via fax. DECA acts as a liaison between commercial organizations and the intelligence community with the goal of increasing awareness about the industrial espionage threat and helping to prevent incidents. (The organization was renamed in September 1996 and is now known as Awareness of National Security Issues and Response). The security manager had always made a point to contact the DECA office whenever his company was visited by any foreign organizations. In his fax, he told the FBI about the NHK film crew, and he asked whether the company should be concerned about the visit.

He was very surprised by the speed of DECA's response. He received a return telephone call almost immediately. The

FBI wanted to know what time the film crew was due to arrive. The security manager replied that the crew was due at 9:00 A.M. the next day. The agent said that FBI people would be at his office by 7:00 A.M.

The next day, the feds met with him and informed him that other companies visited by NHK reported that the film crew had "engaged in very targeted efforts to obtain very sensitive, proprietary information." The FBI advised him to cancel the visit in the interests of company security. He met with his superiors and told them of the FBI's warnings, but the film crew was already at the front door, and the possible exposure in the Japanese market was tempting. Of course, it would be up to the security manager to make sure the film crew got away with nothing of real value.

The security manager did his best to contact everyone scheduled for an interview that morning, warning them against talking about possibly sensitive information and advising them of the FBI's concerns. He met the film crew members and stuck with them throughout the visit.

Riding herd on the Japanese filmmakers proved to be no easy task. There were more of them than anyone expected. Three or four is the usual film crew complement, but the NHK crew included six people: a cameraman, soundman, and director, as well as an assistant cameraman, an assistant director, and a translator.

The first interview went smoothly. The subject was a vice president of research. As the security manager entered the office with the film crew, he noticed that the cameraman began to film the office interior almost immediately. The cameraman was clearly trying to film papers and anything else he could see scattered around the office. The security man busied himself turning over papers on the vice president's desk while the cameraman poked his lens around the room. The interview turned out to be quite uninformative from an espionage perspective.

The next stop was the building in which the company manufactured one of its top products. Since the area was frequently toured by visitors, the company had installed a window into the manufacturing area, which provided a clear view of almost everything going on inside. The security manager noticed the cameraman filming this area for many minutes. Under the circumstances, the exposure was unavoidable—the company had installed the window, after all. The cameraman could have filmed the production rate and a variety of other aspects of the operation, but the area was not particularly sensitive.

The security manager also noticed the assistant director sketching the entire production area and making notes next to some of the sketches in Japanese. During his military service the security manager had been stationed in the Pacific Rim, where he'd picked up a basic knowledge of Japanese—a fact he carefully kept from the film crew. He noticed that the director's notes indicated the types of materials the pipes were composed of, approximate sizes of machinery, and other detailed information about the facility, details that probably would not appear in the film.

At this point, the director, assistant director, and translator huddled together and conversed in Japanese. After a few minutes, the translator turned and spoke to the plant manager, who was also following the crew around the plant. "How many people work in the plant?" he asked. "What is your total workforce? How many total batches of product do you have in production at any given time? What is your total annual volume, in liters, that you produce here? Who is the principle supplier of equipment that goes into this facility?" The plant manager looked at the security manager in disbelief. He had been warned by the security manager about these types of very proprietary questions, but the plant manager couldn't believe the brazenness of the inquiry. He politely declined to answer the questions because of the proprietary nature of the informa tion. Visibly frustrated, the assistant director pounded her fist into her other hand. Apparently, the other biotech firms had been more cooperative.

The filmmakers were then led into a series of labs that housed no proprietary information but were impressive because of the interesting technologies they contained. One of the labs was responsible for generating computer graphics that allowed people to visualize molecules. The technology is widely available, but this company uses it for very advanced applications in biotechnology. In a side conversation, the senior director of the film crew spoke with the person in charge of the lab. They talked for thirty minutes, covering very specific details about the applicability of the graphics technology to biotechnology research. The director seemed particularly interested in why the technology was a critical component of the company's success.

After the film crew left the lab, the security manager quickly went back to talk to the person in charge of the facility to try to find out what they were specifically talking about. The researcher said that the director was a real expert in the field and that it was a pleasure to talk to someone with such specific knowledge of the area. It was becoming clear that the director had much more in-depth knowledge than one would expect a filmmaker to have about a very complex aspect of a highly technical industry.

During a later interview with a senior researcher in a different lab, members of the crew began to wander away from the area. The security manager caught the cameraman trying to film restricted areas of the lab. He, the public relations officer, and other company people had to gather the curious crew back together. The filmmakers tried to make an issue out of the restriction on their movements. The phrase "Is there something that you are trying to hide?" was repeated by the director several times. The PR officer handled the situation tactfully, saying that providing further access was simply beyond her control. The crew agreed to cooperate and restrict its movements.

A short time later, another senior researcher came out to meet with the NHK film crew. The interview began with a few basic personal questions; they wanted to know his name, how long he'd been with the company, and the nature of his job. As the interview progressed, the questions became more focused. The translator commented that compared to the number of people that worked at similar companies, this company seemed to be far more productive. She mentioned that this company was considered the leading biotechnology company in the world. Then she asked the researcher, "What is the specific source of your competitive advantage over other biotechnology and pharmaceutical companies?"

The security manager had warned the researcher about such questions, though he hadn't really needed to. It was obviously inappropriate. After thinking about it for a moment, the researcher smiled and said, "It is our people and their ability to collaborate for a common goal." The filmmakers refused to accept this answer. "How can you be so much more productive in your product yield than other companies with similar products?" the director asked. Again, the researcher said it was the people that made the difference. After that, the questions became, in the security manager's words, "downright nasty." However, the researcher stuck to his guns and the confrontation ended in a stalemate.

That encounter set the tone for the rest of the NHK visit, and the crew members smoothly shifted their line of questioning. During the rest of the interviews, the filmmakers did not badger any of the company personnel, although they probably continued to film things they weren't supposed to and they asked questions they probably did not expect to get answered. The security manager remained with them the entire day.

Towards the end of the day, the security manager decided to try to find out a little more about what the Japanese filmmakers were actually up to. He talked with the assistant director, who was obviously tired. She casually mentioned that the NHK crew had been filming in the United States for an entire month. As a matter of fact, the crew was scheduled to visit one of the company's competitors later that week. He also learned that the filmmakers had been averaging six to eight interviews a day and that their previous interviews included people from the National Institutes of Health and most of the major U.S. biotech firms.

The film crew left the company at around 4:00 P.M., as scheduled. The filmmakers had arranged to spend an additional day at one of the company's sales offices in the San Diego area. The security manager warned the San Diego office about the film crew, though he could not make the trip down to the area. The public relations officer later reported that the film crew cornered one of the sales reps in an office and tried to get him to pose with documents and sales pamphlets that he gives to doctors. The director wanted him to hold the papers up by his face and explain their purpose, on camera. The salesperson demurred and slipped the papers into his briefcase. Throughout the day, the film crew was clearly trying to pick up the company's sales and marketing methods.

This was not the last time the company would hear from NHK. The translation firm called the public relations officer and requested follow-up interviews. This time, the company declined. Later, the filmmakers sent the company a letter requesting answers to a list of questions. The list included all of the very sensitive questions that had not been answered by the researchers during the film crew's visit and was actually quite belligerent in tone. In it, the filmmakers stressed that NHK could not use the footage the crew had shot at the company in their documentary unless the company answered the enclosed questions. What a shame it would be, the letter implied, if all of the company's previous cooperation was for nothing. The letter reminded the PR officer that the documentary would be shown during prime-time television on one of Japan's largest television stations.

The company again declined to provide the information. Later, when the documentary was broadcast, none of the company's footage appeared in the final cut.

The company has since received three additional requests for interviews by different Japanese filmmakers claiming to represent other stations. The company is no longer interested in such exposure. Its employees also receive many requests to make presentations at Japanese professional conferences. One recent request was from a Japanese pharmaceutical company that wanted the company's sales manager to describe how to market biotechnology products and how they differ from pharmaceutical products—not a very subtle attempt to get the company to give away its proprietary secrets.

CONCLUSIONS

Everything the NHK film crew did was legal. All that the filmmakers did was ask for information in a very creative way. From an intelligence perspective, I can't help but admire their creativity. The attack was incredibly simple and easy to put together. John Quinn, a former CIA operative and expert on Japanese business intelligence tactics, theorizes that NHK probably intended to do a legitimate documentary on the biotechnology industry. After the NHK people began doing their research, they might have contacted Japanese biotech firms and struck a deal. The companies would provide the expertise and collection requirements, and probably extra funding; NHK would gather intelligence. This made it possible for the filmmakers to create a better documentary while supporting their nation's industries. To the Japanese government, it was a win-win situation; to the

American firms that were naive enough to participate, it could have been devastating.

VULNERABILITIES EXPLOITED

It is fairly obvious that the intention of the NHK film crew was to get inside American companies by offering prime-time exposure on Japanese television. This is actually a great offer to most companies interested in breaking into markets in the Pacific Rim. The Japanese market is very closed, and any exposure might be helpful. To some companies, it's an offer they can't refuse. It's also likely that the translation firm is a front company for Japanese firms gathering business intelligence in America.

Upon arriving at a company's facility, these "filmmakers" would make the people comfortable with their presence. They would start out by asking nice, unassuming questions. The fact that they also stuck a camera into peoples' faces only increased the likelihood of them being intimidated into giving up very sensitive information.

When they met with resistance, the crew would shift gears, asking questions designed to make the company personnel feel uncomfortable, sometimes goading the people into giving up information rather than risk an international incident. People tend to cave in when faced with a persistent individual who acts with total confidence.

The PR Problem

Another problem in this case comes from the public relations department. PR executives want to get their company's story out there, and they tend to be somewhat uninformed about the malicious intentions and tactics of industrial spies. When they are the ones supervising an interview, they tend to give the

interviewee little guidance. They tend to expect that person to stop himself or herself from answering inappropriate questions, while the interviewees expect the PR officer to set the boundaries of the interview. Under those circumstances, it is not uncommon for an inexperienced employee to blurt out sensitive information. It is a deadly cycle that good spies rely on.

From the initial FBI response, it is obvious that the other companies the film crew visited were not as diligent in their security posture as this company was. Judging by the reactions of the filmmakers, they had been enjoying a consistently deep level of access. After over a month of collecting information, they would never have been as blunt as they were with this company if the other companies had demonstrated similar resistance.

The fact that the security manager was very involved in the filming obviously helped to drastically decrease the information compromise. But, because of typically lax company-wide security awareness, it is very unlikely the people interviewed at the biotech company would have been as diligent if the security manager had not been around during the interview.

Communication Gaps

The security manager lobbied to set up a process at the company that kept him informed about outside visitors to the company. This is an excellent countermeasure. Unfortunately, he was informed of the NHK visit less than twenty-four hours before the crew's arrival. He was able to contact the FBI and develop his own intelligence. Even though he did learn about the threat, it was really too late for him to do much about it. While he was meeting with the company's senior managers, trying to convince them to cancel the film crew's visit, the filmmakers were downstairs signing in at the front desk.

The FBI could have sent out an alert to companies likely to be contacted by NHK. If the security manager had not

contacted the DECA office, he would never have known about the potential threat and the crew's previous antics. Most likely, the film crew caught many other companies totally unaware.

Poor Awareness

The entire Japanese effort was predicated on catching people unaware of major security issues. The filmmakers wanted the people being interviewed to be intimidated into giving up information, expecting them to be overwhelmed by the cameras. People will give up a great deal of information if someone just takes the time to ask them for it. There was very little about this attack that was difficult to arrange. A security manager watching from the sidelines might make interviewees think twice, but what happens when the security manager isn't there? Few firms think of involving their security managers in "public relations" events.

According to John Quinn, the methods used in this case were very unusual for Japanese people and companies. Although they might be shameless in their pursuit of information, they are usually polite to a fault, showing great respect for all other individuals.

Whatever else it did, the NHK film crew broke no laws. Everything it did during, before, and after its visit to the biotech company was completely legal.

12

The Weakest Link

U P TO NOW, THE CASE STUDIES I'VE PRESENTED HAVE DEALT primarily with nontechnical corporate penetrations. This is as it should be, since nontechnical attacks comprise the vast majority of the actual cases of industrial espionage. However, computer-based crimes are still responsible for billions of dollars in losses and tremendous compromises of information. What Scott Charney said is true: "Outsiders do outsider things." In the context of this book, that means attacking computers through external sources, such as the Internet.

This case describes a penetration test performed by Price Waterhouse in 1995 for a large U.S. government agency that uses computers containing a great deal of very sensitive and personal information. George Kurtz, a computer analyst who specializes in performing technical penetrations, led the attack. The executives of the government agency wanted to prove that their computer system was secure despite the fact that it was connected to the Internet.

BACKGROUND

The system in question was a large IBM mainframe computer system that was running the ACF/2 operating system. This type of system has a great deal of security built into it. It has what the National Computer Security Center (an information security arm of the NSA) calls *multilevel security*. The computer has very strong password and user containment capabilities. It also provides for the classification of data and users. A document may be classified as Top Secret, for example; a user with only Secret clearance could not access such a document. Any attempt to gain such access would set off alarms in the system.

The actions of the system's users can be closely tracked. The government agency looked at the computer as a fortress, able to withstand the heaviest attack. Kurtz and his team from Price Waterhouse proved it wrong.

THE ATTACK

In all likelihood, a direct attack on the targeted computer system would have failed. Security is very strong on that type of system; it really is something of a fortress. Therefore, Kurtz began his attack with careful preliminary observations. He examined the system's Internet address. He probed the network the system was attached to by using some standard attack tools available through the Internet. On the network segment, he found a variety of computer systems that had several different types of operating systems. One of them caught his attention. It was a computer from Sun Microsystems running an operating system known to have a number of known vulnerabilities.

The probes told Kurtz that the Sun computer system was configured to allow valid users to log on to the computer without having to give a password. This level of accessibility is desirable in certain types of networks, but when a system is plugged into the Internet, it is a deadly and imminently exploitable flaw.

Kurtz set the user name on his own computer to that of a common system account (bin) that typically has system administrator–type privileges on poorly configured systems. Kurtz then tried to log on to the targeted computer system, and, as expected, was not asked to give a password. He found that he had most system administrator privileges, although not complete control over the system. And though he had established a presence on the right network, he was clearly not yet on the targeted system.

To get more information, Kurtz needed full system administrator privileges. He was allowed to copy the password file but not to change it. He made a copy of the file, then deleted the password for the system administrator in his own copy of the file. He then exploited a widely known vulnerability on this type of operating system and overwrote the normal password file with his own version of it. The system administrator suddenly had no password at all. Kurtz could now log on to the system as the official system administrator, with full privileges. He could now modify this system at will, and he was about two hours into the exercise.

Kurtz still had no access to the targeted system, but he was getting closer. He installed a back door—a way to get back into the system—just in case someone detected his presence and cut off his way into this system. Then he installed a password sniffer. Whenever one computer talks to another, every other system on the same network can see what the computers are saying, but they ignore the conversation, so to speak. Kurtz's sniffer told the system he was on *not* to ignore the other computers on the network. More importantly, he set the sniffer to capture the user IDs and passwords of others logging on to the network. In a typical office environment, in which e-mail is stored on a remote computer system, when employees log on to get their messages, they are actually logging on to the remote system.

After installing the sniffer, Kurtz logged off and let the program collect passwords. The modifications to the system and the installation of the password sniffer took him about three hours. No one had yet detected any of his actions, so it was time to call it a day.

The following day, he again logged on to the system and found that he had accumulated an immense amount of information. During the night he'd collected hundreds of user IDs and passwords. He searched for the user IDs and passwords of possible systems administration accounts on the ACF/2 system but found none. However, he did get many systems administrator passwords for other systems on the network.

Now he began logging on to the dozens of systems he'd compromised to find out exactly what they did, and more importantly, to see whether he could uncover any relationships to the targeted system. During his search, he found that he had compromised the organization's mail server, which made it possible to read everybody's mail. The problem was, the system supported thousands of users, each of whom received dozens and sometimes hundreds of messages each day.

With the help of some common system search tools, Kurtz focused his search through the company's vast sea of e-mail. Specifically, he set the search applications to seek out any mention of the words "password," "user name," "enable ID," "user ID," and the like. One of the messages that surfaced during this search was from one systems administrator to another. The message was about an administration account that had been set up for the message recipient on the targeted mainframe computer. The message was relatively secure, since it mentioned only the name of the account and not the password. But for Kurtz, it might be enough.

He searched through his list and found the password of the systems administrator whose mail he had read. Relying on human predictability, he attempted to log on to the targeted computer system with the name of the administration account he'd found in the e-mail message and the password from the administrator's personal account on another system. The combination worked, and Kurtz connected to the targeted system and established system administrator privileges.

Although the nature of the ACF/2 operating system prevented him from establishing complete control of the computer, he was able to look at and modify files throughout the system. He'd proved that even the strongest operating system could be seriously compromised through the weakest link on its network. He accomplished his security breach in three days.

CONCLUSIONS

Kurtz's attack was very simple and straightforward, yet it yielded an incredible amount of information about private individuals—and virtually anyone with Internet access could have done the same thing. George Kurtz is obviously a gifted computer professional, and he is incredibly proficient at finding, exploiting, and fixing system vulnerabilities. Typical hackers would consider him *elite* because he was able to exploit a very secure computer system, but there was nothing unique about what he did. He only compromised known technical vulnerabilities, the existence of which are widely known throughout the Internet and hacker communities. True, his attack was very disciplined and precise—an amateur would probably have been much sloppier—but it could have been accomplished by lesser thieves. The important point of this case study is that a network, and every computer on it, is only as secure as its weakest link.

VULNERABILITIES EXPLOITED

The results of the penetration test were devastating to the security staff of the government agency. It caused the staff to totally reevaluate its security program's focus, and rightfully so.

Poor System Configuration

The poor configuration of the first system he attacked allowed Kurtz to establish a foothold on the network, through which he was able to enter the target system. Since the first system contained little significant information, it was probably deemed unworthy of much security effort. As this case study shows, that was an extremely poor assessment.

Failure to Fix Known Operating System Vulnerabilities

Although a configuration issue allowed Kurtz to gain access to the first system, it was a system administrator's failure to fix a known vulnerably that let him take control of it. A great deal of information was available about the problems of the weaker system as well as plenty of data on how to correct those problems. Because this information went unutilized, Kurtz was able to capture hundreds of passwords, and he bypassed some of the strongest operating system security mechanisms available.

Overuse of Passwords

It's human nature to balk at memorizing half a dozen passwords, but overuse of the same password is what gave Kurtz entry into the target system. Although the administrator's passwords were not vulnerable to password cracking (guessing), passwords can be obtained through a variety of methods: shoulder surfing (looking over people's shoulders to watch them type their password), password sniffing, or social engineering, to mention a few. Once Kurtz figured out the password, he had access to every system the administrator used.

No One Noticed

Perhaps the most troubling aspect of this attack was that nobody noticed that it was going on. Had the administrator of the first system realized that his password had been changed, he could have prevented the capture of the passwords that compromised the mainframe computer. Likewise, had the administrator of the mail server realized that someone had logged on to the computer as the administrator and was reading everybody's mail, the attack could have been thwarted.

Mr. Kurtz seriously compromised the security of a powerful computer system, and he wasn't particularly trying to cover up his tracks. Because nobody had noticed the attacks, Price Waterhouse had to prove that Kurtz had compromised the mainframe system by showing the government data that could have come from nowhere else. Although the strength of the ACF/2 operating system would probably have allowed the administrators to notice the attack at a later time, the thieves went about their business totally undetected until their mission was complete.

From an administration and security perspective, this case demonstrates the danger of reliance on the security of a computer system on its own strengths. In these days of computer networking, the strength of the security of an individual computer really depends upon the strength of the most insecure system on the network to which it is connected. A computer is not like a bank vault, isolated and secure. Locked up in a heavy enough safe, your money would be protected in the worst neighborhood in town; a computer attached to a network is like a safe with a trap door. Sooner or later, someone is going to find a way in.

13

The Things You Never Hear About

CITIBANK ALLEGES THAT IN 1994, VLADIMIR LEVIN, A SYSTEM administrator from St. Petersburg, Russia, compromised its system security and made financial transactions for his own benefit. The bank was able to stop Levin from absconding with millions, and it actually caught the greedy hacker.

The case attracted a great deal of attention from the press. Many people criticized Citibank for a lapse in security, despite the fact that it recovered almost all of the stolen money. The bank also implemented security mechanisms that made attacking its systems vastly more difficult. Still, other banks were able to use the bad publicity to steal business from Citibank.

Nobody noticed a similar drama unfolding at another large bank just down the street. To this day, no one even knows it happened.

BACKGROUND

There are many stories in the financial world, computer underground, and organized crime circles about major compromises of large financial institutions; we don't hear about these potentially devastating data manipulations on the six o'clock news. In researching this book, I came across a particularly shocking, but expected, story about just such an attack, and I met the formidable hacker who would only admit to *witnessing* it.

My source for this story is one of the world's true computer geniuses. He is one of the gifted few who can find new vulnerabilities like a water witch with a divining rod. He's the kind of hacker who stays out of the spotlight, never wasting his time bragging about his previous exploits and never trying to impress the *lamers* who long to become *elite*.

The bank in this story must go unnamed, since it never knew that its system was ever breached and the hackers involved are not going to admit it. I've also changed the names of the hackers involved.

THE ATTACK

Like most hackers of any sophistication, "Codey" maintained a private Internet account through an Internet Service Provider (ISP). Unlike the popular dial-up services, such as CompuServe and America Online, Codey's ISP provided him with a "shell account," through which he had direct access to the UNIX log-on (the same type of account most college students have through their schools). Like others of his predatory species, he routinely scanned the Internet for potentially vulnerable systems.

In his travels through cyberspace, Codey came upon a likely looking system: a Sun Microsystems computer located at the University of Missouri. The system suffered from a well-known vulnerability in its mail program. As hackers are often inclined to do, Codey exploited the vulnerability to access and control the system.

Codey was a cautious trespasser. The first thing he did was check the system for intrusion detection and system logging software. He found no such security applications running on the computer.

Since he had gained access to the system through a widely known vulnerability, he assumed that the administrator of the system was not very good (a reasonable assumption). However, experienced hackers take pains to avoid being caught, and Codey was no exception. He modified a system process to keep the administrator from noticing any programs he was running. He also modified the directory program to hide his files, should the administrator ever try to look for them.

He then modified the log-in program to capture users' passwords as they logged on to the computer. The new log-in program also provided him with quick access to system administrator privileges. He further modified the logging programs to make it impossible to detect him through normal means. Then he added a few back doors to the system, just in case.

With the system properly bent to his will, Codey proceeded to collect other passwords. He installed a password sniffer program similar to the one George Kurtz used to hack the government mainframe in Chapter 12. While the password sniffer was working, he cast about for interesting information. He left the sniffer to work for a few days; it collected thousands of user IDs and passwords from systems around the world.

At about this time, Codey invited two friends to help him shop around on the newly compromised systems. The young, like-minded hackers were glad to join the raiding party.

Together, they moved on from Codey's point of entry at the University of Missouri to exploit a VAX system at the University of Pennsylvania. They got onto the system using one of the user IDs and passwords Codey had collected, and then they exploited a known vulnerability that allowed any valid user to obtain system administrator privileges. As with the previous system, they checked the level of security and found the system to be virtually unguarded. They then modified the system files to avoid detection and put the password sniffer into place. Of course, they looked around for anything cool.

The sniffer collected thousands of new user accounts from systems throughout the world. The young hackers were deluged with information, but they slowly worked their way through the compromised accounts. They looked for accounts on potentially interesting systems, such as the military systems (.mil), or for large corporations like IBM and General Motors. One of the accounts that snagged their attention was connected to an organization (an Internet address that ended with .org) that none of them had heard of.

They logged onto this organization's system and began exploring. The computer was not a very common one, but they still found many familiar vulnerabilities. They determined the probable skill of the system administrator, secured system administrator privileges, determined the security level, and then modified the system to allow them continued access. They then installed a password sniffer. What they found scared them. Almost every access they saw in the information captured by the password sniffer was to a very large, very well-known bank. They also found connections to international organizations. It appeared that this system provided a bridge from those organizations to the bank and that someone had decided to connect this system to the Internet. This system was supposed to be a jumping point from the international organizations to the bank and the Internet. Probably unintentionally, it served as a jumping off point from the Internet to the bank. Clearly, the mysterious .org computer system was on a network inside the bank.

Three people were working on this enterprise from the first access at the University of Missouri system, each spending about three hours a day hacking. About two and a half weeks after their initial exploration, they had unintentionally obtained access to one of the largest banks in the world.

Using one of the newly captured log-ins, they accessed a bank computer system that seemed to be the center of a great deal of activity. Using a tool that exploits a known vulnerability specific to that computer, they obtained control of the system. They now had control of a minor system inside one of the twenty largest banks in the country. They very carefully examined the system for possible intrusion detection tools and other indications of the level of system administrator expertise. Even here they found little to worry about. They started to modify the bank's system for their own purposes, then they decided that they wanted to see exactly what was going on in the bank's network.

They installed a program called TAP, which allows them to watch user sessions as they occurred. With this program, they were able to "eavesdrop" on sessions going on across the network. They witnessed actual financial transactions being performed, and they observed the specific key stroke sequences required to make a transaction. They learned which passwords to give to authorize transactions and the order of the necessary commands. They also learned how to modify the transactions as they were occurring and to disconnect users from the system.

In order to figure out exactly what was going on, they had to watch when "unusual" commands were sent across the network and then see what types of responses came back. The hackers determined that the users they were watching were actually tellers or account representatives using special terminals with special keys. Because the bank used special terminals, the hackers had to write a program that emulated the terminal's unique actions. Common programs are available that emulate most terminal types, but there wasn't one for this bank's terminals, so the hackers had to write a program to create one. The programming was not difficult for someone with Codey's expertise, but it was above the skills of the majority of hackers. It wasn't long before they had learned exactly how to conduct transactions of their own and had the capability to do it.

Apparently, this capability was too much of a temptation for one of the hackers. "Jed" decided that as long as he was inside the bank, he might as well scoop up some money.

Jed supplemented the group's electronic activities with a little social engineering. He wanted to determine the best times to get more account information and to hide his actions. He phoned the bank and, posing as a customer planning to make a large deposit, asked when bank business was slowest. He claimed that he wanted to avoid crowds while carrying large sums of cash. Then he asked when the bank was busiest, thinking, he said, that maybe he'd be safer when more people were there. (He was intending to conduct his thievery during the bank's busiest hours.)

Jed began spending more and more time on the bank's system. He searched for accounts with very large balances. These, he reasoned, would be the best accounts to steal from, because they were involved in more transactions and were least likely to miss the money.

During this time, Jed began setting up a number of bank accounts around town to facilitate the laundering of his planned ill-gotten gain. He used fake identification to establish the accounts, stealing IDs in some cases, making up a fake cards using a computer graphics package like CorelDRAW, and even buying fake identification cards from criminals.

Two events threw a monkey wrench into the master plan. First, Jed was arrested on charges unrelated to his hacking activities. Since he was the only person in the group who was seriously interested in any financial gain, the impetus to rob the bank was lost. (Although many people don't believe it, the hacker culture frowns on profiteering and theft; purists never realize any profit from their hacking.)

Second, the password on the system that provided access to the bank was changed. In theory, Codey and the other hacker could have gotten back into the system, but they decided such a move would only lead to trouble; besides, they had already done just about everything that could be done to the bank's computers (and maybe Jed would try to plea-bargain his way out of his current problems by giving the other two hackers up to the cops).

They did not return to this particular system, and the bank continues its business, never knowing, or admitting, that its security had been breached so severely.

CONCLUSIONS

The hackers involved in this case study made all the significant accomplishments in their attack within a two-month period, working part-time and with no financial resources to support their activities. And they found the bank *by accident*. Is it likely that criminals with minimal funding could have done the same? The answer is obvious. Were any skills required here that someone with tremendous financial incentive could not acquire? Was this banking compromise simply not preventable? The answers are just as obvious.

While this case seems to involve more advanced techniques than the case study in Chapter 12, there was very little sophisticated computer work in this action. The hackers methodically compromised one system after another. They modified those systems to cover their tracks, and they made sure that nobody could see what they were doing. Although they did show an unusual amount of discipline compared to other hackers, they used no resources that are not freely available to any hacker—or to any other person with Internet access for that matter—on the planet.

The only task the hackers performed that required any kind of real sophistication was the creation of the terminal emulator program. This step did require some above-average programming skills that are beyond the typical hacker. My source for this story says that a third-year computer science student should have the required skills.

VULNERABILITIES EXPLOITED

From all indications, this case went totally unnoticed, yet the compromise was very serious. If the hackers had been malicious, they could have ruined the bank. They did have the capability to destroy all the data on the computer system, and they could have made off with millions.

Poor System Configurations and Known Vulnerabilities

The hackers compromised sophisticated computer systems around the country and the world. Although they secured many system access points through a password sniffer, primarily they exploited the system configuration and vulnerability problems. By the hackers' own admission, they could have been easily stopped by good system administration. They could never have installed that first sniffer unless the system was poorly configured. Every system compromise was critical only after they were able to get system administrator privileges. This was only possible because of the existence of the known vulnerabilities and configuration problems on the system.

Not Knowing the Existence of Internet Gateways

Many organizations don't recognize how many connections to the outside world run into their computer systems. In this case, the bank had the .org system installed directly on its network. It's possible that the bank didn't know it had a system connected to the Internet, but that is no excuse and demonstrates poor network control. If bank administrators did know that there was such a system, they should have been very carefully monitoring it.

Organizations must identify all of the connections to systems beyond their own and secure them. Every bank has dozens of connections, including modems, commercial networks, banking networks, Internet connections, and others. Although this case demonstrates that perimeter security is no single method of defense, a good perimeter security mechanism is a must. These hackers literally stumbled onto this bank's system by accident and were able to infiltrate to the point of making their own transactions. The people who actually intend to compromise banks are bound to be even better at it.

Poor Administration

The hackers in this case were performing better administration than the actual administrators. They modified log files, changed system programs, and modified user permissions. All this activity should have been noticed by *somebody*. According to Codey, it seemed as though the real systems administrators never logged on to the systems at all. The systems seemed to have been left to administer themselves.

This is unacceptable. If administrators never intend to properly maintain the system, they should at least install some form of automated intrusion detection. A properly monitored system is much less vulnerable to attacks of all kinds.

Another aspect of administration is checking for the alteration of sensitive files. There are intrusion detection and administration tools that watch key files to see if someone has changed them. Administrators can also do this manually.

Social Engineering

When Jed called the bank to find out when heavy volumes of transactions were made, the teller gave him some very sensitive information without even thinking about it. Although it might have seemed harmless, it was critical, and it could have helped Jed to clean out a few accounts. Bank robbers want the same information so that they'll know when to stop by for a quick withdrawal. The bank does have to give out certain information, but some things are better left unsaid.

PART III

WHAT YOU CAN DO

Countermeasures

THE CASE STUDIES CITED IN PART II INCLUDE A WIDE range of incidents and perpetrators, from the most diabolical intelligence agencies to callow hackers. Each example illustrates the typical, modern foreign and corporate espionage methods and tactics. As I have pointed out, in all instances the crimes should have been prevented with simple, low-cost countermeasures.

You'll be surprised at the number of things you can do with the resources currently at your disposal. I don't recommend relying on your present security plan if it leaves you open to attack, but if at the very least you develop more effective applications of existing security systems, then I will have done my job.

The biggest problem you'll face in your efforts to implement further countermeasures in your organization is simple ignorance. Most people and organizations tend to be unaware of the most common threats to their security. When they think about these matters at all, they imagine superspies and high-tech wunderkind. They buy into the hype of the information warfare bogeyman and industrial espionage spooks. They feel helpless and they do nothing. It is my fervent hope that the preceding case studies have at least begun to dispel these misconceptions. The fact is, an individual can do a great deal to prevent attacks from even the most well-equipped intelligence operation.

In almost all cases where attacks cannot be prevented outright, measures can still be implemented to effectively reduce their damage. People see the signs of corporate espionage all around them: a computer log in in the middle of the night, desks left in subtle disarray, strange telephone calls—all are possible indications of an attack. If everyone inside your organization would just *look* for signs of intrusion and report them, you'd increase your security a thousandfold. The countermeasures proposed in this chapter will help tremendously with the task of detection, which can be even more critical than just stopping an attack.

No security strategy can prevent every loss, but that fact shouldn't stop organizations from taking action. Countermeasures are never perfect; accidents and mistakes are unavoidable, but their effect on an organization can be greatly minimized.

As you read through this chapter, consider carefully which tactics best suit your organization and your specific security needs. It is unwise to put a countermeasure into place just because everyone else is doing it. Take a look at the following recommendations and consider carefully how they will affect you and your situation. You don't want to end up spending more on countermeasures than your information is worth. The goal is an effective strategy that addresses your particular threats and vulnerabilities appropriately.

As always, consider the *risk*. Some vulnerabilities are negligible, while others can ruin your business. Consider each of the following countermeasures and ask yourself these questions:

- Does my organization have vulnerabilities that the countermeasure addresses?
- Is the countermeasure relevant to my industry?

- Can I easily implement it?
- How much work will implementation of this strategy require?
- Do I currently have access to the money and/or resources necessary to effectively implement the countermeasure?
- Will the countermeasure be worth its cost?

Another factor to consider when choosing countermeasures is the culture of your organization. Some groups depend on an open environment to facilitate research. Depending on the value of your information and the nature of the threat, your organizational culture may have to change to make your environment more secure. Think and compromise; you don't want your organization to suffer significantly in the process of securing it.

All the countermeasures discussed in this chapter—both basic and sophisticated—are widely available. I've broken them down into the same categories I use to define vulnerabilities: operations, physical, personnel, and technical. However, you won't necessarily be using them to counter weaknesses in identical categories. You might address many operations vulnerabilities with technical countermeasures. For example: The vulnerability presented by computer users in your organization who don't know that they should not download certain types of files from the Internet can be countered with firewalls, technical countermeasures that prevent the downloading of certain types of files, or with anti-virus software, another technical countermeasure.

Many of the countermeasures I'm recommending in this chapter are the same strategies routinely employed by the U.S. Intelligence Community. Despite occasional splashy headlines of espionage, it suffers very few losses compared with the threats it faces.

I want to emphasize that I do not discuss all possible countermeasures in this chapter. I have, however, included a substantial

list of the most useful and cost-effective steps you can take to protect your organization. If you only implement the strategies discussed here, your organization would certainly be much, *much*
more secure. These countermeasures will deter almost all attackers, making your company an expensive or difficult one to target,
and in most cases, not worth the effort and expense required to
attack you. Once you have put the countermeasures I've described
here in place in your company, please don't hesitate to consult
other resources on this subject. I don't know everything, and you
can never be too safe.

Some of the countermeasures detect attacks more than
they prevent them. Detection can be more important. Even if
your countermeasures repel 1,000 attacks, if you do not know
about them, then you won't know to look for the next attack,
which might target an unprotected vulnerability. Focused
attackers will keep coming at you until they get in. If you can
detect them, unsuccessful attacks can tell you that you have a
threat and will cause you to be more alert. Even if someone
does compromise you, detecting the attack tells you how to
strengthen your security.

OPERATIONS COUNTERMEASURES

Operations countermeasures are nontechnical procedures
designed to blend with an organization's day-to-day operations. The idea here is to create a corporate culture in which
security is subtle but second nature. Most of the countermeasures described in this section are easy to implement and
are inexpensive. They won't work, though, unless the employees are well informed about the procedures, the purpose of the
procedures, and the consequences of ignoring them.

For the most part, these countermeasures are nonintrusive.
No company should have to place itself under martial law to

keep its information safe. However, when the stakes are high, more intrusive measures may be necessary.

The problem with operations countermeasures is that they easily may be taken for granted by even security professionals. Security professionals tend to focus on computers or facilities, ignoring operational solutions. The types of countermeasures discussed here provide an incredibly high payback. It's usually worth taking a small amount of resources from the other security disciplines to help create an organizational culture that supports security as a whole.

Awareness Training

There is probably no more effective countermeasure, dollar for dollar, than a good security awareness program. In all the case studies presented in Part II, better user awareness could have significantly minimized or prevented the attacks. In every case, someone should have noticed the unusual behavior of coworkers, the irregular access to computer accounts, or the social engineering tactics employed. If the victims had just been more aware, the attackers could have been stopped dead in their tracks.

Many security awareness programs are considered to be worthless by security professionals, and I'm inclined to agree with that assessment. In researching the problem, I've discovered that far too many so-called awareness programs are nothing more than speeches informing employees of the consequences of illegal activities. The focus is on employees' misbehavior, and the emphasis is on penalties.

Threatening to fire people caught stealing secrets is not only a waste of time, it's counterproductive. It's no wonder "security" has such a negative connotation for so many. People learn to fear the word, and they report incidents to the department only as a last resort—and sometimes only when they believe they are being set up. Some security people believe that threatening workers acts as a deterrent; I believe such threats destroy morale and reduce overall cooperation. You want your people to start perceiving your security department as a resource they can turn to when they have or see a problem. Don't present it as an oppressive force that they have to avoid at all costs.

Programs that focus on penalties do nothing to educate, and that should be the primary purpose of any awareness program. You should work to inform your people of the threat their organization faces. Obviously, you have to tell them about your policies, and people should be made aware that criminal actions are dealt with harshly. Keep things in proportion; most of your employees have no criminal intentions.

One of the most effective ways to educate your people about security issues is to tell them about real cases. That's why I created Part II of this book. All too often, organizations try to hide the truth about previous attacks in the misguided belief that knowledge of a breach will make them more vulnerable. It is only when people hear about real cases, however, that they believe the threat is real. Organizations can filter out sensitive details of a case and still use it to get the point across. If a company does not have a case of its own to talk about—which is extremely rare—company officials can use a case from a similar organization. Stories of corporate espionage affecting organizations of all sizes fill the newspapers and can be found easily on the Internet.

Your people must also be made aware of the value of information itself. Employees honestly don't know that a list of customers is critical to both your company and others. They don't realize that a competitor can ruin your entire software development efforts if it gains access to certain phone numbers. They don't know about the cascading effect of small compromises of the data they handle each day. Show them how the information they control affects your organization. And don't forget to mention the countermeasures your organization uses.

An effective awareness program stresses the usefulness of simple and basic countermeasures. You'll want to give examples of how the little things stopped, or could have stopped, major corporate espionage cases. Show your people how their seemingly small contributions can make a major difference. Let them know that *they* can be the ones to stop those mythical (hopefully you now see them as mythical) James Bonds and evil computer geniuses.

Remember that you have to tell employees exactly what they should be doing, and what you tell them should be clear and simple. You have to let people know about the threats, but you must also tell them what to do about it. They should know exactly what their actions should be in different circumstances and what you expect of them. The other countermeasures discussed here should be clearly understood by all employees.

A good security awareness program is an ongoing program; it doesn't start and stop with the new hire briefings. At least twice a year, organize presentations about new security topics. At those sessions, revisit the basics to keep everybody sharp. The tone should be friendly and informal. When possible, include new case studies of actual attacks.

Security awareness materials can play an important role in your ongoing educational program. Security departments can publish their own newsletters and distribute posters and fliers. The National Security Agency's Security Awareness Division puts together posters on a monthly basis. They are distributed around the intelligence community and to its contractors. In some cases, employees like the posters so much that they steal them (one of the more popular posters was a Santa Claus with a finger at his lips in a shushing motion; around Christmastime, people were fighting for them). In most U.S. defense and intelligence installations, all telephones are tagged directly with reminders that others can listen in on conversations.

One of your security people could write a regular column for the employee newsletter. The content of such a column should be not only entertaining but also informative. Posting stories from newspapers, magazines, and the Internet about security breaches is another good way to remind people about their responsibilities and the dangers around them. Along with each story, include a review of your own countermeasures. Show how they could have prevented the incident.

Unless security managers want to go it alone, they must increase the security awareness inside their organizations and create an environment in which people want to help. I was once hired to conduct a penetration test at a company that, for political reasons, sent around a note warning employees about my impending attack. The note asked everyone to keep his or her eyes peeled and follow established procedures, including reporting unusual incidents. For weeks prior to my arrival, the security manager received a striking increase in reports of incidents requiring his attention. Unfortunately, most people seemed more interested in detecting a penetration test as opposed to a security incident, but the exercise did help to increase awareness and got employees to start reporting those types of incidents.

When people know what to do, what to look for, and how to respond to a variety of common situations, they usually do their part. An increased level of awareness among the people in your organization will counter most operations vulnerabilities and help counter physical, personnel, and technical weaknesses as well. Instead of depending only on your security personnel, you could be utilizing thousands of people in your organization to detect espionage activities. Employees could have stopped the attacks in nearly all of the case studies cited in this book.

Classifying Information

It's a simple and unavoidable fact of life: businesses must exchange information, both within their own organization and among their customers and suppliers. However, all information is not created equal, nor should it be equally available. It is perfectly reasonable and even advisable to categorize some of your company's information for the purposes of controlling its distribution among different groups. You can restrict access to certain customers, different levels of employees, various project teams, senior management, and specific individuals. You get to decide which information is available to which groups.

Most organizations already classify their information. Usually, however, they have few if any formal processes in place, which means that lots of data slips through the cracks.

Also, companies rarely utilize fine distinctions for sensitive materials. They don't often stop to think about the *relative value* of information. For example, in general only employees should have access to a company's telephone directories. The same may be said about the organization's business plan. However, the business plan is easily much more sensitive than the telephone directory—the compromise of the former could certainly hurt your organization; the compromise of the latter could destroy your organization. If both are classified merely as "sensitive," your employees are going to treat the documents as equally valuable.

For this reason, I recommend utilizing an extra level of control for certain types of information. For example, some information could be restricted to employees only, but it may also be designated as controlled in a library and protected by limited removal procedures.

You must also decide who in your organization will actually be doing the categorizing. In many companies, the people creating the information are responsible for categorizing it.

Although this is probably the only realistic way of implementing this countermeasure, I strongly advise establishing some clear organizational direction in the process. Don't leave something so important to individual caprice.

Make sure that your corporate policies on this subject are widely available to anyone who will be classifying information in your organization. Without direction, people will tend to take the path of least resistance. They're bound to classify your valuable information in a way that minimizes their personal aggravation, rather than in a way that keeps it safe.

Here are three common policy statements used by other companies and organizations to guide the classification process:

- Any document containing the name of an employee is restricted to company employees.

- Information concerning product development is restricted to people working specifically on the development.

- Corporate financial information is restricted to senior officials and others responsible for compiling the information.

Special measures should be put in place to regulate the flow of information that is classified as especially sensitive. At the very least, access to such data should require a signature on a log sheet, and someone should be designated to check the logs on a regular basis.

Thoughtful classification of information would have prevented the theft of the manufacturing instructions described in Chapter 7 and the theft of many chip specifications described in Chapter 8.

Security Alert System

People have to know who to tell when they discover potential security problems. The only thing most people think to do is tell their supervisor. If they have a bad relationship with the boss, they might be disinclined to bring up a problem. If they do tell their supervisor, then the supervisor must know what to do with that information. In most cases I've investigated, the supervisors have no clearer idea about what action to take than the people they supervise.

Not wanting to seem stupid, many managers ignore critical situations. In other cases, they believe it to be their jobs to handle the situations themselves and act accordingly, never letting upper management and the security department in on the problems. Some managers believe that going to security will create problems for them and their groups. Yet managers do their employers no favors when they try to handle possible industrial espionage situations without outside help. They also let indications of more serious problems go unnoticed.

To facilitate communication within your company about potential security breaches, I strongly advise establishing simple and easy reporting procedures. The simpler and easier, the better. Company e-mail is a wonderful vehicle for this. It provides a very fast, cheap, and reliable method of contacting security. Users can type up a quick message at their desks and fire it off to the security account, hopefully named "security." There is a small risk that an attacker who has compromised the mail server might see the message, but the resulting increase in communication throughout the company makes the risk well worth taking. To increase the confidentiality of your company e-mail, you might enable the use of encryption (described later in this chapter).

E-mail also lets the security department post company-wide alerts about possible problems. The attacker in Chapter 6 who telephoned people and asked for their passwords could have been thwarted handily with a company-wide security e-mail warning, assuming that someone first detected the unusual call.

Reward Programs

One of the best ways to encourage employees to cooperate with security is to show them that you appreciate their efforts. A useful way to express this appreciation is by offering rewards for employee cooperation. Make certain, however, that you are rewarding people for awareness and proper action, not snitching on coworkers. You don't want to give the people in your organization the impression that you pass out rewards for eavesdropping.

Cash rewards work best, in my opinion, but when money is tight, a small gift might suffice. Gift certificates are always good. You might also try a special, personalized mug. If no money at all is available, then you can use a graphics package to create a certificate of recognition. When possible, you'll want the company president or other senior official to sign the certificate. The cash value of the reward is not as important as the act of recognition. In this case at least, it really is the thought that counts.

Call Backs before Disclosing Sensitive Information

For practical purposes, sensitive and controlled information should be given out on a face-to-face basis only. The information might also be given out over the telephone under special circumstances, say, to people you personally recognize. Sometimes employees have no choice but to release information to anonymous strangers, but when an unknown caller asks for any sensitive data, his or her identity should be verified before even the most seemingly innocuous information is handed over. In Chapter 6, all of the attacks would have failed utterly if the people contacted by phone had simply tried to verify the caller's identity.

If an employee is asked for information that is clearly sensitive, and he or she doesn't know who the person is but thinks that the reason seems valid, then the employee should ask for the person's name and telephone number. The employee should then hang up, confirm the telephone number with a company telephone directory, then call the person back at that number. Or, if the person says that he or she is not at the listed directory number, then the employee should check with someone (like a secretary) to verify that the person is indeed at the location he or she claims to be at. This whole process normally takes about fifteen seconds. Anyone can claim to be someone else, and a quick telephone check can prevent major compromises. This process should be part of normal company procedures. If a caller balks, then he or she just might be an attacker. If the complainer claims to be the CEO, for example, then the employee can say, "If you are who you claim to be, I might be fired for doing my job. If you are not who you claim to be and I give you the information, then I will definitely be fired." This will usually quell any resistance.

This countermeasure is a no-cost solution that is simple to implement. It sets up a tremendous hurdle that every anonymous attacker must clear. It can be used for any release of sensitive information, but it can also be used in response to requests for sensitive services, such as the changing of passwords. In all organizations, people forget their passwords from time to time and call the company help desk to reset it. Before giving out any password information, the help desk personnel should either personally recognize the callers or take the time to call them back at their assigned numbers. As Chapter 6 demonstrates, simple identification verification procedures can be a very effective security countermeasure. If it were implemented properly at banks and credit companies, this strategy could also decrease a tremendous amount of credit card fraud. Individuals should also do this with their own affairs. If you are going to be giving out your credit card number or other sensitive information, make sure that you initiate the phone call (after all, you should be calling the Home Shopping Network, and not the other way around).

Verifying the Need for Information Access

Almost as important as establishing a procedure for verifying the identity of persons seeking information from your organization is verifying that that person actually needs access. In most organizations, there are really very few people who need access to very sensitive information. In most cases, verification will take no more than a few minutes and require little more than a single telephone call, but even a few hours' delay should not be considered a major problem. The inconvenience is minor when compared with the potential for loss. The attack in Chapter 7 would have been prevented entirely, and I would have actually been caught, if any of the people I met with had sought to verify, through my supervisor, my need for the information. Failure to ask a few simple questions could have resulted in a multibillion-dollar loss.

When it comes to very valuable information, consider designating a member of the security team as the project security officer (PSO). The job of the PSO is to keep track of who is authorized to access information about a particular project. The PSO also acts as the primary point of contact between security and the project team. The PSO position does not have to be especially time-consuming. Essentially, the PSO is contacted only when someone new wants access to the data for which the PSO is responsible. The PSO also typically attends project meetings, to keep abreast of project status and pending security issues.

You must allow for exceptions in your security plan, but they should not go unchallenged. When exceptions arise, the need for the exception should be verified.

Verifying Identities and Purposes

Unfortunately, putting a name on a list just isn't enough. That personable gentleman standing in your office doorway, asking so winningly for access to sensitive information, may or may not actually be who he says he is. (He might even be *me*.) In organizations in which the employees don't know each other personally—a common situation in most large companies—your people must fall back on identity verifying procedures. These procedures need not necessarily be complex. Something as simple as looking at the person's access badge or calling his or her boss can make all the difference.

Your identification procedures should even apply to your security personnel. In the course of my work as a penetration tester, I've had occasion to venture into restricted territory at the client companies, often after regular working hours. Whenever people stopped me and asked what I was doing, I'd just tell them I was with security. Invariably, they'd say okay and be on their way.

Industrial spies come up with very creative stories to facilitate their larceny. Professional liars are supposed to sound and look good. It's their job. Whether they claim to be a security officer, the president's personal assistant, or God Almighty, make them prove it!

Removing Personal Identifiers from Access Badges

Most companies that utilize access badges put their employees' names and ID numbers on them. Then, there they are, on hundreds of shirt pockets for all the world to see, providing any observer with enough information to perpetrate a simple impersonation or a key transaction. After all, employee numbers are inevitably used for other purposes throughout the company. In the attack against the investment banks in Chapter 6, employee numbers were used to verify identities over the phone. Although in that case the attackers secured the numbers directly from the employees, they could just as easily have gotten the information by hanging out in local bars at quitting time.

There's really no reason to display an employee's ID number on his or her access badge. The practice serves no purpose. Removing them eliminates a major vulnerability.

In some situations, it may be desirable to display ID numbers but not names. Police in some countries display only numbers on their badges to prevent invaders from identifying and killing the local police to suppress resistance. (Prior to countries being invaded during World War II, Nazi sympathizers collected the names of policemen from their name tags and handed lists over to the Nazis after the invasion.) Although you are unlikely to find yourself in situations quite this extreme, the point is to keep the names and numbers apart—the combination causes the problems. Similarly, all paperwork that combines this information should be protected.

Nondisclosure/Noncompete Employee Agreements

In the Ann Landers letter reprinted in the Introduction, we have a case involving an employee who learned specific information about a business and then turned around and used that information to directly compete with her former employer. This particular case involved a family member, but this phenomenon is by no means strictly a family matter. Employee use of information acquired during the course of employment to further personal entrepreneurial goals is common throughout the country. It is virtually impossible to prevent someone in your employ from taking information and using it for other purposes; however, you can minimize your losses.

By requiring all employees to sign nondisclosure/noncompete agreements, you create a legal recourse should that person use your information against you. These agreements vary in content and extent, but their basic purpose is to keep your organization from becoming a training ground for competitors. The nondisclosure aspect of the agreement binds your employee contractually against disclosing your company's information to a

competitor (usually, a new employer). The noncompete component ensures that an employee cannot take your information to
start a business that competes directly against yours.

Employers must place reasonable limitations in these
agreements. For example, you cannot prevent an employee
from ever competing against you; you may only state that he
or she cannot compete against you for a period of time, usually months. The agreement can further restrict a former
employee's ability to actively market products or services to
your established customers, also for a specific time period.

When the agreement is a reasonable one, most employees
will sign it willingly. When people do balk, express indigna-
tion, or find the agreement insulting, pull out the Ann Landers article.

These agreements are usually signed by employees during
the new hire orientation process. Keep in mind that nondis-
closure/noncompete agreements don't directly prevent the
compromise of sensitive information, but they can make it
more difficult for former employees to profit from their
actions, which does discourage this kind of betrayal.

Prepublication Reviews for Employees

Most people who work in technical and scientific industries
routinely attend professional conferences at which they and
their peers present papers. Some highly skilled professionals
also write articles and books about their work. This kind of
information exchange is usually good for an organization.
Companies benefit from employing experts who are known
and respected in their fields, and interacting with peers at conferences is one way reputations are built.

Unfortunately, professionals usually write about what they
know best: their work. Without meaning to, a scientist or
technician in your organization could reveal sensitive or proprietary information you wouldn't want your competitors to

know about. This type of information compromise is usually unintentional and arises because employees don't understand the damage they could be doing.

To prevent potential compromises of this nature, you'll want to institute a formal review process that requires your people to submit articles and speeches for review before publication. The content of such material should be reviewed by peers and security personnel to ensure that it is nonproprietary, but you'll also want the process to be quick and not overly restrictive. You don't want your creative people to feel as though they're on a short leash. An effective awareness program should help explain the need for such a review process; widely disseminated publishing guidelines will help to keep people on track from the beginning.

Review of Corporate Releases

Although employees release potentially sensitive company information through speeches and articles, the organizations themselves release much more information than any employee ever will. Companies are required by law to publish detailed financial data as well as a wide variety of other information, but most organizations go well beyond these requirements. John Quinn, a former CIA operative and vice president of the Operations Security Professional Society, studied recent Securities and Exchange Commission (SEC) filings. He found that companies produce much more revealing documentation than is legally required. Besides creating a major vulnerability, this overcompensation probably doubles the cost of producing the documents.

This phenomenon is true not only of legally required information disbursements but of corporate releases in general. Companies discuss an immense amount of information in their press releases and marketing materials. The Lockheed

Martin help wanted ad shown in Chapter 5 illustrates this seeming generosity.

Companies must take special care to monitor the tendency of PR departments to give out more information than is necessary or even healthy. The content of press releases, brochures, and advertising must pass a test of reasonableness. Most organizations can get their message across by putting out much less information. The security department should definitely be in the information release cycle. You'll want to require security people to offer their input in a timely manner, and you'll also want to take into account the promotional needs of your company, but a judicious application of moderation in this area could yield a big security payoff.

Ultimately, your PR and security departments should work together to protect the sensitive information in your organization. A spirit of cooperation between these two departments can be invaluable to a company. The case study in Chapter 11 illustrates how helpful public relations people can be and how a coordinated effort between the two departments can effectively thwart a potentially serious attack.

Strict Guidelines for Marketers and Salespeople

Marketers and salespeople exist for one purpose: to sell products or services. Their companies judge them, reward them, and penalize them on their sales records. When they make their quotas, they're heroes; when they fail to hit their targets, they're in the unemployment line.

In the heat of battle, salespeople can lose perspective. When facing a sale that can go either way, they will naturally be very tempted to say whatever it takes—to release whatever information they think is necessary—to close the transaction. Marketing people are always searching for the right words and pictures to promote your company, even if those words and pictures reveal sensitive data. You can't really blame these hardworking folks for their voluble natures, but you must implement policies that effectively zip their loose lips. They represent a potentially dangerous information leak that you can plug with strictly enforced information dispersal guidelines. These guidelines should specify the types of information they can release and especially the types of information that they *cannot* release. Companies should also find ways to spot-check their sales and marketing staffers to ensure that they are following the rules.

Reporting Unusual or Frequent Contact with Competitors and Others Especially Interested in Your Work

Most companies want to stay out of their employees' personal lives for a wide variety of reasons. Not only is employee surveillance difficult and time-consuming, it lowers morale; no one wants to work for Big Brother. Yet, industrial spies often contact employees outside of work to collect information and set up penetrations. They show up at company social functions, attend conferences, and hang out at the local watering hole. This sort of thing happens more frequently than businesses want to admit.

Although most casual contact with competitors is probably innocent, the cases in which it is not usually prove to be very costly, as Chapters 9 and 10 clearly show. Therefore, I believe that it is reasonable to request that your employees contact security whenever a competitor's employee starts asking about the work of your organization.

The object here is to look for patterns, not to monitor your own people. If they're running into the same competitors on a regular basis, you have reason for concern. Such patterns are rarely coincidental. An interested outsider insinuating himself or herself into the lives of your people is a sure sign that your organization has been targeted. It's in the best interest of your employees to report such contact before they are sucked into the tangled conspiracy of a professional manipulator, as was the lonely woman in Chapter 10.

In many cases, the adversaries do not reveal their true employer. For that reason, people should report the activities of anyone who seems to be unduly interested in their job or company.

Companies in high technology and other sensitive fields should also ask that their employees report contacts by people working for foreign governments and companies. As Chapters 8, 9, 10, and 11 show, foreign governments and companies specifically target American technology, and they will use tactics most people believe are reserved for the acquisition of government secrets.

Information compromises perpetrated through unsuspecting employees can be effectively thwarted with simple reporting procedures. Make sure your people know what to watch for with a list of clear signs that the relationship is something other than what it seems to be.

Nondisclosure Clauses for Business Partners

Every company has suppliers and customers. To do business with these people, you must disclose a certain amount of information about yourself, which can result in others having as much information about your organization as you do. Manufacturers need materials, and so they must provide lists to suppliers. If they take bids, they might find themselves providing sensitive lists to people with whom they won't be doing business. Customers have to know details about the products and services they're buying. New products must be marketed, which requires the expertise of a marketing firm, to whom you must tell many of your secrets. A donut shop has to buy flour, and the amount of flour it buys tells somebody, somewhere something about how many donuts it sells.

In most cases, your competitors have the same customers and suppliers you do, and some of them are bound to use those relationships to gather information about your company. Seemingly innocent and casual conversations can draw out a great deal of information from unsuspecting suppliers. The last thing you want is to pay someone else to gather information for your competitors.

To prevent this kind of information compromise, you should specifically require confidentiality from all of the people with whom you do business. You can put a confidentiality clause in your business contracts. Although this countermeasure doesn't directly prevent information compromise, it does create a financial disincentive as well as a legal obligation.

Obviously you have more leverage in this regard with your suppliers than with your customers, but it never hurts to ask for confidentiality from everyone.

Monitoring Internet Activity

The growth of the Internet and our increasing dependence upon it presents special information security problems. Whenever your employees send a message to Internet mailing lists or bulletin boards (BBSs), they release information about your organization, albeit unintentionally. Postings to BBSs can tell a potential attacker a lot about your system vulnerabilities. When a programmer posts a message to a BBS about hardware or software issues, for example, attackers can reasonably deduce that you use that particular piece of hardware or software in your company—most of which have widely known vulnerabilities. Employee postings can also subtly indicate details about your company's future plans and product directions that a careful eavesdropper can use against you.

Even when your people go to nontechnical BBSs, the messages themselves reveal the location/identity of your mail and news systems, along with information about the software running on those systems. The same is true for mailing lists. Also, a great deal of financial information is readily available about your company on the Internet from other sources. For example, all SEC filings are available on the EDGAR Web site.

All companies connected to the Internet should browse it regularly, using widely available Internet search engines to keep up on the information out there about their operations. Your goal is not to monitor your employees but to stay abreast of potential problems. In most cases, you'll find that your organization creates the bulk of this data. If you do see indications of a vulnerability, you'll be able to fix it. If you find an excessive amount of information on the Internet about your company, say, from your employees' activities, you can establish a policy to reduce it.

You'll also see what others are saying about you. I have personally spotted postings from hackers detailing how to attack my clients. Once I found these postings, I was able to advise them on how to close up the vulnerabilities (hopefully) before the hackers and other criminals had a chance to exploit them.

Regular Internet monitoring can also reveal the identities of employees who are spending too much time in cyberspace. There are valid reasons to use the Internet, but employees requiring a great deal of time on-line should be given personal accounts they can use to gather information without indicating that they are from your organization. Employees who are apparently wasting time should, of course, be told to stop.

If your organization does not have the time or the resources to perform its own Internet monitoring, then services are available to do this, including the NCSA IS/Recon service (1-800-488-4595).

Monitoring Technical Vulnerabilities

Although many people find this hard to believe, technical vulnerabilities are best combated with operations procedures. Hackers and other criminals attack your computer systems by exploiting known vulnerabilities and poor configurations. New vulnerabilities appear with annoying regularity about all types of computer systems. As some holes are plugged, new holes appear. Barriers are erected; routes around them are plotted. It's the nature of the beast.

Known technical vulnerabilities allow attackers to steal billions of dollars' worth of information annually from banks and other organizations around the world. Fortunately, almost anything you know about, you can fix. Updating for known vulnerabilities and poor system configurations would have prevented or minimized the penetrations described in Chapters 7, 12, and 13. Ferreting out these weaknesses could prevent at least 98 percent of all computer hacking–related crimes.

The only effective way to cope with the ebb and flow of system vulnerabilities is to establish regular monitoring procedures for weak spots and the fixes for them. The mailing lists of legitimate security organizations, such as CERT, the Department of Energy's Computer Incident Advisory Capability (CIAC), and Purdue University's COAST laboratory, can provide invaluable resources in your search efforts. These resources list the most recently uncovered vulnerabilities and the latest fixes. Unfortunately, fixes are typically published only after they have proven themselves, which means the vulnerabilities may be known for months before the CERT and CIAC issue an advisory.

Fortunately, advanced Internet advisories are also available. Perhaps the best of these is the Best-of-Security mailing list, a "moderated" list for which the moderator actively solicits information on vulnerabilities from list subscribers. The messages usually include information on the vulnerability and crude fixes for the problems. Although there is no guarantee that the fixes work, in almost all cases they do prevent people from exploiting the problems. The IS/Recon service summarizes all of this information on a biweekly basis.

At a minimum, you should read these advisories and take the corrective actions as quickly as possible on all of the vulnerable computer systems in your organization. Keep in mind that you are protecting yourself against not only outside hackers but especially malicious insiders.

Maintaining Contact with ANSIR

If your organization is in a high-technology industry, you should establish an ongoing relationship with your local FBI ANSIR (Awareness of National Security Issues and Response) office. For that matter, any corporate security manager should maintain a relationship with the local ANSIR office. ANSIR has a wide range of information available about the types of threats your organization faces. With the advent of new presidential initiatives, ANSIR may become more proactive in its warning of organizations about ongoing penetration activities. Maintaining close ties with this group could provide quicker and more efficient responses should you discover an attack against your organization.

Traveling Separately

In 1983, an Air Florida jet crashed into the Potomac River; on that flight were several of the top executives of Fairchild Industries. The company was strategically devastated. After that tragic accident, many organizations established policies that prohibited senior company officials from traveling together. It's a good policy. Look what happened in 1996, when the plane carrying Secretary of Commerce Ron Brown crashed in Bosnia. Not only was Secretary Brown killed, but so were about a dozen CEOs of major U.S. companies. Notice that the President and Vice President of the U.S. never travel on the same planes.

A separate travel policy may create an additional expense and some inconvenience, but it serves to minimize critical personnel losses when disaster strikes. You might also want to consider encouraging executives to take separate cars, especially when you consider that automobile travel is many times more dangerous statistically than is air travel.

Separate Telephone Numbers

Telephone records can divulge a tremendous amount of information about an organization and its operations. For this reason, I recommend that companies install at least a few separate telephone lines outside the existing company telephone exchanges. These numbers should be reserved for sensitive business, and their use should be limited. Adversaries know your typical telephone exchanges, and they will search their records. Special numbers that are not typically allocated to your organization are much harder for adversaries to find. This minimizes the likelihood that they will see your telephone patterns and pick up on highly sensitive conversations and projects.

Limiting Telephone Conversation Topics

No matter what telephone lines you and your people use, you should try to limit the sensitivity of the topics discussed over the phone. Phones are relatively easy to bug and could provide a lot of information to eavesdroppers.

If you are traveling overseas, especially in hotels, assume that your top competitor is listening to your phone conversations. It's probably true! Choose your words wisely, because multimillion-dollar business deals have and will be compromised. The National Counterintelligence Center has reported that a multimillion-dollar deal was compromised because the

French government tapped a hotel telephone call and used the information against the target. The threat is very real, and you must act accordingly.

Minimizing the Use of Cellular and Portable Telephones

If a regular telephone is a vulnerable medium of communication, cell phones and cordless phones are an open line to your competitors. Everything you say on a cellular or cordless telephone can be heard by anyone with the right equipment. If you must use one of these types of telephones, never talk about sensitive issues. If you must talk about sensitive issues, try to use code words, or better yet, hang up these types of phones and go to a pay phone.

Limiting Conversations Away from Work

It's natural for people to discuss their work outside the office. Work dominates our lives, takes up most of our time, and, if we're lucky, engages us in satisfying ways we want to share with others. If you're getting together with coworkers, the tendency is even stronger.

However, for security's sake, people should avoid discussing work-related topics away from the office. Companies should help their employees to understand the potential dam age they can do with these kinds of conversations. They should establish strict policies and work to gain their employees' cooperation by explaining why they are in place. Even spouses should be reminded that what they hear can be very sensitive, and they should avoid repeating casual comments about their spouse's work. United Parcel Service requires the spouses of its employees to sign confidentiality agreements. In some companies, you find signs posted in the elevators reminding people not to discuss work outside the facilities.

Changing Patterns When Conducting Sensitive Business

One of the biggest operations vulnerabilities is predictability. When potential attackers know the patterns of your life, they can exploit them. If you regularly call your customers at a specific time, the bad guys will know when to tap your telephone. If you leave your office at the same time every day, the spies will know when to begin following you. If you eat breakfast at the same pancake house every morning, the spooks can be in the next booth, listening.

I worked with one client whose competitors simply hired private investigators to follow their salespeople around, compiling a list of sales calls. The next day, the competing company sent out its own sales people to call on the very same people. I have a feeling that this case is not unique.

If you are at some risk, it is important to vary your patterns deliberately. Take a different route to work on Wednesdays. Make your calls in the morning this week instead of the afternoon. Zig one day, zag the next.

Also, consider your paper trail. Companies might want to issue multiple corporate credit cards and advise their people to use them only for sensitive projects. Never put down your frequent flyer number when you are traveling on a sensitive trip. When possible, use cash. Competitors and foreign intelligence agencies have compromised many computer records in an effort to put together profiles of the activities of targeted organizations. Many companies hire private investigators to do this. Seems a little like we've entered the world of James Bond here, but when the stakes are high and the vulnerabilities are many, these are reasonable precautions that can help enormously to minimize certain exposures.

Security Working with Other Departments

For some reason, security people tend to work as lone wolves. They tend not to involve other departments, and they sometimes let problems continue while they're conducting their investigations. This tendency allows problems to get worse, giving attackers more time to perpetrate even more critical compromises, as was the case with Bill Gaede in Chapter 8.

When security people work with others in an organization— especially managers, human resources personnel, and the information systems (IS) departments—they simply do a better job of circumventing problems. They have an opportunity to study the extent of the problems more thoroughly while minimizing potential losses. Others can bring additional skills to an investigation, allowing for earlier detection of other problems. To address their privacy concerns, extremely safety-conscious security people can require those assisting their investigations to sign confidentiality statements, in which they promise not to disclose anything they learn to others.

Disaster Recovery and Incident Handling Procedures

The only guarantee a security department can give to management is that there will be problems. Even the most comprehensive countermeasures cannot eliminate risk and losses altogether. Therefore, your organization must establish disaster recovery and incident handling procedures.

Disaster recovery procedures are emergency plans that help overcome service outages. These outages can be caused by hackers but are usually the result of equipment failures, natural disasters, programming errors, and power crashes. You should consider the different types of system outages and decide on strategies for recovery from each of them. For example, you could hire a company with a computer system that resembles yours so that you could switch over to its facilities in the event of a major equipment problem; this way, you may suffer a temporary outage, but the other company lets you use its computers to get you back up and running.

Incidents are security breaches that do not necessarily cause outages but nevertheless represent a danger to the organization. These could include hacker incidents, computer viruses, thefts of computers, and information thefts, among other things. Your organization should categorize the different types of incidents and decide exactly how you want to respond to each of them. You should consult with your company's general counsel on your prosecution policies and also to determine whether the security department may sometimes let the problems continue as a means of catching the attackers. You must assess the potential liability from such action. You'll also want to consult with your PR department on how to deal with the press should the news get out that you have a problem.

One of the most critical decisions organizations have to make is whether to let the incident continue. Although some people contend that you must intervene immediately, there are several factors to consider. If you close up the holes, the attackers will know that you have spotted them and close up shop. You've stopped their information collection activities, but you've also impeded the collection of evidence against them. You may never learn their identity or the extent of the breach. Letting the incident continue allows for the compromise of more information or additional thefts, but it also allows you to track down the attackers and see how far they are entrenched in your organization (they might have installed a few back doors into your organization).

Organizations should also acquire the resources necessary to fully investigate potential incidents and correct them. This involves an investment in hardware, software, and personnel. It can also involve contracting with consulting firms that offer an emergency response service.

The most critical success factor in dealing with incidents is preparation. Part of that preparation should include testing your security procedures to see if they actually work. You should hold "fire drills" to simulate all types of problems, including disasters. The time to find weak spots in your security is before, not after, an actual incident.

Perform Periodic Vulnerability Assessments with Penetration Testing

Despite your best efforts, some vulnerabilities are bound to go unnoticed. It's almost inevitable. However, you need to discover *all* of your weaknesses to accurately assess your risk and to know which countermeasures to put into place and where to put them. Even a small nick in your armor can be exploited by wily attackers, and any attackers worth their salt will try to get at you from more than one angle. The key is to find all of your vulnerabilities before the attackers do.

That's why many organizations perform penetration tests, similar to those conducted in Chapters 6, 7, and 12. During a penetration test, a trusted team of espionage or technical experts simulates an attack for the purposes of exposing weak spots. The results of such a test tell you not only where you need to spend the greatest effort bolstering your security but where to place detection mechanisms as well.

Deciding who should perform a penetration test can be a tricky matter. Many people within an organization like the idea of performing a penetration test because it sounds like it might be fun, but poorly trained testers can leave behind more holes than were there before they started. Many amateurs just don't know how to clean up after themselves, and they can ruffle a lot of feathers in the process. A good penetration test doesn't point fingers or take down individual names, but it does provide a summary finding that companies can use to accurately assess their risk and prioritize countermeasures. A good tester can also spot-check specific countermeasures and evaluate their efficacy. Companies are well advised to consider hiring outside consultants to perform this kind of work. A qualified outsider is less likely to have political agendas than people with stakes in the organization.

With accurate penetration test results, you can tailor your security program to the specific needs of your organization.

PERSONNEL COUNTERMEASURES

Personnel countermeasures address vulnerabilities in the many ways that companies hire, maintain, and terminate employees. Most of these countermeasures involve the human resources (HR) department. HR is the company gatekeeper, so to speak, responsible for hiring competent and trustworthy people. That department is also responsible for your workers at the time of their termination. HR is there at the beginning and the end, and that's where most of these countermeasures are most frequently implemented. (Once a person enters the workplace, the local manager becomes the responsible party, and operations countermeasures are more applicable.)

Some of these countermeasures should be implemented with or by the security department. There is a great deal of crossover between responsibilities here, and both security and HR should work together for the betterment of the entire organization.

Background Checks

Perhaps the most effective task HR can do to increase security is require background checks of employees. In many market sectors, this is a common requirement. Background checks should include a criminal records check, verification of previous employment, and validation of educational claims. Recent surveys indicate that over 80 percent of employment candidates lie about their backgrounds on job applications. In most cases, the lies are inconsequential, but some people, who are not qualified for the jobs they apply for, talk their way through interviews and into positions of responsibility. Other studies show that concerns about background checks deter many people from lying on their applications.

Depending on the types of positions applied for, companies might also want to conduct psychological testing on prospective employees. This kind of screening procedure is usually reserved for very sensitive positions and senior managers. Some companies hire an organizational psychologist to assess the suitability of certain candidates for key positions.

Most companies cite the cost of background checks as a reason for not performing them. A basic background check costs between $30 and $50. The total cost of hiring a new employee almost always exceeds $3,000. In some cases, the cost of a new hire is above $10,000. When the cost of the background check is compared with total hiring costs, it is inconsequential. For more senior employees and people in sensitive positions, you might want to consider more extensive background checks. These are more costly, but they're worth the expense since the stakes are high.

Background checks do not guarantee that employees will never commit illegal acts against your organization, but they do weed out many undesirables. One company that recently started performing background checks found that the organization was rejecting 5 to 10 percent of applicants based on the checks; upper management believes its new policy will save the company a tremendous amount in future legal and regulatory problems. If the company I penetrated in Chapter 7 had done a background check on me, it would not have lost billions of dollars (luckily, it was only a test). If either AMD or Intel had checked up on Mr. Gaede (Chapter 8), it could have bounced him before he did any damage at all.

Checks on Spouses

Although most organizations don't extend their background checks beyond the employment candidate, some companies do perform background checks on immediate family members as well. Spouses in particular have come under the scrutiny of some HR departments.

Usually the extent of this background check depends on the position for which the candidate is applying. Besides a standard background check, you could ask spouses to sign nondisclosure agreements.

If the resources are available, this deeper level of inquiry can sometimes yield important information. Simply because a husband or wife happens to work for your competitor doesn't mean he or she will necessarily use his/her insider connection to gather information, but such a connection must be considered a vulnerability. Spouses have been know to influence their better halves to commit industrial espionage, as Gaede did.

Employee Hotline

The human resources department should establish a hotline that allows people to report problems that are not specifically security-related. A hotline could allow workers to point out disgruntled coworkers or to request assistance with personal problems. The idea is to facilitate the exchange of information outside the security loop. People are sometimes hesitant to go to security because of the stigma attached to it, but they might call up someone in HR.

Maintaining Contact with Information Systems Departments

One of the most pervasive problems among companies and organizations that utilize computer systems is that people who leave the company often have accounts on the system long after their termination. In Chapter 7, I exploited the accounts of several people who had left the company. In other cases, former employees access the computer network remotely and steal information.

The root of this problem lies in a lack of communication between the human resources people and the technical departments. HR should contact IS *before* anyone is fired. It should deliver as much advanced warning as possible when it knows people are scheduled to leave the organization. The quicker, the better. This gives IS a chance to remove accounts the day the person leaves the building.

IS should also be contacted when there is trouble with employees. It should know which accounts might need special attention. That way, it can increase auditing of the specific accounts and watch for suspicious activities. The IS department people can't do it if they don't know about it. This countermeasure hinges on HR's willingness to take a minor extra step.

Maintaining Contact with the Security Department

Information systems is not the only department that needs to know when personnel actions occur. HR should also inform the security department whenever someone leaves the company. Security should always monitor employees when they are about to leave an organization. The department will want to be prepared to remove an employee's physical accesses the minute he or she leaves the company.

One of the problems with former employees is that the security guards are familiar with their faces. In large organizations, former employees often find that they can walk right through the gate. After an employee has departed the company for good, security can distribute photographs to the guards, which will let the guards know which one of those familiar faces should no longer be welcomed.

The exchange of information between the HR and security departments should be a two-way street. When security people discover an employee problem, they should contact someone in HR. Security should resist the urge to act in a vacuum, which only hinders investigations and exacerbates problems.

Tracking Information Accesses

Often, after an employee has left a company, no one knows for certain which information that person had access to. Someone inside the organization should know, definitely, which facilities and projects are available to which people. This knowledge allows for damage assessment and control when people are involved in security incidents or when they leave the company. With a formal access policy in place for sensitive information (as I recommended previously), tracking information access should be a simple matter. Such a policy would have prevented my success in the NCC penetration test (Chapter 7).

Reviewing Visitors

While you're scrutinizing your employees, don't forget to take a long look at your visitors. Anyone who comes into your company is a potential threat. Their physical presence gives them a certain amount of access, which real pros can often exploit and turn into greater access.

Start by letting security know about the visit. The earlier the better. This countermeasure won't work without them. Security will probably want to make a few phone calls to verify the reasons for the visit and the identities of the visitors. As the security manager did in Chapter 11, you can call the FBI ANSIR office to see if anything is amiss. In his case, he learned some very valuable things about his Japanese visitors.

Once your visitors are on-site, limit what they see. Even if the visitors are customers you are trying to impress, be careful where you take them and what you reveal. There's usually no need to go overboard.

If the visitor is going to have access to extremely sensitive information, you should perform a public records background check. Also, many firms have the capability to perform overseas background checks when dealing with foreign visitors.

Categorize Employees

Employees within any given organization fall into three basic categories: regular employees, contractors, and temps. All three categories should not enjoy the same access to information in your company. Although you must place full trust in your regular employees, there's no reason to trust the others at quite the same level. Temporary and contract employees don't have the same investment in your company as regular employees. That doesn't mean they are necessarily more criminally inclined, but spies are much more likely to assume the guise of a contractor or a temp because they go through less scrutiny.

Contract employees are usually specialists hired for specific projects, which eventually come to an end. They will need greater access than a temp because they have greater responsibilities, but they should never be allowed too deeply into the inner sanctum.

Temporary employees should never be placed in positions of trust unless they have a long-standing relationship with the company and are well known to their managers. When I penetrated NCC (Chapter 7), I gained my initial access as a temp. As you'll recall, my ruse yielded fantastic results.

Differentiate the different categories of your workers in all forms of company identification. Access badges for temps and contractors should be strikingly different in appearance from regular access badges. Make them a different color, or write TEMP or CONTRACTOR on them in big, bold letters. The idea is to allow for the immediate determination of that employee's status.

Companies that use caller ID should enter an employee's name and status into the system from the first day of employment. In Chapter 7, if my name had been indicated as "TEMP-Name" on the internal caller ID system, the people receiving my calls would have known instantly that I was not actually the supervisor for information security as I claimed.

These kinds of differentiation techniques are even more important in large organizations, where all of the employees don't know each other on sight. These relatively simple steps can remove some of the most commonly exploited organizational vulnerabilities.

Imposing Your Requirements on Contracted Services

Companies often hire other firms to provide security guard and janitorial services. These people, whom you have neither screened nor interviewed, have nearly full access to your facilities at times when everyone else is gone from the premises. Some companies outsource some or all of their secretarial and technical staffs, putting relative strangers into critical positions.

All the personnel countermeasures I have described in this section are utterly useless if you open your doors to companies with lower hiring standards than your own. You must contractually specify that any companies from whom you hire on-site services use the same personnel screening measures that you employ. The *very* same. Anything less, and you might as well scrap your own program.

These contracted service positions constitute a major vulnerability. Recall the article published in *2600: The Hacker's Quarterly* describing how to get a job as a janitor (Chapter 4). The target mentioned in the article was a very large company and would probably not have hired the person as a regular employee.

If hackers know how to use this vulnerability to avoid your security measures, you can bet that more profit-motivated individuals know it, too. Don't allow careless contract service providers to become security back doors into your organization.

Coordinating Terminations

When employees leave an organization, whether under good circumstances or bad, other people within that organization need to know about it. Unfortunately, many companies have no clear lines of communication for this critical bit of information. The job is often left to harried managers with no clue of whom to inform. In very large organizations, this is a job that often simply goes undone.

To correct this situation, human resources should take on the responsibility of coordinating the termination process. HR can develop a contact sheet for each terminated employee and inform all relevant parties. The list should include security officers, PSOs, systems administrators, and project teams within your organization with whom the employee had a relationship. Everyone should know about that person's change in status.

If many people leave your organization on a regular basis, then you may want to publish a periodic summary report. Although many people receiving the reports may not be affected, it is much better to alert more people than necessary on this matter.

PHYSICAL COUNTERMEASURES

All the cases cited in Part II that involved on-site thefts of information were successful primarily because of poor use of physical countermeasures. Physical countermeasures deal with the security of information that exists in a physical form—such as documents, computer disks, or product prototypes—and with facility security. Usually, these two categories are tightly coupled.

Physical countermeasures may seem like the most obvious steps people could take to secure company data, but in my experience, they are the most frequently overlooked. I suppose these strategies seem too simple and too obvious to be very important, but the fact is, time and time again, attackers exploit lapses in physical security to make off with priceless information. Perhaps most surprising to many is that most of these countermeasures are already available.

Lock Up All Controlled Information

Sensitive information must be protected. Although operational procedures control its distribution, the disks, files, and documents on which it is stored must be physically protected from theft or compromise. To that end, your organization must require your people to lock up their papers and other material while they are unattended.

This seems so obvious, so simple, but without a clear message from management, people just won't do it. In Chapters 7, 8, and 10, most of the compromises of information involved collecting physically unprotected data. Exploitation of this vulnerability is part and parcel of almost all cases of industrial espionage.

Use Available Locks

In the cases cited in Chapters 7, 8, 9, and 10, the thieves came upon many locks that could have thwarted their activities, but the locks were simply not used. Almost all desks, doors, and file cabinets have locks. They provide readily available, cost-free physical security for information of all types. If people would actually use them, many incidents of espionage would be significantly reduced in scope. Although a very determined attacker might try to pick a lock or track down the keys, locks prevent a significant amount of casual theft and force an attacker to take more easily detectable steps.

If there are places that need locks within your facility, get them installed, and see that they are used. It's a small inconvenience that could save you a bundle.

Using Password-Protected Screen Savers

Another counterespionage tool that is readily available to nearly everyone is the screen saver. These computer utilities were originally developed to prevent burn-in problems with computer screens left on the same page for too long (after a certain number of minutes of inactivity, the screen saver comes on, sending patterns across the screen, which stops the burn-in). Many people don't realize that these programs almost always include a *password protection* feature. When this feature is activated, users must enter a password to "unlock" the screen saver image and gain access to their computers. This means that when people leave their desks for any significant period of time, their computers are automatically locked, preventing others from taking advantage of their absence. Chapter 7 provides an excellent example of what can happen when this feature is not utilized.

People should remember that they usually leave their mail logged in all day. This means that anyone who goes by their desk could read their mail and everything else they are working on. Password-protected screen savers are standard on most major PC operating systems, including all Microsoft Windows operating systems available over the last five years.

Clean Desk Policies

Whenever I'm performing a penetration test, I get very excited at the sight of a messy desk. It's an unvarying sign that sensitive information will be all over the office.

Corporate-wide clean desk policies can help to discourage people from allowing their desks to become too messy to be safe. This is an absolutely essential, no-cost countermeasure that every company should implement. It might even help your business be more efficient. It would certainly have hindered my penetration efforts at NCC (Chapter 7) and Gaede's thefts at AMD and Intel (Chapter 8), and it would have helped to prevent a certain amount of information from being compromised in the case of the Japanese film crew (Chapter 11).

In-Box Security

While your employees are cleaning up their desks, don't let them forget about their in-boxes. They're often the weak links in your physical security chain. People will leave extremely sensitive documents in open in-boxes without a second thought.

Short of banning this practice, you can reduce your exposure a bit by insisting that people seal sensitive documents in envelopes before leaving them in in-boxes. The envelopes should have plain, standard covers with no attention-getting labels, colors, or graphics. If you're going to print "Top Secret" on the envelope in bold magenta letters, you might as well leave the documents out for all to see.

Conduct Facility Walk-Throughs

To ensure that the above countermeasures are being implemented, managers should take on the responsibility of checking the desks and areas of their employees. They should walk around periodically and try the locks and see whether anyone

is leaving sensitive information out in the open. They should make sure that keys are not readily available to anyone who walks by the desk, file cabinet, or office door (sometimes keys are left in drawers or in small containers on the desk). Managers should also make sure that passwords are not written on scraps of paper taped to monitors or under keyboards. During a recent vulnerability assessment, I found a cipher lock combination written on the side of a picture frame near the locked door. The walk-through should focus on what a hostile adversary could get if he or she were to walk through the facility.

People on corporate security staffs should also check for messy desks and unused locks. If managers or security people find isolated cases of this, they should lock up the materials and request that the offender be more careful in the future; if it happens repeatedly, then more drastic actions should be taken. If this is a company-wide problem, then managers should be required to do regular walk-throughs until the problem is cleared up.

Watch for Strange Postings

Creative attackers have posted misleading bulletins throughout targeted organizations. Recall the incident described in Chapter 5, in which a hacker infiltrated a company and posted a fake announcement of a new help desk telephone number— the attacker's own telephone number was listed as the new help desk line. Although this was a rare attack, corporate security personnel should periodically check bulletin boards, just in case.

Locking Cables

Almost all companies experience the theft of computers from time to time. For the most part, the thieves are stupid burglars only after the hardware. However, you can still lose access to the information on the stolen machine.

Many companies sell cables and other mechanisms that lock a computer to a desk. These devices are far from perfect, but they do make the theft of equipment much more difficult.

Place Controls on Copy Machines

As the case cited in Chapter 8 illustrates, a copy machine is a spy's best friend. It allows thieves to tromp through your resources, make off with vital information without actually stealing it, and leave nary a footprint. Bill Gaede told me that he could never have stolen as much information as he did if the copy machines had been monitored in any way.

The monitoring can be done in several ways. Gaede himself recommended that companies put video cameras near the machines. This would certainly work, but it might seem intrusive to some people, and it might be expensive.

Another countermeasure that is both cheaper and more readily available utilizes an existing feature of most modern commercial copy machines: the accounting feature. Employees using machines equipped with this feature must enter authorization numbers before they can make any copies. The machines then record the number of copies that the employee makes. Organizations using this countermeasure typically review the copy logs on a monthly basis for the purposes of charging the copy costs back to specific projects or departments. The procedure also provides a ready means for detecting an employee making excessive copies.

Even if the thief uses another person's authorization code, someone is eventually going to notice that an unusual number of copies are being made, prompting an investigation. Even if the procedure doesn't prevent all illegal copying, it will be a probable deterrent and definitely helps in detecting thefts.

Library Control

Most large companies maintain some kind of in-house library facilities—places where sensitive information is stored. These

company libraries provide one-stop shopping for astute spies. Bill Gaede was able to abuse libraries virtually at will at two organizations unlucky enough to employ him.

To prevent the abuse of company libraries by on-site attackers, organizations should restrict access and lock the doors. When the library is opened, a librarian should be on duty at all times. People wanting access to information should be required to sign and date a log and list the specific documents they borrow. Library logs discourage people from abusing these rooms and taking out documents for nefarious purposes. The logs create tracks, which investigators can follow.

Security Reminders

The Department of Defense posts reminders on every telephone in every office—right on the telephones themselves—reminding its people that their conversations can be monitored by outside entities. In commercial organizations, you can also remind people that competitors can monitor your telephones. Some companies use awareness posters in the break rooms. Other companies remind people not to talk business outside the company in newsletters, articles, or e-mail bulletins.

Whichever method you use, the countermeasure is a simple but effective one: remind your people constantly to pay attention to security issues. They need to know about information value, the threat, the vulnerabilities, and the countermeasures, and they need to be told over and over again.

Make Shredders Widely Available

Almost all documents produced by your organization, even the most seemingly innocuous notes and memos, could contain something sensitive or something that an attacker could use against you. Allowing your people to dispose of papers by simply tossing them in the trash is a very dangerous policy.

The solution here is relatively simple: make shredders widely available throughout your organization's facilities. Ideally, there should be one beside every desk or for every person or group of three, but you can get away with providing one for every work group; at a very bare minimum, you should have one next to every copy machine in your company. Remember: the further away the machine is from the individual, the less likely it will be used.

Many shredders cost less than $30 and may be significantly cheaper when purchased in bulk. The cheapest ones shred the paper into ribbons, which may be pieced back together, although this is extremely difficult. For slightly more money you can buy a cross-cutting type of shredder, which cuts paper into ribbons and then cuts the ribbons into smaller pieces, which are nearly impossible to piece back together. If a shredder is centrally located, it should be a high-capacity machine.

Some companies hire an outside service to shred their documents. The company provides bins in which people are to place their sensitive materials. The service then collects the materials and brings them to a central facility for shredding. The efficacy of this type of service depends on how liberally the collection bins are distributed in your organization. It's also a good idea to send someone out to follow the shredder's trucks once in awhile, to make sure they are properly disposing of the papers.

I've noticed that people naturally tend to put their papers in the company recycle bins, which are not secure in any way. It's up to you to let your employees know that they should use the shredders.

Lock Dumpsters

No matter how widely shredders are distributed, people will place sensitive materials in the regular trash. Although you can minimize this problem, it is still cause for concern. "Dumpster diving" is a tried-and-true corporate espionage technique. As I mention in Chapter 5, the Masters of Deception hacker group used this technique to secure superuser passwords to the national telephone system—which shows how much damage can result from a little diligent trash shifting. To counter this vulnerability, simply put a good lock on your dumpsters.

Perimeter Locks

Unattended, unmonitored, and unlocked doors provide opportunities for thieves to sneak out equipment and to let accomplices into the buildings. All entrances to your facilities should be locked or manned. When doors must be unattended, they should not only be locked but also wired with alarms that sound whenever they're opened. If it is not practical in your organization to guard all entrances, then consider monitoring them with closed-circuit cameras. Also, don't neglect the gates to storage yards.

Log Unusual Accesses and Removal of Equipment

These days, very few of us can get away with working a forty-hour week. Consequently, it's not unusual to find honest, hardworking employees staying late at the office and taking work home. Unfortunately, this behavior is also a warning sign of potential espionage activity.

As we saw in Chapters 7, 9, and 10, attackers will enter your facilities late at night when their actions may go unnoticed. To counter this vulnerability, require your people to sign in and out of your buildings after normal work hours. The hard workers won't mind, and the spies will leave tracks.

When you do notice that an employee is putting in frequent late hours, don't hesitate to investigate. In the case study in Chapter 10, the woman was caught stealing the information because her employers checked up on her. Bill Gaede told me that he made it a point to leave the buildings by six o'clock every evening so that he would not have to sign out and leave evidence that he was there.

You should also require your people to sign for equipment they carry out of the building, even during the day. Loading dock areas should be closely monitored, because people can drive right up to the door and drive away with truckloads of equipment.

Using logs is an excellent deterrent, but bold thieves may simply sign a different name and number. Your guards should verify the identity of every person signing the log.

Access Badges

Most companies with security interests use access badges. Unfortunately, many fail to use them correctly. An access badge should indicate employee status—regular, contract, or temporary—as well as to which facilities the person has access. Most important, the badges should be worn at all times. During my penetration of NCC, I simply hid my temp badge and told people what I wanted them to believe. No one challenged me, and many people gave me very sensitive information. Organizations should encourage employees not only to wear their badges but also to challenge others who don't.

Card Access Locks

One of the most effective physical countermeasures available today is the electronic door lock. Electronic locks are opened with access cards fitted with magnetic strips. The card readers in the locks identify the card holder and record the date and time he or she entered the building. The access cards can be programmed for specific entrances at specific facilities at specific times, effectively restricting access. Perhaps the most valuable feature of this technology is that the cards can be deactivated. This means that terminated or suspect employees can be denied access to particular facilities instantly. The card readers also record attempts at access with deactivated cards, leaving records of the number of times a person has tried to enter restricted buildings during restricted time periods. Companies can use these records to identify employees who try to get into restricted areas.

Properly Trained Guards

Most modern companies of any size employ security guards, and they can serve as very important deterrents to illegal activities on-premises. In my experience, however, the guards in most organizations rarely do the job they should. It's not usually their fault; often they're poorly trained, either by the contract service provider or the company itself. Either way, it's up to you to make sure your guards are providing the physical countermeasures your company needs.

Guards should look closely at access badges. They should also search unusual packages and bags. They should patrol facilities, looking for things that are out of place. They should notice people in the buildings at odd hours, and they should question them and ascertain whether they are in the "right" areas. They should keep track of unusual incidents, late-night visitors, and odd details in logs. (The purpose of the log is not to compile data on people but to make it possible to see patterns of behavior.)

Most important, guards should be trained to know which items are of value. The guards at AMD were told to watch for blue binders, which indicated that the materials were of a sensitive nature. But when Bill Gaede absconded with sensitive AMD documents, he just put them in a different binder. To the guards, if the material was not in a blue binder, it was not important. Your guards must be trained to recognize the things they should really be looking for.

Security Patrols

Companies should also have their guards patrol outside their facilities to search for unusual cars and especially vans. Besides safety concerns for employees, the vans can be loaded with TEMPEST receivers, which can pick up the data on a variety of electrical devices, and/or receivers that pick up the signals from bugs planted inside of your facilities. Security patrols might also pick up investigators that are trailing your salespeople.

Choose Locations Wisely

Security must be involved with the choice of corporate locations. Along with considerations of space and comfort, you must think about such factors as the location of your competitors and the physical aspects of the area. You don't want to set up shop in a place that allows your competition easy access. Neither do you want to put your headquarters on a flood plane or an earthquake fault line. You will want to locate in an area with a reliable power supply and a low crime rate. All of these considerations should be second nature to your security department. Use their safety-consciousness to avoid built-in problems.

Watch Where You Conduct Business Outside Your Facilities

When you are conducting business outside your facilities, you must consider the vulnerabilities around you. Expect that people will overhear your conversations. Count on the person next to you on the airplane to look at your notes and computer screen while you are working. Be aware of your surroundings and the likelihood that all of your actions can be seen by others. Basically, you have no privacy outside your facilities, and you must act accordingly.

Fire Suppression

Fire protection is very important around computers, but the most common fire suppression systems tend to destroy the data copmuters contain. Companies usually rely on standard sprinkler systems to suppress fires. In an office environment, sprinklers are probably the best solution. However, in computer rooms, they can be disastrous.

Computer rooms should be equipped with gas fire suppression systems. These systems use inert gases to smother fires. These gases also smother people, so they are only used in certain situations, but they are very effective. I strongly recommend considering this type of system for your computer rooms.

If you've chosen, as so many companies have, to locate your computer facilities in the basement, your equipment might be even more vulnerable to the damage of a sprinkler system. If there is a fire in any of the upper floors, the sprinkler systems will activate, flooding the area with hundreds of gallons of water. The problem is, all that water will eventually seep down into the basement and your computer room. This could lead to millions of dollars in losses. Therefore, you might want to consider moving your computer facilities to an upper floor.

Uninterruptible Power Supplies

Uninterruptible power supplies (UPS) provide backup power when your primary power source goes off-line. The sudden loss of power can damage computers and result in a loss of service and vital data. Depending on the industry, this loss can cost billions of dollars.

Computers and peripherals plug into the UPS, which is plugged into an electrical outlet. Some UPSs also connect to computers through computer cable ports and instruct the computer to shut down gracefully when there is a power outage, saving all your work in the process. Other systems simply keep things going for varying lengths of time to allow you to save your data and shut down your machine. Depending on the type of UPS, they can keep your computers running for hours.

UPSs also act as surge protectors. The strength of electrical currents vary as they travel through power lines. Occasionally, there are power spikes that can literally fry your computer. These spikes naturally occur and can be amplified by lightning strikes. To prevent these power spikes from ruining your machines when you don't use UPSs, you can use power strips that have surge protection capability.

Modem Surge Protectors

Telephone lines are also subject to power spikes that can ruin sophisticated telephone systems and modem boards. Fortunately, some surge protectors now include telephone jacks, which prevent power spikes from reaching your telephone equipment. Since these telephone spikes have also caused deaths, these surge protectors can save lives as well.

TECHNICAL COUNTERMEASURES

Technical attacks account for tens of billions of dollars in corporate losses annually. Although an operational process for updating systems for known vulnerabilities can repel many attacks, there are still additional technical steps that must be taken to repel both technical and nontechnical attacks. As a matter of fact, a strong technical security foundation not only repels attacks, it is the best detection mechanism. Technical countermeasures, when properly implemented, can more than pay for themselves, and they provide the final and most difficult hurdle for an attacker to overcome.

I have not discussed every possible technical countermeasure in this section. You can find several books on this subject; also, technology by its very nature is ever changing. I have included the most commonly available and readily applicable countermeasures, all of which will serve you well. It's a good idea to continue your study of technical counter-measures with other books and possibly a consultant.

Anti-Virus Software

In a recent survey conducted by the National Computer Security Association, 98 percent of all organizations reported being victims of computer viruses during 1995 alone. Although the average loss in the survey was approximately $8,000, many companies reported losses in excess of $100,000. I don't believe any large company can honestly claim never to have suffered a significant loss from a virus.

Anti-virus (AV) software is widely available, and site licenses are easily acquired. All organizational PCs should have AV software loaded on them. When possible, they should be configured to run in your systems' background, automatically seeking out viruses whenever a disk is loaded into the system or when a file is downloaded from the Internet. AV software can prevent viruses from spreading into an organization. Once you acquire the AV software, you should require your technical departments to update the application approximately once a month. Vendors update their software whenever a new virus is discovered, but it is incumbent upon you to get the new version. You should also verify that your software is certified by the National Computer Security Association (NCSA) to ensure that it does what it claims.

Backups

The most important thing any individual or organization can do to protect computerized information is to back it up. Computer backups won't prevent breaches, but they will make it possible to recover from almost any damage inflicted by an

attacker or unintentional disaster. With no backups, you have few
if any recovery options, and you could suffer even a total loss.

Backups can be automated so that no manual intervention
is required. You can buy tools that assist with the backups, or
you can create backup tools for yourself. Ideally, every system
should be incrementally backed up once a day—at the very
least, once a week. Incremental backups save only the files that
were changed since the last backup. Full backups should be
performed weekly.

On a regular basis, organizations should make extra copies
of their backups that can be used as evidence if criminal incidents arise. When you do detect problems, you have the old
backups on hand to study to determine how far back the
problem goes.

This really is an essential countermeasure. No matter what
problems you have with budgets or staffing, you must assign
people to perform regular backups.

Firewalls

Although I contend that organizations put too much faith in
firewalls, they are critical for preventing a wide variety of
problems that originate from the Internet. Firewalls are devices that secure one network segment from another; the
device can be either a single-purpose computer or a computer
with application software loaded. Good firewalls can prevent
many attacks from outside an organization, as long as they
are properly configured. Before choosing a firewall, you must
determine your specific needs. You should also make certain
that any firewall you install is NCSA-certified. This ensures
that it is a versatile, secure, and established product.

Organizations should also consider acquiring firewalls for
internal use. There are many parts of your internal networks
that do not need to be generally accessible. The HR department and research departments almost always will not be
accessed from outside those departments. Internal firewalls

can prevent a variety of technical attacks that originate inside of your organization. Although they will not prevent all types of attacks, they could aid in detection of attacks and will give your organization a warning that they should look for other attacks.

Vulnerability Scanners

Hackers seek out vulnerable systems. There is no reason why you shouldn't do the same. Hackers have no special skills or talents that lets them find the holes in your system; they have vulnerability scanning tools to do the work for them. SATAN (a vulnerability scanning tool developed by Dan Farmer for Systems Administrators) made the headlines when it was first released, because it supposedly made hacking easy. While it did make vulnerability scanning more user-friendly, hackers already had such capabilities. The tool was designed primarily for administrators who did not know how to perform scans for themselves. The need is there.

Besides SATAN, other commercial vulnerability scanners are available that are well supported by their vendors. These scanners allow administrators and security personnel to find the vulnerabilities before the hackers do. This way, they can fix the holes before the holes can be exploited. An example of a vulnerability scanner is the Internet Security Scanner (ISS), used to compromise NCC in Chapter 7. If the administrators in that case had used it on their own systems, I would never have gotten control of them. Ironically, the SATAN controversy was based on the fear that hackers would have the run of the Internet with such a tool. Since everyone should have heard about SATAN, however, they should have run the tool against their own systems and fixed the vulnerabilities that they found—then they would have been safe from anyone running the tool against them.

Concerning freeware scanners versus commercial scanners: you get what you pay for. When the freeware tools (such as SATAN) are first released, they are probably as good as the commercial tools, if not better. However, they are not updated for new vulnerabilities as they are found. The commercial tools (such as ISS) are updated as new vulnerabilities are discovered, which means you can get a software update and make sure that you are secure against the latest round of hacks.

War Dialing

As Chapter 6 describes, a war dialer searches ranges of telephone numbers to find those telephone numbers specifically connected to a computer. These connections present back doors into your organization. Organizations should periodically use a war dialer to search their telephone exchanges for computer connections to see exactly what potential attackers would find.

If you find an unauthorized connection, you should investigate how easy it is to exploit. Does it require a password or a call-back mechanism? After you find it, you should also check telephone records to see who has been trying to access it. Modem connections should be kept to a minimum because of the vulnerabilities that they present. Any unnecessary modem lines should be disconnected.

Intrusion Detection Software

Despite all your efforts to prevent intrusions, attackers will probably breach your perimeter security mechanisms from time to time. If you can detect these breaches early, you can respond, stop them, maybe even catch the attacker. The case studies in Chapters 7, 12, and 13 illustrate what can happen when there is no intrusion and abuse detection software. The software could have alerted the security departments and prevented the intrusions from continuing, saving billions in losses.

Although it can be time consuming to put intrusion and abuse detection software on all your systems, you should at least install it on the systems inside of your organization that contain very sensitive information. Start with those systems, and then work on securing others. It might take some time to identify all relevant systems, but you should know where all your sensitive information is kept.

Many of the commercially available intrusion and abuse detection tools are excellent, but they can be expensive. However, you can download a very good basic tool, called Tripwire, free from the Internet.

Most organizations today would notice significantly more problems if they had this kind of protection software installed.

Access Controls

Most computer systems contain many security features that people simply don't realize are there. In most cases, all your systems administrators have to do is turn them on.

One of the most common security features is *access control.* Access controls are intended to prevent users from accessing files they shouldn't be accessing. You can give your people default accesses, and then specific individuals can be provided with additional access as it becomes necessary. The system administrator should set up default permissions that are restrictive.

Administrators should also ensure that certain system files are properly controlled. A tool called COPS, available for free from the CIAC, helps check access permissions to sensitive files. Several commercially available tools provide advanced checking features.

All of the technical penetrations in the case studies could have been minimized if better access controls had been in place.

Password Checkers

Many computer intrusions, including the one described in Chapter 7, exploit the widespread existence of poor passwords. Many passwords are remarkably easy to guess. If it's a word that can be found in a dictionary, a cracking program can figure it out. The default passwords distributed to employees by many companies are extremely easy to figure out. Cracking programs can be tailored for an organization to search for passwords that might be specific to an organization, such as project names. They can also be robust enough to search for word and number combinations.

To prevent password guessing attacks, systems administrators must run password crackers against their user accounts. Hundreds of password crackers are available on hacker and legitimate Web sites for all major types of computer systems. There is a reason that these tools are so plentiful, and administrators who don't use them are dangerously negligent. It's up to you to find the weak passwords before the criminals do. Other tools are available that force users to enter strong passwords that are not readily susceptible to password crackers.

Perishable Passwords

You can set all the passwords on your system to expire after a certain period of time. This is an important countermeasure that minimizes the vulnerability presented by password sniffers. If the password changes before the attacker can get to it, then he or she cannot compromise the account. Generally, passwords should be set to expire every twenty-one days. This feature is usually available on all major operating systems.

Account Lockouts

Most operating systems include account lockout features, which I believe are critical for good security. One type of lockout takes effect when a user has not accessed the system for a certain period of time. This is desirable because it locks out accounts that are not used.

The other type of lockout kicks in after a designated number of failed log-in attempts. An employee might forget a password, and after a few unsuccessful guesses, activate the lockout, but it's more likely that someone trying to guess their way into the system is to blame. This type of lockout requires the administrator to reactivate the account and prevents the intruder from continuing to guess passwords unhindered.

Audit Logs

The one essential feature all server systems must have is an auditing program. Auditing programs record the activities of each system user. At a minimum, all systems in your organization should record the dates and times of each log on and log off. But they should also record any security-related events, such as failed log ons and attempts to access restricted files. Most systems can also keep track of the files and functions each user accesses. This information can be critical to any investigation of both compromised accounts and insider abuse. You will want to know whenever an employee seems to be accessing an excessive number of files or database records. With that information, you can circumvent an incredible amount of illicit activity. It also helps you investigate incidents after they've occurred.

In the case involving the Social Security Administration (SSA) employees who stole the personal information of tens of thousands of people, the SSA and Citibank investigators were able to study the extent of the problem thoroughly after checking the SSA audit logs. They were able to learn exactly who had looked at the compromised accounts, to identify the rogue insider. They were then able to view that person's records to see what other records had been looked at.

Although that case was a security success, it also underscores a failure of sorts. The abuse went on for over a year before someone noticed it. In order for this countermeasure to work, you have to review the audit files regularly. For this, you need *audit reduction tools*, which filter out unremarkable log entries.

Audit logs could have helped to detect and thereby minimize some of the incidents in Chapters 7, 12, and 13. In each of those cases, someone logged on to a computer system as someone else and performed many unusual actions. In each case, the actions went undetected for a long enough period to allow very important compromises of information.

Mirrored Logs

In Chapter 13, the hackers modified the audit logs to cover their tracks. This is a common practice among the better hackers and criminals, but fortunately, few of them are quite that good. However, to detect the intrusions of attackers who *are* that good, I recommend utilizing mirrored logs. When you are using this, each time your audit program creates a log entry, an identical entry is created in a separate mirrored log, preferably on a separate computer. When attackers attempt to erase their tracks, they will delete the entries in the primary log, but the mirrored log remains unchanged. You'll be able to see virtually every step they took.

Administrators should compare the mirrored logs to the primary logs on a regular basis. When discrepancies appear, it indicates that someone has tried to modify the logs, and the security department should be alerted.

An advanced security feature, mirrored logs do require a skilled administrator. However, it's a countermeasure that I believe is well worth the effort.

Write-Protect Disks

When hackers took over the CIA and Department of Justice Web pages in 1996, the incidents made front-page headlines around the country and the world. But these intrusions could easily have been prevented if the Web masters had write-protected the disks on which the Web sites were stored. Just as floppy disks and VCR tapes have write-protect tabs, many hard disks have write protection capabilities that make it impossible to overwrite files. If those government files had been kept on write-protected disks, the hackers could not have overwritten them, no matter how much control over the computer system they had secured. They would have had to gain actual physical access to the servers to do the save level of damage.

Similarly, your organization could place some sensitive data on write-protected hard disks, but it might not be practical in most cases, since you cannot modify the files.

Write-protected disks are useful primarily for protecting static Web sites and other computer files that are not modified regularly and some sensitive data that never needs modification.

Adequate Software Testing

Software programming errors cause more damage than malicious intruders ever will. To minimize this vulnerability, organizations should establish very strict software testing standards. Too often, developers are in such a rush to meet the demands of tight schedules that they fail to adequately test their programs before releasing them into operational areas. The Bank of New York incident is one of the more notorious examples of this situation. In that case, a one-line programming error caused an electronic funds transfer system to crash, resulting in the bank incurring millions of dollars' worth of losses. The 1991 crash of ATT's long-distance service was the result of a programming error, costing the company millions. The 1996 crashes of the western U.S. power grid also involved programming errors. The inadequate testing of the Hubble Space Telescope caused billions of dollars in losses, as did the underreported loss of a NASA satellite.

Organizations should insist that software developers use structured software testing methodologies on all their efforts.

There are tools available to help automate this process.
Organizations should also require that the testing phase of
development not be cut to meet deadlines. This may seem
like a costly requirement, but the potential for losses due to
programming errors is enormous. Quality assurance must be
treated as a critical part of your information security effort.

Bug and Wiretap Sweeps

Bugs and wiretaps are traditional tools of espionage. To
counter this, periodic bug sweeps should be performed. When
you see any other signs of espionage activities, such as a competitor consistently beating you to the punch or other indications of major leaks, you should consider performing a bug
sweep immediately. Many companies claim to perform this
service, however, they vary greatly in quality and scope. A key
part of a bug sweep should be a scan of the telephone lines to
see if they are tapped. Since many high-quality bugs use the
electrical circuits as a carrier, the power outlets should be
examined for unusual signals. This requires special equipment
that many services do not have. The better services will even
use metal detectors to search behind walls for old bugs.

These services are expensive, so companies should consider developing in-house capabilities. If you do decide to
contract with a service, you want to define your critical areas
and have the services check only those areas. These companies
charge by the room or the square foot, and costs can add up
quickly. You should always consider performing a bug sweep
when you are having a sensitive meeting, such as a shareholders' meeting, away from your corporate locations.

Encryption

Encryption technology could make it possible to prevent
nearly all electronic information compromises. It's relatively

easy to encrypt both stored data and sensitive information you wish to transmit over networks. Many commercial encryption tools are available to secure both voice and computer transmissions. For small-volume data transmission, Pretty Good Privacy (PGP) is a freeware encryption tool available from sites on the Internet (commercial organizations should purchase commercial versions). PGP is relatively simple to use and is the most common tool utilized for e-mail security. Commercial, user-friendly versions are also available at retail stores.

Commercial tools for encryption can be integrated into your communications devices, such as your routers and firewalls. You can also buy special-purpose devices, such as Virtual Private Network devices. These devices allow you to connect securely to other parts of your company over the Internet. These encryption programs are invisible to your users and provide a tremendous amount of security.

To encrypt user files, you'll need one of a number of readily available commercial tools (PGP also does this). In some cases, the encryption function can be made invisible to the user. In other cases, the user may be asked to enter a password when accessing files. I strongly recommend encrypting all of your highly valuable information.

Encryption of telephone communications is now possible, and some hardware is commercially available. For those who regularly call specific people, you can acquire and distribute telephones with encryption built right into them. You can also buy encrypting devices that plug into a telephone jack.

Companies that discuss sensitive issues with other parties over the telephone should very seriously consider acquiring some form of telephone encryption. This is especially true if you are calling or doing business in foreign countries. It's no coincidence that when Motorola was testing its new telephone encryption system in one of its Japanese offices, Nippon Telephone and Telegraph (the Japanese equivalent of ATT) sent a repair person over to its facility within two hours, claiming a problem with the telephone lines. The telephone and fax calls of all large American companies are extremely likely to be monitored at their international locations by the host countries and foreign competitors.

One of the most annoying arguments I hear against encryption is that the code can be cracked. These naysayers also claim that the U.S. government only lets people use encryption that the NSA can break. Whether or not there is any truth to those arguments, they are profoundly short-sighted. The use of any encryption—even relatively weak encryption—makes the situation much more difficult for eavesdroppers and intruders. Sure, someone will eventually be able to break any encryption, but for now only the most sophisticated attackers can do this efficiently. More often than not, an attacker will simply move on to an easier target. By using an encryption program, you are probably cutting out over 99 percent of the technical threats to your electronically stored data and transmissions.

As to the argument about "Big Brother" reading your encrypted information, I say he'd be reading anyway. Most of those cynical people out there are using nothing while they're waiting for Big Brother–proof encryption. Assuming that for some bizarre reason the U.S. government does want to read your files, I am much less worried about one Big Brother than 50,000 little brothers who are *already* out there reading your unencrypted information while you are waiting for an encryption that Big Brother cannot read.

Digital Signatures

Digital signatures represent a special use of encryption technology that allows you to authenticate the identity of a person sending you an electronic message and the content of that message. This feature is available with most encryption software. The application of digital signature technology could have stopped the intrusion in Chapter 7. The company in that case depended heavily on e-mail for the exchange of information. The Smart Card application was originally e-mailed to the attacker, and the company would have preferred to keep the whole process on e-mail. However, they needed a hard copy signature to approve the application, which was easily forged. If a digital signature process had been in place, it would have been almost impossible to get the Smart Card without being detected.

Organizations that implement enterprise-wide encryption should utilize the digital signature capability.

One-Time Password Tools

Password sniffers and guessers—favorite tools of hackers (as shown in Chapter 13) —would be all but useless if companies employed one-time password mechanisms, such as the Smart Cards described in Chapter 7. The company's modem banks were compromised only when the attacker secured an official card. Passwords that are used only once present virtually no vulnerability. An adept social engineer might secure a password once, but it will be useless for further espionage. The fact that an attacker must continually acquire new passwords exponentially increases the difficulty of the attack.

There have been a few technical compromises against some one-time password mechanisms, however, this countermeasure will serve you well under most circumstances.

It is no coincidence that Citibank began the use of Smart Cards after the Vladimir Levin incident. The incident in Chapter 7 could have been significantly minimized if the company had used Smart Cards internally. The incidents in Chapters 12 and 13 could have been prevented altogether.

Off-Line Data Storage

If you have any information that is extremely valuable, used rarely, and not shared, it should be stored off-line. Sensitive data that does not have to be shared should never be stored on your system. Save it to a floppy or tape, take it off-line, and lock it up when it's not in use.

This countermeasure is simple, cheap, and very effective, yet it is surprisingly seldom utilized, even by the experts. Tsutomu Shimomura, whose personal computer system was thought to be compromised by Kevin Mitnick, claims that the attacker was after some reverse-engineered software, which he could have stored off-line. He had no reason to keep the information on his system, which was connected to the Internet. If it was as valuable as he claims, and very likely it was rarely looked at, it should have been stored on a tape or floppy disk.

CONCLUSION

When it comes to espionage and high-tech countermeasures, your goal, as always, should be to minimize your risk. To do this, you must understand the threat to your organization and you must know your vulnerabilities. You should select your protective strategies according to your specific needs. Never use a cookie-cutter approach. There's too much at stake for templates.

People frequently ask me which countermeasures I would start with. First and foremost, I strongly recommend implementing backup procedures, acquiring surge protectors, and installing anti-virus software. These things are basic and critical, and they address the most common problems. They are also incredibly inexpensive when compared with the potential losses. Next, I would utilize the tools you already have but aren't using, or aren't using properly; locks and screen savers come immediately to mind.

Frankly, any one of the measures listed in this chapter could be the most important for you, depending on your situation. I would strongly recommend using any of them where appropriate. Almost all of the countermeasures in this chapter are simple and relatively easy to implement, requiring few sophisticated tools or techniques. But they yield tremendous paybacks. Even if those James Bond types and supposed genius hackers do exist, you can stop them dead in their tracks.

15

Taking Action

B Y NOW, YOU SHOULD HAVE A CLEAR IDEA OF WHAT you're up against and the steps you can take to protect yourself. You've read case studies of some of the best-planned and executed industrial espionage attacks available to the public. You've seen that each one of those attacks could have been prevented if simple countermeasures had been in place at the target organizations. You know now (if you didn't before) that all the hype about information warfare and industrial espionage is just that—*hype*.

You don't have to implement martial law in your organization. You only have to take the precautions that are commensurate with the value of your information. I've presented many countermeasures that will have a tremendous impact on your organization and that will cost you little or nothing.

Now it's time to take action.

DETERMINING VALUE

To get any management support at all, you must show that the money put into information security is well spent. Good managers want to take as little as possible from the company's bottom line. It's often difficult for them to see the value of high-tech countermeasures—if they're working, nothing happens.

As you approach management with your security plan, you should have some value in mind. What is your company's information worth? This is not an easy question to answer. Begin by determining the physical value of your information assets. Corporate accounting departments and CFOs will often be able to provide you with the approximate value of the company's property—but they often don't usually have a clue what your information is worth.

Financial analysts might have an idea of the value of corporate intellectual property. Of course, your company's information is probably worth much more than that. Information, by its very nature, has a hidden value, which can be difficult to pin down. What would your information be worth if it fell into the wrong hands? This hidden value can sometimes be illustrated in an all-or-nothing type of loss scenario. For example, a lunatic tampered with some Tylenol packages, causing the deaths of several people. The physical loss to the manufacturer included the costs of a product recall, new packaging, and the inevitable litigation. However, the loss of trust among consumers almost put the company out of business.

You might also look at the security-related losses of organizations similar to your own, though getting accurate figures from your competitors could be difficult.

Remember: it is unlikely that you will ever lose everything to an industrial spy or high-tech criminal. If you claim total losses in your information valuation, management will view you as an extremist paranoid unaware of the real business issues, and they won't take you seriously. Estimate that you could lose a portion of your market share, not your entire market share, and so on. As the Coca Cola example in Chapter 3 shows, even if the company's secret formula were released,

Coca Cola would not go out of business; it would, however, lose a portion of its customer base.

DETERMINING THREATS

Most organizations already know who the bad guys are. Most companies have suffered losses from competitor espionage actions or employee theft. So you probably already have some indication of the level of threat your company faces. You might want to review Chapter 4 to consider other possible threats.

You'll probably have to do some additional research to make the case for improved security. Are any others interested in your company? Are you on the Internet? Exactly how closely tied to national defense is your operation? Are you on the verge of developing any new breakthroughs? Ironically, the security department might not be in on these kinds of internal secrets.

You might want to ask around about incidents that may have gone unreported. In many cases, managers have intervened and handled situations themselves without reporting them to security. Look for one-time happenings that could be part of a coordinated effort. Emphasize to managers and other employees you talk to that you are not trying to get anyone into trouble; you just want data. You'll be surprised at what you'll learn on this kind of fishing trip. When you put your findings together, you will be shocked to find what really goes on inside your company. You could be giving management its first clear picture of the true level of threat your company faces.

DETERMINING VULNERABILITIES

As you compile your lists of actual suspicious and criminal activities within your organization, note the weaknesses exploited and the methods used. When you begin to examine exactly how spies and malcontents have actually attacked you, a pattern of vulnerabilities could emerge, which should help you predict how you will be attacked in the future. Wade through the details of the actual attacks and focus on the basic vulnerabilities exploited by the attackers. You must conduct a complete vulnerability assessment (you may want to read through Chapter 5 again). You don't know what you don't know. The good thieves don't get caught, and they don't leave evidence of their activities behind. It's the stuff you don't know about that they are the most likely to exploit. Your enemies are searching for your Achilles' heel; you should be, too.

DETERMINING COUNTERMEASURES

You cannot approach management without a plan, which means you will have to take some time to select the countermeasures you wish to implement. As I explain in Chapter 14, some countermeasures are very easy to implement and require no extra resources or even much management support. It's often just a matter of letting people know what they should be doing. Encouraging people to use already available locks and computer password protections can yield tremendous payback. The simplest countermeasures make the biggest difference.

Beyond basic countermeasures, you'll probably want to implement some of the absolutely essential security strategies recommended in Chapter 14. Your initial investigations should have shown you where the major breaches are and where you are most likely to be attacked in the future. Once your most basic procedures are in place, move immediately to address your most pressing security needs with the stronger measures you've selected.

You should also choose a few strategies that fall somewhere in between. Many countermeasures address security issues that are not absolutely critical to your company's survival but will cost you in the long run. You don't want a security plan composed entirely of must-do measures—you've got to include something for the higher-ups to turn down. Put some lower-priority options in your plan that will give you room to negotiate.

GETTING SUPPORT

No matter which corporate espionage countermeasures you hope to implement to protect the information in your organization, to have any real impact, they must have company-wide support. Unfortunately, the kind of support you need is not always readily available. You may find that you have to justify even the simplest and most commonsense measures to senior management. You might find second-tier managers resistant to change or line workers hostile to what may seem to be intrusions on their privacy. Without everyone's support, you're really working with a handicap.

Management might talk about something called "due diligence." The concept is a somewhat misty standard used to legally justify all manner of losses. When companies take the position that they have satisfied due diligence requirements, they are saying, "We did everything that similar organizations have done to prevent the loss." In other words, they did as little as possible while satisfying legal requirements. They are, in essence, admitting that they are safe only from claims of negligence by shareholders.

I've seen guards making rounds through buildings, not to satisfy true security requirements but to satisfy insurance requirements. They're there to look for physical hazards—wet floors, broken electrical outlets, cracked glass—not to protect your company's valuable information.

So, be prepared: the process can be quite discouraging.

When you seek support for your security plan, keep in mind something that I've stressed throughout this book: you can never have perfect security—and you shouldn't try to sell it as such. What effective countermeasures will do is minimize the risk to your organization. You can, in effect, make attacking your organization too difficult and too expensive for many likely attackers, and you can improve your company's ability to detect attacks in progress.

To do that, you'll have to invest some resources: money, time, and personnel. A phased implementation approach can spread out the costs so you feel the impact less. You might want to develop a timeline for your plan.

Be patient. You're probably asking a lot of people to make some pretty annoying changes in their routines.

First- and Second-Line Management Support

Gaining the support of first- and second-tier management is critical. A company-wide letter from the CEO stating that security is important is not going to do much—it'll just end up in the trash with all the other policy letters. The managers, however, who see the employees every day are the ones who will actually be there to notice when people are following security practices and when they are not. These are the folks who can influence security the most. When they start checking everybody's doors and file cabinets to see that they're locked, then you will start seeing the rank and file following procedures. Senior management support is only useful when it produces the required funding and gets the lower managers to enforce policies.

Your best hope is to get their voluntary support and cooperation, but sometimes force is your only option. I personally do not like having to intimidate people into being security-conscious, but it frequently works if senior management supports it. Until managers start to consider security to be part of their responsibility, you'll get a lot of lip service and very little follow-up.

THE CULTURE FACTOR

Before you seek to implement any countermeasures, try to get a sense of how people will react to them in your particular organization. In some corporate cultures, the security people are the bad guys; "openness" is paramount. In others, naiveté reigns: "We're safe. No one's going to get in here." I hate to say it, but if you work in an open, trusting environment in which people help one another without question, then you've got a problem. Lock up a few storerooms, and they'll think you're instituting martial law.

Try to describe your corporate culture. Is management weak? Are its edicts usually ignored? Are coworkers more security-conscious than in other organizations? Is secrecy an integral part of your industry? Do the people working in your company know that? You must know the answers to these and similar questions, so you'll know how to approach your organization with your plan. Whether you are the CEO, the head of security, or just a well-meaning employee, your plan must fit your corporate culture.

CREATING AN AWARENESS PROGRAM

Security awareness programs have the highest payback when compared with almost all other countermeasures. When the people in your organization become truly security-conscious, they will come up with countermeasures that you never thought of. Security should always be a bottom-up program, with every employee performing security functions throughout the company. You want your entire organization to be aware of the problems. When that happens, your organization is much more secure than most attackers expect. Most important, you have thousands of people detecting security problems, not just the two people in a typical security department.

Telling everyone to be "security-conscious" is pointless. You've got to let your people know *specifically* what you want them to do. They have to hear "Lock your doors" or "Log out of the computer," and they have to hear it *a lot*. If an awareness program does not specify exactly what employees should do when they notice a security breach, then it is assuming a common knowledge that just doesn't exist (remember, *there is no common sense without common knowledge*). You should distribute bulleted lists specifying exactly what people should do. You should include brief reasons why these procedures are necessary. You should emphasize that managers will be held responsible for enforcing the specific procedures.

ASSESSING THE SUCCESS OF YOUR COUNTERMEASURES

After your countermeasures have been in place for a while, you'll want to begin assessing their effectiveness on a number of levels. Are people using the countermeasures? Do they seem to be accomplishing what you want?

Your people are one of your best resources for assessing the effectiveness of your countermeasures. Talk informally with "typical" workers. During ad hoc conversations, see if you can find out which security procedures seem to be working and which are turning out to be bad ideas. Make the interview a little longer than necessary, to give the person time to relax and think about your questions.

You should seriously consider performing a vulnerability assessment and penetration test. Once your plan has been in place for several months, test it with a professional. Even if the news is bad, it's better to find it out before an attacker does.

When things don't seem to be working, don't be afraid to make changes and modify your strategy. You'll have to do this whether your plan is working or not; once you've taken care of your current set of problems, others are sure to rear their ugly heads.

CONCLUSION

Every company is at risk of penetration. There is simply no way around it. If you have anything of value, somebody else wants it. You are sticking your head in the sand if you think that nobody will try to steal from you. Industrial spies and high-tech thieves steal from mom-and-pop shops and multibillion-dollar corporations every day. No one is immune.

But you don't have to lie back and make it easy for them. As I hope I've demonstrated in these pages, you're not fighting James Bond or unstoppable computer geniuses. Even if you were, you *can* stop them.

Fire can be a devastating force; we're all vulnerable to it. Yet, by incorporating the proper countermeasures into our lives, we can protect ourselves from fire and even use it to make our lives better. In much the same way, we can take the steps necessary to protect ourselves from corporate espionage. Fire and espionage: both are potentially devastating, and both are prevented by known countermeasures.

Index

passwords and user IDs *(continued)*
overuse of the same password, 258
password "sniffer" software, 130, 173–174, 255–256, 262, 330
password protected screen savers, 313
poor passwords, 129–130
Smart Card, one-time password, 174, 202, 337
success rate of trying every word in dictionary, 129
system administrator privileges, 255
when password and ID are same, 164
patent, filing for, 163
pattern (changing), to avoid surveillance, 300
payroll, sabotage of program, 45
PBX corporate telephones, 120
penetration testing, xii, 303–304
Pentium, foreign interest in, 203–204
People's Express, 51
PETA (People for the Ethical Treatment of Animals), 38, 49
phreakers, 84
Piech, Ferdinand, 46
planning. *See* intelligence process
police department (NYPD) "give-away" ploy, 95

policies. *See* vulnerability
Pollard, Jonathan, 72
postings (fake) on bulletin boards, 315
presidential campaigns, donations to, 82–83
pretext phone calls, 94–95
Price Waterhouse, 253
Prime Time Live (ABC) report on industrial espionage, 102–103
procedures. *See* vulnerability
Proctor & Gamble, 3
programming error, Bank of New York mishap, 40, 333
Project Rahab, Germany (BND), 73
proposals. *See* bidding process, and requests for detailed information
proximity of offices, 115
PSO (Project Security Officer), 286
psychology. *See* social engineering
public relations
as area of vulnerability, 99
role of PR officer, 251
training of personnel, 291
publications, reviewing before release, 289–291

Q

questioning, the art of, 145
questionnaire, collection ploy, 66–67
Quinn, John, 67, 249, 290